5/13

D0457496

Brotherhood

"Open, honest, and brilliantly written, *Brotherhood* reaffirms why our arms, hearts, and policies must remain open to welcome those who are eager to live in the land of promise. Every page contains a thoughtful gem that will enlighten the reader about the universal truths that bind us together. Read this book and take comfort in the knowledge that dreams still matter in America."

—William S. Cohen, former secretary of defense and chairman and CEO, The Cohen Group

"In *Brotherhood,* Deepak and Sanjiv beautifully articulate their birthright and the intoxicating and permeative influence it had on their lives as doctors and spiritual practitioners in the Western world. Through their entertaining storytelling, they thoughtfully and humorously depict how, in India, chaos and order, the ancient and modern, and faith and disbelief collide to create enduring influence. I, too, discovered that you can leave India, but that she never leaves you."

—Jacqueline Lundquist, author and former first lady of the U.S. Embassy, New Delhi, India

"Deepak Chopra and his younger brother, Sanjiv, have written an extraordinary and compelling account of their life's journey from a privileged upbringing in India to careers in medicine and spirituality in America. It is a story of tradition, of sibling rivalry, of the responsibility to 'give back at every conceivable opportunity,' and of immigration to another world to fulfill their respective dharmas. But most of all, it is a story of family, which was their lodestar and remains the touchstone of their lives."

—Ambassador Elizabeth Frawley Bagley

"The story of Deepak and Sanjiv's lives easily unfolds, bringing us full circle to the knowledge that brotherhood is universal. *Brotherhood* takes us on an epic journey discovering the heart of life."

—Marc Benioff, founder and CEO, Salesforce.com

Brotherhood

Dharma, Destiny,
and the American Dream

Deepak Chopra

and

Sanjiv Chopra

New Harvest
Houghton Mifflin Harcourt
Boston • New York
2013

This edition published by special arrangement with Amazon Publishing

For information about permission to reproduce selections from this book,
write to Permissions, Houghton Mifflin Harcourt Publishing Company,
215 Park Avenue South, New York, New York 10003.

www.hmhbooks.com

Library of Congress Cataloging-in-Publication Data
Chopra, Deepak, author.
Brotherhood : dharma, destiny, and the American dream / Deepak Chopra and
Sanjiv Chopra.
p. ; cm.
ISBN 978-0-544-03210-1
I. Chopra, Sanjiv, author. II. Title.
[DNLM: 1. Chopra, Deepak. 2. Chopra, Sanjiv. 3. Physicians — India — Auto
biography. 4. Physicians — United States — Autobiography. 5. Cross-Cultural
Comparison — India. 6. Cross-Cultural Comparison — United States. 7. Delivery of
Health Care — India. 8. Delivery of Health Care — United States. 9. Emigrants and
Immigrants — India. 10. Emigrants and Immigrants — United States.
11. Siblings — India. 12. Siblings — United States.WZ 100]
610.92 — dc23
[B]   2013001928

Book design by Brian Moore

Printed in the United States of America
DOC 10 9 8 7 6 5 4 3 2 1

To our amazing and loving parents,
Krishan and Pushpa Chopra

Contents

Brotherhood

To the Reader

Writing a double memoir was uncharted territory for us. We had no model to follow. When two people write together, they combine their voices as one. Why didn't we? Deepak could have controlled himself and not bossed his little brother around (he promised). Sanjiv knows how to hold his own and stick out a gentle elbow when in danger of being pushed out of the nest.

Instead, we chose this novel way of presenting the story of our lives, because it proved more exciting for us and, we hope, for the reader. One brother is free to tell how he remembers early days in Jabalpur and Shillong, seeing through his set of eyes memories, nostalgia, denial, and fantasy. Then a second viewpoint is offered. The facts, as it were, don't change. A big colonial house in Jabalpur where our father saw a stream of patients every day and our mother quietly fed the poorest ones is what it is. Facts are no more than the seed of a memoir. It was better to let each brother sow his own seedlings, free to let the past unfold in its own peculiar way. We didn't look at each other's chapters along the way. There were no arguments over who was right.

Another reason to write as separate voices came from our publisher, who felt that beyond the Chopra brothers lay the larger world of immigration and the American dream. The two of us chose to leave India with no money or property except the intellectual property of a medical school diploma and some dreams. Not many Americans were aware of Indian immigration in the Seventies, much less an

"Indian diaspora." They were focused on their own troubles, for one thing, especially the Vietnam conflict that created a severe doctor shortage and opened the door for two young foreigners to practice medicine here. The general view, to be blunt, was that foreign doctors were necessary but not welcome.

India didn't want us to leave, either. The government had banned the written examination that a doctor needed to pass before America would grant a work visa. Only a pittance was allowed to be exchanged into dollars for travel abroad. There was a much deeper resistance at work, however. India is a mother culture that actually mothers, that holds its children tight and very reluctantly lets go. As young — and eager to prove ourselves — as we were, we heard tears being shed behind us at the Delhi airport, and not just by our parents. Our choice to step away made us neither fully Indian nor fully American. We had seized a double fate.

At birth, a pair of identical twins shares the same genes, but by the time they turn seventy, their genetic profiles are dramatically unalike. The actual DNA hasn't changed, but its activity has, rising and falling, recombining thousands of on-off switches. This divergence happened to us, only it was a set of cultural genes that we shared. As you will see, our lives took drastically different paths. Deepak played a major role in bringing Indian spirituality and the medical tradition of Ayurveda to the West. Sanjiv continued on the path of Western medicine to become a professor at Harvard Medical School. There have been times, frankly, when we wondered whether we understood each other's reality. Such is the fascination and pain of beginning so close.

Today a double fate is more common than ever. By current estimates from the U.S. Census Bureau, 20 percent of Americans have at least one parent who was born abroad. The fabric of America has changed, bringing mixed feelings on all sides. So a double memoir made sense for the Chopra brothers. Doubleness remains true for us forty years on, piling up richness and loss, consternation and clarity. Like everyone else, we can look back on lives unlived. The life we did live feels symbolic, however. Brotherhood is universal. A self gets built, two selves find an orbit around each other, a society absorbs them into a collective fabric that is never the same tomorrow as it was yesterday. We wanted to share our journey with everyone who is building a self in the same complex and often mysterious way.

DEEPAK CHOPRA
SANJIV CHOPRA

1

Sacred River

Deepak

Deepak as a toddler with parents, Krishan and Pushpa Chopra, 1949.
Krishan was an army doctor at the time.

H ERE. NOW. YOU GO."

If the priest didn't mumble these exact words, then his gesture told me to take hold of the stick in his hand. It was time. I was the oldest son. By rights the oldest son is the one to poke a hole in the father's skull, releasing his soul from this life to the next.

Only vaguely did I know about this ancient ritual. I'd never seen it. Hesitating, I glanced over at my brother, Sanjiv. Being the younger son, he would go next.

This is totally bizarre.

My thought stayed with me. The priest was running everything. Sanjiv and I were almost irrelevant: two modern bystanders caught up in ancestral ways. We had flown back to New Delhi the moment we received news of our father's sudden death.

The smoke from burning bodies raised an indescribable smell around us and dirtied the sky. It must have been a strong stench, but at that moment I was immune to it. Each pyre occupied its own small plot in the burning *ghat,* or cremation ground. Women were keening. The logs for cremation formed a social order — cheap wood for the poor; expensive, fragrant sandalwood for those who could afford it. Orange marigolds were also scattered over the bodies of the well-to-do before the fire was lit.

The priest was eyeing me, wanting to move on; this was his daily business. Meanwhile I felt a strange detachment. Centuries of tradition said, "You must not forget us," and I obeyed, taking the stick from the priest's hand.

In the flames, which were transparent in the noonday sun, I could glimpse the shape of my father's body. The shroud had burned away, and the remains were more skeleton than corpse. No horror overcame me. A part of my mind stood apart, admiring the efficiency of the ghat. The fires burned very hot and finished their work with dispatch.

Daddy had been alive thirty-six hours ago. He had sat up late to watch, with no enthusiasm, George W. Bush take the oath of office. It was 2001, his first inaugural. That morning, he had walked grand rounds at Moolchand Hospital as usual, with a line of young doctors in tow, and had mentioned to my mother as he kissed her good night that he was feeling a bit of discomfort. Better call K. K. in the morning, one of the young doctors who worked with him, just in case. Now there was empty space where once a person had vibrated with life.

How is an adult defined? Someone who knows the value of doing what he doesn't like to do. So I did it, driving the pointed end of the stick into my father's skull. I once read a medical memoir by Michael Crichton that began with a shocking sentence: "It is not easy to cut through a human head with a hacksaw." Poking a hole in one is easy, though, if it has crumbled nearly to ashes.

How long would I remain this detached?

I passed the stick to Sanjiv and managed to keep my eyes on him without flinching after what I had done. When we're together, I'm the quiet one. But we both occupied a somber silence at that moment, and a shared bewilderment.

Death is bewildering. The survivors confront something worse than deep sadness — sheer emptiness. A void in the vicinity of the heart holding a place for pain to fill in later. In Buddhism it is said that there is no alternative to emptiness; it only matters how you face it. Unknown to me, I would face it very differently than I imagined.

The priest nodded matter-of-factly when the two brothers had done their sacred duty. The chanting continued for hours. Our legs grew rubbery; we were exhausted and bleary with jet lag.

There is a native people in the desert mountains of western Mexico, the Huichol, who take peyote every day, starting when, as babies, they drink it in their mothers' milk. Are they in a walking hallucination that feels normal to them? At that moment, Sanjiv and I were two Huichols.

For a long time I didn't know when I was actually born. Looking back, it might not have mattered. None of us is truly present at our own birth. We are barely prepared to arrive. A newborn's brain is still manufacturing new neural connections at the rate of one million per minute. It has a few primal reflexes, like grasping with the fists, obeying life's command of "Hold on tight." On the African plain a wildebeest or giraffe must know how to walk the instant it drops from the womb to the welcoming, dangerous earth. Survival is at stake. The mother gives a few licks to encourage her calf to stand up, and then the parade of life proceeds on its way, with a wobbly infant bringing up the rear. A human baby isn't like that. It is a half-finished product, a sketch waiting to be filled in. To remain alive, a baby needs all the care it can get.

Indian families have gotten the message with a vengeance. I opened my eyes that day—in April? October?—to see half a dozen female members of my family, and that group of anxious, beaming aunts, cousins, midwife, and mother would be the smallest group I saw in one room for many years. I was the first child of Doctor Krishan Lal and Pushpa Chopra, born at 17 Babar Road in New Delhi. Perhaps because I was born in a crowd I've never felt existential loneliness. It was a pleasure to be named Deepak, because hearing my name made people smile. *Deepak* means light, and I arrived during *Diwali,* the festival of lights. Firecrackers were going off in the streets, which helped mask the sounds of my grandfather firing off joyous shots from his old army rifle while standing on the roof of his house. The city was sparkling with thousands of oil lamps to celebrate the victory of good over evil. To name a baby Deepak is a cause for smiling.

The only anxiety was that my father wasn't present. In 1946 the war was still winding down, and he had been on the Burma front, where it was thought he might still be during my birth, although his exact whereabouts were unknown. It would be another twenty days before he set eyes on his newborn son.

But it wasn't turmoil or anxiety or superstition that made my parents change my actual birthday from October 22 to April 22, only a technicality around when I was allowed to start school. Moving my birth to the spring of 1947 allowed me to attend school when the family moved to a new station. I'm not sure I have the details clear in my mind even now.

It's inborn for Indians to look on any day as either propitious or ill-favored. Being born on Diwali is auspicious enough to satisfy anyone, but doubly so for a doctor, since the festival celebrates Lakshmi, goddess of prosperity and healing. (The word "goddess" can be misleading. I was brought up to worship God in the singular. All the Hindu gods and goddesses stand for God, without a plural.)

Every morning my mother lit a lamp and recited daily *puja*, the household religious ritual, Sanjiv and I at her side, our main fascination being our mother's singing of the prayers, which was lovely.

Our home was full of visitors and patients from every faith, and my mother cared for all of them. My father's religion was medicine. An army doctor like my father was allowed to maintain a private practice on the weekends. I became aware early on that Daddy was a special kind of physician. Cardiologists rely on readouts from EKGs to tell them what a patient's heart is doing, but my father gained a reputation for gathering the same information using only a stethoscope and the sound of a heartbeat. He could time the intervals between the contraction of the two chambers of the heart — the auricle and ventricle — by ear, down to fractions of a second. The EKG only came into general use in the Forties, and, in fact, my father had trained under one of the British doctors who pioneered it when he did a tour of medical duty in India. A doctor's recollection from that era says that cardiology "was nothing more than having good hearing through a stethoscope," but my father's accuracy was considered uncanny.

When he was stationed in Jabalpur, we lived in a huge colonial house with a sweeping drive lined with mango and guava trees. Patients came from all over India as Krishan Lal's reputation grew.

My mother would station herself on the veranda, knitting. She kept an eye out for how each patient arrived, whether on foot or by car with a driver. There was no fee for anyone, but when a poor patient was leaving, she'd quietly tell a servant, Lakshman Singh, to make sure he had something to eat and, if the need was great, a train ticket home. It seems extraordinary, looking back, that Lakshman Singh came with my mother as part of her bridal dowry. He was fourteen. (The last I heard, he is now in his eighties, having outlived both her and my father.)

When I was ten and we were leaving the post in Jabalpur to go to the next in Shillong, a sizable crowd gathered to see my father off at the train station, touching his feet, laughing and weeping. I held Sanjiv's hand, wondering at this crush of humanity, so many people so deeply moved.

My mother lived through her children and through her husband's work. She would wait up for him to return from the hospital and quiz him about his cases. Did you rule out a pulmonary edema? Did you exclude atrial fibrillation? She became quite expert at this, and would predict how a case was likely to progress, shaking her head with a mixture of satisfaction and regret if she had been right and the patient didn't recover. She would also pray for the patients and become vicariously involved, not just in the detective work of diagnosis but in their personal lives as well. My father did the same. I had no way of knowing that this kind of medicine had no future. No one knew any other way at the time.

On the day after the cremation Sanjiv and I returned to the ghat and helped sift through my father's ashes. The smoldering heap could be touched gingerly, and every fragment of bone that could be picked out was put into a small pouch. The atmosphere was less eerie than the day before. We had woken from our hallucination. A new crowd of pyres was blackening the air. The wailing women had different faces, if grief ever wears a different face. At one point the priest held up a piece of sternum with two ribs attached. This somehow delighted him.

"Ah, your father was enlightened! See, this proves it," he exclaimed. To him, the fragment looked like a figure sitting in *Samadhi,* or deep meditation.

My mother, who was arthritic and confined to a wheelchair, hadn't attended the cremation. It's fairly usual for some of the family who are closest to the deceased to stay away. I hadn't had time to know what was coming over me emotionally, but I could faintly smell it —an acrid bitterness that had no name. Perhaps the constant activity surrounding death in India is a wise old way to keep shock from paralyzing us. The only person who had burst into tears since my arrival was Shanti, the live-in servant who greeted me at the door when I was driven to my parents' house, on Link Road in Defence Colony. That area of South Delhi took its name because the houses were built by Indian veterans of World War II who had each been given a free lot in gratitude for their service.

This house, built on the parcel given to my maternal grandfather, is three stories tall, made of brick with one wall faced with river stones. My grandfather had camped himself on the building site, sorting the stones for choiceness and telling the workmen where to place them. This kind of facade was an unusual touch then. A small patch of manicured lawn and a few rose bushes decorate the front, but it's not a tranquil setting. Link Road is full of traffic, and the noise presses on you almost constantly inside the house.

Shanti's anguish made me cry as we embraced. I don't remember tears after that. (There was no wailing at the cremation, either. We have strong women in our family.) My mother was in her bedroom, sitting up, waiting. Because she had become more and more an invalid, none of us had expected that she would be the parent left alone. There were arrangements to be made about where she would live now. We had to face the creeping signs of dementia. But none of that came up the first night. My mother was somber and lucid. I remember only one sentence from her: "Your father's upstairs. Spend the night with him."

His body lay on the floor in a third-floor bedroom. It was wrapped in a winding sheet that left his face exposed. When I saw it, there was no sign of Daddy in the grayish skin and masklike expression. I sat until dawn, letting my mind wander through memories that came randomly. My brother and I were well loved as children; none of the images that ran through my mind were troubling, and for that reason none were exceptional. The army camps we lived in, called cantonments. My mother sharing a meal with the kitchen maid; she and my father had no tolerance for the traditional caste system. A procession of anonymous sick people coming through the door. My father as a young man, striking in his uniform with a blaze of medals across his chest. He was comfortable being our household god, modest as he was.

Flying in from Boston, Sanjiv had arrived at Link Road before me and had been sent to bed to soften the edge of exhaustion. He was waiting when I came downstairs after dawn. Nothing dramatic was said—few words at all, in fact. The extended family would arrive soon. Sanjiv's wife, Amita, had flown over with him, but it was agreed that my wife, Rita, would come later, after the four days of immediate mourning were over, to help my mother settle my father's affairs and sort out his papers.

On the third day Sanjiv and I took the car to Haridwar, four or five hours north. The bits of bone from the cremation were to be immersed in the Ganges. Cultural genes taking over again. The city of Haridwar is one of the seven most holy places for Hindus. The name translates as the Gateway to God; it is where the Ganges tumbles out of the Himalayas and the steepness of Rishikesh, the valley of the saints, before it broadens out on the plains.

The city is sacred chaos. The minute we stepped out of the car a gaggle of priests converged, assaulting us with questions about our family: my father's name, my grandfather's, and so on. Temples line the river, and countless people wade into the water for holy ablutions. At night a flotilla of burning lamps is launched, creating an incandescent mirror of the starry sky.

Once we had answered enough questions, Sanjiv and I were guided down a narrow alley filled with pilgrims, putt-putting scooters, and sweetshops. Inside a small courtyard a priest unrolled a long parchment scroll. Before ashes are scattered over the Ganges, the deceased's family marks their visit by entering a message on the scroll. The event doesn't have to be a death. For hundreds of years this has been a place where people have come to mark important passages in their life, such as a birth or a marriage.

The days of mourning for my father had scattered my energies. Now, looking at the messages left by my ancestors, my mind was suddenly thrown into sharp focus.

In that dim, airless room I saw that the last few entries on our family scroll were in English: My father coming to scatter the ashes of his father. My grandfather arriving right after World War I with his new bride to "bathe in the celestial pool." The record turned into Urdu and Hindi before that, and if the family line had held strong, the record could have stretched back to one of the earliest Vedic *rishis,* the seers who began the spiritual lineage of India before there was even a religion labeled Hinduism.

I was unusually moved, even though I had had no real interest in our family tree. Impulsively I added a message to my own children: "Breathe the scent of your ancestors." That moment lingers in my memory. Later a folded note was found in my father's room, bidding a final farewell. We don't know when he wrote it, or if he had a premonition that he would die. As much as he had enjoyed his life, the note said, he didn't intend to come back again. My mind flashed to lines from the Persian mystic poet Rumi: "When I die I will soar with the angels. When I die to the angels, what I shall become you cannot imagine."

Yet that moment of fullness fled quickly. If a life is contained between its most ecstatic moments and its bleakest, then for me the two collided into each other. I became subdued and downcast.

I wanted to talk to Sanjiv about this feeling of doom. I wanted to hear what he would say. But as the days passed, I held back. This wasn't a topic that we felt sympathetic about when we shared our conflicting views. I was the medical maverick, he the establishment. Brothers can share genes, a family, and a culture that weaves them into its complex fabric. That much was unspoken between us. Yet twins who are born with identical genes are not clones. At age seventy their genetic profile will be completely different. Genes switch on and off. They listen in on the world and eavesdrop on a person's every thought, wish, fear, and dream. Twins diverge as much as the rest of us, although they may retain a subtler bond. Did Sanjiv and I have that? Daddy had abandoned us to our dream of life. Did he wake up from his or simply vanish?

The scattering of the ashes done, my brother and I arrived back at Link Road after midnight. The pouch that held our father's ashes was empty, left discarded in the backseat. On the way home neither of us had said what was in his heart. The extended family dispersed after four days. I passed Rita when she arrived, and as quickly as I had entered the province of death, I was back home under the California sun. But the province of death is portable, it seems. I became haunted by an overpowering sense of gloom: My father doesn't exist anymore. There is nothing left. He is leading where one day I will have to follow.

Spiritual awakening begins when you realize a simple fact that most people spend their lives avoiding: Death is stalking us at every moment. I cannot say that I felt it as vividly before Haridwar, but as a child I had literally been woken by a death.

I was six at the time. My parents had gone to England so my father could complete his advanced training in cardiology. Sanjiv and I remained behind, living with our paternal grandfather and two uncles in Bombay. (Sanjiv and I lived with various members of our family as our parents studied or traveled for work, or when we left home to attend private school. Our aunts and uncles were considered our second parents. It has always been that way in India.)

For an Indian to travel to London for medical studies was rare in those days. In this case, my father had been medical adviser to Lord Mountbatten, the last viceroy of India. In 1947 Mountbatten was ordered to liberate the country in a matter of months. Events moved swiftly and with barely a look behind; three centuries of colonialism unraveled.

In the mad confusion that ensued, Mountbatten didn't forget my father, and it was through him that the path of Krishan's medical training was smoothed. This wasn't enough to overcome ingrained prejudice, though. At the British army hospital in Pune, my father trailed behind the white doctors during grand rounds. He pored over his textbooks late into the night so that he would be prepared when the attending physician called on him to answer a question, but he was never called on. He was ignored, frozen out. He became a silent attendant to a procession of British superiors. One morning at a patient's bedside, however, the other young doctors were stumped by a tricky diagnosis. The attending turned and repeated his question to my father, who knew the answer. In a single stroke, he had earned respect.

As gentle and tolerant as my parents were, there was never a doubt about the line drawn between whites and "brownies." Most colonials assigned to India had come out in Victorian times to make their fortune or else to escape disgrace. It was a time when the oldest son inherited everything, the middle son went to university to become a clergyman, and the youngest or most hapless son became a soldier. India was an escape route and a chance to rise higher socially than you could have back home. Salaried clerks lived like rajas. The colonial clubs were bastions of pretentiousness, stuffier than any club in London. The British were out-Britishing themselves.

By the time my parents were growing up, this fixed hierarchy may have shifted, but the attitude of contempt and indifference to Indian culture hadn't. Which is understandable when you have conquered a people and want them only for looting and profit. India was a jewel in the crown for mercantile reasons. There was no real military use to occupying the country, only a vast potential for profit.

The Chopras attached their fortunes to the British because there was no other ladder to climb. My great-grandfather was a tribal chieftain in the barren desert landscape of the Northwest Territory and had held out with cannon rather than accede to the British army when they came to call. So family legend went. He was killed, but his son — my grandfather — accepted a position as sergeant in the

British army, which guaranteed him a pension. The linkage with the white colonials became second nature. England was the other place where tea, chutney, and kedgeree featured in daily life. Both countries stopped everything when the cricket scores came over the radio and worshipped cricket stars more devoutly than gods.

Still, when my father was ready to set sail, my mother, who wouldn't follow him for a while, got him to promise one thing: As soon as he landed at Southampton, he was to go and have his shoes polished by an Englishman. He did and reported back the satisfaction of sitting in a high chair with a white man bent down before him. He remembered this incident in later years without pride, but without regret, either. While the British saw a benign empire (no one was legally enslaved after a certain date), the subjugated people experienced their psychological scars being rubbed raw every day.

My father traveled to Edinburgh to sit his medical license exams —it was riskier to take them in London, where the test was supposedly more difficult—and when he sent word back to Bombay that he had passed them, my grandfather was overjoyed. As when I was born, he went to the rooftop of our flat with his rifle and fired several rounds into the air. Then he took Sanjiv and me to see *Ali Baba and the Forty Thieves* at the cinema, which thrilled us. Even better, he was in such a jubilant mood that he took us to a carnival and lavished us with sweets.

In the middle of the night I was awakened by the anguished cries of the women of the house. Servants rushed in and swept us up in their arms. Without explanation, we were left with a trusted neighbor. Our grandfather, we learned, had died in his sleep. At six, I had no concept of death. My confused mind kept asking, "Where is he? Somebody tell me." Sanjiv, who was three, reacted with a sudden outbreak of a mysterious skin condition. He was taken to the hospital; no credible diagnosis was made. But one doctor hit upon an explanation that still satisfies me today: "He's frightened. The skin protects us, and he feels vulnerable, so it's peeling off." This man predicted that Sanjiv would recover as soon as my parents arrived, and he did.

A day later we heard that my grandfather was being cremated.

Two small children wouldn't be taken along, but one of my uncles attended, returning with a bitter scowl on his face. He was a journalist, someone I was in awe of. He didn't know I was in earshot when he blurted, "Bau-ji was celebrating with the kids yesterday, and now what is he? A handful of ashes in a jar."

I'm wary of assigning defining moments to a life. Too many influences swirl around us, and secret ones percolate inside us from the unconscious. Experts in memory say that the most striking ones we carry from childhood are likely to be deceptive; they are actually amalgams of many related incidents congealed into one. Traumas blur together. Every Christmas adds to a single joy. But Uncle's words may well have set my course. If so, they lay submerged for years while death stalked me and I kept intent on not looking back over my shoulder.

I cannot leave that moment without saying that old people seem to time their deaths, as some research now has confirmed. They wait for a significant day, a birthday or perhaps Christmas. Death rates among the elderly go up after major holidays. Years before any statistician thought to look, I had a moving experience of this. An elderly husband and wife had entered the hospital together. The husband was dying, in the late stages of cancer, as I recall. The wife's condition was much less serious, certainly not grave. But she declined rapidly, while he seemed to go on, no matter how deep the ravages of his disease became.

I was a young doctor assigned to check on them every day, and one morning I was shocked to hear that the wife had died during the night. I went and told her husband, who seemed strangely relieved.

"I can go now," he said.

I asked him what he meant.

"A gentleman always waits for a lady to go through the door first," he said. He passed away a few hours later.

Now I'm launched into telling my story and how it crosses and collides with Sanjiv's. Some part of me considers it a strange enterprise, even though I make my living with words. The drawback of being in the public eye, which is also its great attraction, is that people feel as though they already know you. I've lived for a long time with this misperception. I arrived at a hospital in Calgary once to deliver a talk and saw a small group of nuns protesting with signs that read, DEEPAK CHOPRA, THE HINDU SATAN. Anyone can go to blogs run by scientific skeptics, where I'm castigated as the Emperor of Woo Woo (I'm not quite sure what that means, but it sounds a bit endearing, like something out of Dr. Seuss).

Other people look favorably on me and smilingly tell me that I am a guru (a label I would never apply to myself, not because of its odor of charlatanism in the West, but because the title is revered in India). Yet no one has asked me to my face who I really am. Indian by birth, American by choice. Part of the great postwar diaspora that flung South Asians around the world from Africa to the Caribbean. A physician trained at the All India Institute of Medical Sciences thanks to Rockefeller largesse and a stream of visiting professors from the U.S. As with anyone, my luggage is plastered with stickers from every stop I've made in life since the moment I was born. Do you want to know me? Look at my labels.

Telling your life story can be simply an exercise in riffling through labels. It can be the meeting of a writer's insatiable vanity with the public's idle curiosity. I have decided that telling my story can benefit the reader only if we share something so deep that we cherish it equally. Not love of family, dedication to work, a lifelong vision, or even walking the spiritual path.

What you and I deeply cherish is the project of building a self. Like a coral reef that begins as bits of microscopic organisms floating in the sea, gradually coalescing and finally erecting a massive edifice, you and I have been building a self ever since "I" meant something. As reefs go, ours is sticky. Almost any passing experience can glom on to it. There is no plan to this edifice, and for many people the self is built by accident. They look back to find that the person they've become is half stranger, half grumpy boss. Its quirks rule everyday life, veering between "I like this, give me more" and "I don't like that, take it away."

Lives are founded on the whims of "I, me, mine," and yet there is no getting around the need to build a self and cling to it. Otherwise you might wash out to open sea. I wouldn't make so much of India except that it gave me the abiding sense that a self is built for a paradoxical reason that is at once wise, impossible, thrilling, and desperate. You build a self in order to leave it behind. A great philosopher once remarked that philosophy is like a ladder that you use to climb to the roof, and then you kick the ladder away. The self is exactly like that. It's the little boat you row until it bumps on the shore of eternity.

But why would anyone kick the ladder away? We are proud of "I, me, mine." Yes, but it is also the source of our deepest suffering. Fear and anger roam the mind at will. Existence can turn from joy to terror without warning, in the blink of an eye. When life seems like a prison, nothing is more enticing than the Indian teaching that life is play (or *Lila*). I'm telling my story to show that reaching the state of pure play, which carries with it freedom, joy, and creativity, means that you must give up the illusions that mask as reality. The first illusion is that you are free already. Actually, the self you have spent so many years building is a prison, as surely as the microscopic organisms that build a reef are trapped inside its rigid skeleton.

Sanjiv has his own voice and his own world. I will know only how much he agrees or disagrees with me by reading his chapters. I can foresee that he will not agree with my conclusions about spirituality. Modern Indians are eager to break the bonds of ancient traditions and a restrictive culture. America became an escape route for stifled Indians as much as India was once an escape route for stifled British — you can substitute the word "ambitious," "restless," or "alienated" for stifled. I've heard applause when I tell an audience that they are children of the universe. Those words may not exactly mesh with Sanjiv's scientific point of view.

We will not know what it means to creep out of the self until we examine how we built it in the first place. I've asked many teachers what enlightenment is, and one of the best answers — certainly the most concise — is that in enlightenment you exchange the small ego for the cosmic ego. The higher self exists in everyone, waiting to emerge. What holds it back can be seen in my past as much as anyone's. Walls have to be smashed, all the more because we built them ourselves. I bow to the Buddhists who say that there is no alternative to emptiness. But there's another strain in India, going back centuries before the Buddha, which attests to the contrary: that life is infinite fullness, once you awaken to reality and drop the mask of illusion.

2

Blind for a Day

Sanjiv

Five-year-old Deepak and three-year-old Sanjiv
outside their home in Pune, 1952.

MY NAME IS SANJIV CHOPRA and I was born in September 1949, in the city of Pune, India. This was about a year after India had gained its independence from Great Britain. The entire world was recovering from the devastation of World War II, and it was a time of great change. I was the second child of Dr. Krishan and Pushpa Chopra and the younger brother of Deepak Chopra. Our father was a legendary physician and wanted to ensure that we received an excellent education. He never tried to influence Deepak or me into going into medicine. But when I was twelve years old, an incredible incident occurred that set me on my path.

At the time, Deepak and I were living with our uncle and aunt while attending St. Columba's School in Delhi. Our parents were more than three hundred miles away in Jammu. They were keen that we finish our high school education at this preeminent school run by Irish Christian Brothers.

One Saturday afternoon I fell asleep while reading a book. I woke up less than an hour later to discover I was blind. I opened my eyes and the world was completely black. I blinked again and again, but still I could see nothing. I was twelve years old and utterly blind.

Deepak was nearby, reading a book. I nudged him.

"Deepak, I can't see."

He waved his hand in front of my eyes, and when I didn't respond, he started to cry. I remember him calling out to our aunt and uncle.

"I have only one brother and he's blind!"

My uncle Rattan Chacha rushed me to the military hospital. Senior physicians, among them a respected ophthalmologist, examined me and were unable to determine the cause of my blindness. They suspected I was suffering from hysterical blindness, but that made no sense to me or my brother. Why would I suddenly, out of the blue, be experiencing hysteria? I was a good student, a talented athlete, and a happy kid.

The physicians were able to locate my father, who was on a military field trip visiting a rural hospital. My father listened calmly and then started taking a detailed history. "Please tell me what has happened to Sanjiv in the last month. Has he been well? Has he had any illnesses? Has he incurred any injuries?"

The doctors relayed these questions to me and my brother. I replied, "Just a small puncture wound to my thigh when I nicked it with the sharp end of a cricket wicket."

"What treatment did he receive?" my father asked. "Did he get stitches? Antibiotics? Did he get a tetanus shot?" They looked at my records and told him that I had indeed gotten stitches, an antibiotic, and a tetanus shot.

"Was it tetanus toxoid or serum?" The serum, he was told. After a pause, my father said, "Sanjiv is having a rare, idiosyncratic reaction to the tetanus serum: retrobulbar neuritis. It's affecting the nerve in the orbit of each eye. Start an intravenous at once and give him massive doses of corticosteroids."

The doctors followed these directions and within several hours my vision had returned. It was an incredibly scary experience. Had my father not correctly diagnosed this condition, I might well have remained blind for the rest of my life.

Even as a young person, I was amazed at my father's diagnostic skills. All the other doctors, even the specialists, had been stumped, while he, a cardiologist, had almost immediately zeroed in on a rare reaction and ordered the correct course of treatment. It was a moving and unforgettable experience. Prior to this incident, I had vaguely considered following my father's footsteps into medicine, but that experience left an indelible mark. From then on there was not a shadow of doubt in my mind: I would become a physician. I wanted to help people. Although I made that decision when I was very young, I have never regretted it for a moment.

Because my father was a well-respected physician, my family led a privileged existence in many ways. Every three years we moved around the country as my father's military hospital assignments changed, but we were affluent and always lived in nice houses with plenty of servants, and Deepak and I always attended the best schools. We lived in Bombay, Jabalpur, Shillong, and Delhi. We traveled extensively throughout India on pilgrimages or sightseeing trips. The India in which I grew up was a vibrant, complex society finding its own identity as a newly independent nation in the post–World War II world. It was a place where cows roamed freely in the streets, sometimes valued more highly than people, while behind the high walls of opulent estates the wealthy lived charmed lives. What I remember most from my childhood were the sounds, the smells, the colorful chaos, and the daily contradictions.

We grew up surrounded by the cacophony of endless traffic: buses and trucks and cars, bicycles, scooters, carts, and rickshaws, and somewhere in the distance, the railroad. One thing we did not often experience was silence; wherever we lived, the world was always rushing by directly outside my window. I remember being awakened very early many mornings by loud speakers blaring from the mosques reciting the Muslim prayers, or by the street merchants hawking their goods as they walked along: *Alu lelo, kela lelo!* Buy potatoes, buy bananas! The songs of the street vendors were the background music of our lives. And oddly, against that constant chatter, I also clearly remember the beautiful sounds of the birds singing during the day and the crickets chirping at night.

By now I've traveled extensively throughout the world and, as a consequence of the world growing smaller, the easily identifiable smells of a society have become much less distinctive. There really does seem to be a McDonald's on every corner, even in India, where they sell veggie burgers. But once, it was possible to know exactly where you were by smell alone. The spicy, pungent aromas of India are still very much alive in my memory. The fresh smell of rain soaking into dry parched earth is, to me, the scent of life itself. When we traveled by train, hawkers at each stop would come aboard selling *Pakoras, Samosas,* and fudge-like sweet *Barfi*. The aromas would fill the train compartment. Certainly one of the most memorable smells of my childhood was hot tea served in clay pots. One whiff and I'm back in India.

Admittedly not all the smells were pleasant. There is a smell to poverty, and we knew that odor, too.

The poverty around us was so much a part of our lives it was taken for granted. We barely even noticed it. When I asked my parents how it was possible that people could live and die in the streets, survive by begging and have nothing but rags to wear, they explained the concept of karma to me. Karma is an important aspect of the Indian culture, a part of Hindu and Buddhist philosophy; in a sense, karma is your path in life, and it is determined by your actions in previous lives. Hindus believe that a spirit has many lives and that after each death it is reincarnated in another form. Your actions in one life determine your status in the next. If I'm a good person in this life, then I'll be rewarded in this or my next life; if I'm wicked, I'll pay for it in this or my next life. This belief in karma is one of the reasons that the poor in India don't seem to have much resentment against the wealthy; they accepted their poverty as their fate, in the sincere belief that they were paying for their past sins. But my parents also told me that your karma did not have to be your fate, that by working hard you can change your destiny.

The belief in reincarnation has always been very common among most Indians. We had an amazing story of reincarnation in our own family, in fact. My mother had a brother named Shukra, who was four years older than she was; before he could even read or write, he could recite long passages from the Bhagavad Gita, the Hindu scriptures. When my mother was born, her parents named her Suchinta. Her brother objected to this decision. He told them that the name Suchinta incorporated the word "*chinta,*" which means worry in Hindi and therefore had a negative connotation.

"What should we call her then?" they asked him.

"Pushpa," he answered, Pushpa means beautiful flower. And so my mother was known by this name throughout her life.

When my uncle was four and a half, he admonished his father for shooting a pigeon with a BB gun. "What harm did that innocent bird ever cause you?" he asked. "The harm you did will now return to you." This from a child.

The stories about this young boy have been passed down in our family. According to my mother's oldest sister, Bare Bahenji, he would be eating a meal in the kitchen, pause suddenly, and dash outside to the front gate just in time to greet a wandering monk he had somehow sensed. Then he would invite the monk into the house and have a servant prepare him lunch.

Before he reached his fifth birthday, my uncle went to Bare Bahenji and asked for sixteen rupees, then the equivalent of about two dollars.

"Why do you need so much money?" she asked him.

He needed it, he explained, to repay a debt to Daulat, a family servant whose name, ironically, means wealth. My uncle explained that he had incurred this debt in a previous life. He continued to pester Bare Bahenji until she relented. Daulat refused to accept the rupees until my grandparents insisted. A few days later Shukra told Bare Bahenji he would prefer to sleep on the floor. In India this is a common request made by adults who believe they are going to die and want to be connected to the earth. Bare Bahenji was dismayed and disturbed and refused to make his bed on the floor. Instead, she made his regular bed, carefully tucked him in, and sang him a lullaby.

The next morning the family found Shukra's lifeless body on the floor. My uncle had accurately predicted his own death and wanted to repay the debt from a previous life to Daulat the servant before he passed away. For me it's hard not to believe in reincarnation when all this occurred in my own family.

Stories like this one are not unusual in India. The founder and chancellor of Banaras Hindu University, Pandit Madan Mohan Malviya, was a very learned man. He devoted his entire life to the university. On his deathbed he said, "Take me to the outskirts of Banaras."

They were puzzled. "Pandit Ji, you have given your whole life to Banaras. You're now going to pass away and go to heaven. Why would you want us to take you outside Banaras?"

Among Hindus, there is a widely held belief that if you die in Banaras you achieve *Moksha,* an end to the cycle of birth, life, death, and rebirth.

"My work on earth is not complete," Pandit Ji said. "I do not want to achieve moksha. I must come back and finish my work."

India has always been a country where people — no matter how educated, sophisticated, or wealthy — accepted some element of mysticism, understood that some events in life couldn't be easily explained. For example, there was a story several years ago that statues of Ganesha, the elephant-headed Hindu god who dispels all obstacles, were drinking milk. People were pouring milk over the statues and into a bowl at their bases as offerings late in the evening. By the morning the milk would be gone. I thought it was nonsensical, but there were many educated people who believed it. It actually turned out to have some scientific basis; the statues were made of a material that absorbed liquids and did soak up some of the milk.

Unfortunately many people were taking milk their children needed and leaving it for the statue. I asked my mother if she believed the statues were drinking milk. My mother, an intelligent, sophisticated woman, said she did. Then I asked some of our other relatives, and several of them told me it was happening in their own temples. They had seen it!

That was the tradition in which we grew up. There was more to life than what we could see in front of us.

In the India of my childhood, we were exposed to a variety of religions and philosophies and taught to respect all of them. While we were Hindu, we had friends who were Muslim or Parsi and we went to school with Christians and Jews. For me the best part was that we had days off on all of the holidays. We were off for the Hindu festival of lights, Diwali; Easter; the Muslim holiday Eid. When Pope Pius XII died in 1958, we were living in Jabalpur attending St. Aloysius, a school that had classes from kindergarten through grade twelve.

Our school was closed for three days. I was nine years of age and a six-year-old friend of ours stayed with us during those days off. We spent that time running around, playing cricket and games. It was a wonderful short vacation and we really didn't want to go back to school. The night before classes resumed, we were lying in the dark when this young friend spoke up.

"Sanjiv, can I ask you a question?"

"Of course."

"What are the chances the new pope will die tomorrow?"

We were raised as Hindus, which is as much a culture and a way of life as it is a religion. Unlike the major Western religions, there is no formal structure to our worship; we don't have to go somewhere at a specific time to take part in a specific ceremony. We go to the temple when we want to. There isn't even any accepted definition of what a Hindu is or any agreement on whether Hinduism is a religion, a culture, a philosophy, or a way of life. The chief justice of the Indian Supreme Court once said, "Unlike other religions in the world the Hindu religion does not claim any one prophet; it does not worship any one god; it does not subscribe to any one dogma; it does not believe in any one philosophic concept; it does not follow any one set of religious rites or performances; in fact, it does not appear to satisfy the narrow traditional features of any religion or creed. It may broadly be described as a way of life and nothing more."

We were raised in a rich tradition, a mythology filled with hundreds of gods and warriors and moral tales, taught to us from a very young age. During summer vacations our mother would read and sing verses from the two major scriptures, the Bhagavad Gita and the Ramayana, sometimes while playing a small, hand-pumped organ called the harmonium. Many of these stories were thrillers at heart, and as she read them or sung them we could visualize the wars, the chariots, the gods and demigods, the beautiful heroines and the courageous heroes. Usually she would stop reading at a cliff-hanger: Sita has been abducted by the Great Demon and an army is being assembled to rescue her. Deepak and I would ask her to explain the story she'd read and tell us how it applied to our lives. And, of course, like almost all educated young Indians, we read the comic books that retold these stories of gods and epic battles, monsters, myths, and legends. Our mythology was also our popular entertainment. There were hundreds of these comics, and every kid read them. We read about Buddha, Ravana the Demon King, Brahma, Vishnu, Shiva, and Krishna. We read the Bhagavad Gita. We read the Mahabharata, the epic tale of India and Ganesha, the god who is the remover of all obstacles. Together with all this, we read everything from *Superman* and *Archie* to the writings of Gandhi and the works of Tolstoy.

India is a nation in which the reality of daily life and the influence of mystical forces are commonly accepted as equally true. In addition to karma, many Indians also believe in the concept of *Dharma*. In Hinduism and Buddhism, dharma has various connotations, but generally it means cheerfully fulfilling your moral and ethical duty. Doing the right thing.

In a village in the foothills of the Himalayas, there was one family that had refused the smallpox vaccine. The Indian government and World Health Organization had successfully vaccinated the rest of the population, but the head of this family, Mr. Laxman Singh, steadfastly refused. The Indian government decided for the good of the country that the Singhs had to be protected against this terrible disease, so they sent a medical team and law enforcement to their house.

"Why won't you be inoculated?" Laxman Singh was asked.

"God ordains who will be diseased and who will be healthy," he responded. "I don't want this injection. If I have to get smallpox, I'll get smallpox."

The team restrained him, forcibly pinning him to the ground. Singh fought them while screaming bloody murder, but they successfully inoculated him and then did the same to the rest of his family. When this was finally done, Laxman Singh calmly said, "Now please sit down in my hut." He went to his plot, picked some vegetables, cleaned them, and served them to the medical team along with some fresh tea his wife had made.

"What are you doing?" one team member asked. "We came into your house, violated your beliefs, and now you're treating us as guests. Why?"

"I believe it is my dharma to not get inoculated because God ordains who will be diseased and who will be healthy. You obviously believe it is your dharma to inoculate me. Now it is over and you are guests in my home. This is the least I can offer you."

This story is the best demonstration of dharma I have found. For me the word "dharma" incorporates the elements of duty, creed, and ethics. As a child I certainly never suspected that my dharma would bring me to America and Harvard Medical School, but I followed the path that was laid in front of me. My family's roots in the Indian soil can be traced back centuries; planting new ones in another part of the world was never part of my plan. But the actions of fulfilling my dharma have brought me honors in my profession and in my life. As a result, I embrace both Eastern and Western traditions. I speak American slang with an Indian accent. I've spent my life in medicine, relying on the tools of science — experimentation, discovery, testing, and reproducible results — but being brought up in my culture also left me open to other possibilities, ones that might not be scientifically proven or easily understood. I am privileged to lecture annually to as many as fifty thousand medical professionals in the United States and around the world, and each time I do so I feel I am fulfilling my dharma.

When my parents first traveled from Bombay to London, it took them about three weeks by ocean liner. Now I can get on an airplane in Boston and be anywhere in India in less than a day. When I'm there, walking the streets of what is now Mumbai, I see many of the same international chain stores that I'd passed hours earlier in Boston. Growing up, we didn't have television, but now I can turn on the set in India and watch some of the same shows I enjoy in the United States. Once, the only news we got was from All India Radio or the BBC. Now I can simply log onto Twitter, where I follow CNN, NBC, and the *New York Times,* instantly receiving the latest news from around the world. Because of advances in travel, communications, entertainment, and business, the world has gotten much smaller; the once distinct cultures of the world are blending, perhaps too much. But I've always found great comfort knowing that the core values I was taught by my family as part of our Indian culture still make an impact. They have allowed me to become a successful husband, father, grandfather, physician, and lecturer, in America.

3

Charmed Circle

Deepak

Deepak and Sanjiv win first and second prize at a fancy-dress
competition, as a snake charmer and as Lord Krishna, Jabalpur, 1958.

I MUST HAVE BEEN ABOUT THREE and a half when my earliest memories were formed. Being frightened and abandoned sticks in the mind. I was sitting alone in a city park, guarded by a magic circle drawn around me in the dirt. I watched the trees, not yet terrified, even though it was certain that, if I crept outside the circle, demons were waiting in the shadows.

The family had hired an *ayah*, or nanny, to look after me and my infant brother, Sanjiv. One of her duties was to take us to the park every afternoon so that my mother could have a few moments of peace. Was our ayah named Mary? Names are easily lost, but not feelings. In Pune, where my father was stationed (he hadn't yet traveled to London for advanced training in cardiology), the ayahs were often young girls from Goa, a part of India settled by the Portuguese, where Christianity strongly took hold.

Whomever she was, our ayah kept looking over her shoulder every time we arrived at the park. At a certain point she would plunk me down on the ground and draw a circle around me in the dirt. She would warn me not to stray—outside the circle were demons—and then disappear. With or without Sanjiv's baby carriage? That detail is lost. Half an hour later Mary would return, looking flushed and happy. Then she would take us home, reminding me to say nothing about her vanishing act. It would be our little secret. It was several years before I pieced together what was really going on.

First, the circle and the demons lurking outside it. Mary picked this up from a mythic story. By the time I was five or six, my mother began telling me tales from the two treasure troves of stories in Indian scriptures. One is the Mahabharata (*Maha* means great, and *Bharata* is the Sanskrit name for India), an epic saga of a war for succession in the ancient kingdom of Kuru. Its immortal centerpiece is the section known as the Song of the Lord, the Bhagavad Gita. If India is the most God-soaked culture on earth, it is also Gita-soaked. From childhood one hears verses taken from the conversation between Lord Krishna and the warrior Arjuna as they wait in Arjuna's war chariot for the climactic battle to begin. The Gita is a cross between the Trojan War and the New Testament, if one had to give a thumbnail description. When Krishna tells Arjuna the meaning of life, he speaks as God made flesh.

But my mother was keen on the other primary collection of stories, the Ramayana, also an epic that involves a battle, this time between Lord Rama, a handsome prince who is an incarnation of Vishnu, and Ravana, king of the demons. Any boy would be transfixed by Lord Rama's adventures. He was a great archer and had a devoted ally in a flying monkey, Hanuman, whose sole purpose in life was service to Lord Rama.

Blending the human and mythic worlds comes naturally to every child. In my family, though, Rama had a special meaning. Rama was banished into the forest for fourteen years by his father, the king; his father wasn't angry with him but was forced to keep a promise made to a jealous wife. Leaving tears behind, the prince was followed into exile by his beloved wife, Sita, and, what particularly caught my mother's attention, his younger brother, Lakshmana.

"You are Rama, and Sanjiv is Lakshmana."

No sentence was repeated to us more often, although it took awhile before I absorbed its implications: It gave Sanjiv a lower rung on the pecking order than me. Rama was as devoted to his younger brother as Lakshmana was to him. But it was clear who issued the orders and who followed them. This set a selfish precedent in the Chopra family. My mother was adding a religious overtone to our relationship, as a Christian mother might tell her sons, "You are Jesus, and your brother is Simon Peter."

I felt protective toward Sanjiv, but I didn't hesitate to play the Rama card when it suited me. One such incident backfired badly. I was ten and the family was living in Jabalpur. My brother and I were in the backyard, practicing with an air rifle; this was a cherished present my father had brought back with him from London. The target was an empty can sitting on a five-foot post.

A whim entered my head. I stood directly behind the post and told Sanjiv to fire at the can.

He hesitated.

"It's like William Tell," I said. "Go ahead. You never miss."

In school I had just learned the story of William Tell shooting an apple off his son's head with a crossbow. At the time, standing behind a post while Sanjiv shot an air rifle in my direction seemed pretty much like the same thing. When I finally convinced him to do it, Sanjiv was so nervous he accidentally hit me with a BB right in the chin. It started to bleed, but I was more worried about getting into trouble with our parents than a minor wound.

"We have to lie," I decided. "I know . . . let's go home and say that I fell while climbing a fence. Some barbed wire nicked my chin, that's all."

"A lie?" Sanjiv looked distressed. He set his face stubbornly.

"You have to. I'm Rama and you're Lakshmana."

Still distressed but less stubborn, Sanjiv reluctantly agreed to go along with my plan, and our parents accepted the concocted story. But my wound refused to heal, and days later when my grandmother felt around my chin, she made a suspicious discovery.

"There's something in there," she announced.

A rush to the military hospital revealed the BB lodged in my chin. It was removed without leaving a scar (in family legend, however, this is how I acquired the dimple in my chin). I was sent home with antibiotics and a stern lecture from Daddy about the dangers of tetanus. I was relieved to be caught, actually. This incident was one step in a development that became part of my character growing up: a hesitancy to confront authority. A desire to please my father blended into a stronger desire not to displease him. But I was just at the beginning stages of this trait.

Back to our ayah's disappearing act. She may have been a Christian, but Mary knew one of the most familiar tales about Lord Rama's beloved consort, Sita (the two are a centuries-old model for ideal romance in Indian lore). One day Rama sets out to fetch Sita a magnificent golden deer he glimpsed in the forest. He swears Lakshmana to guard Sita, telling his brother on no account to leave her side.

But when hours pass and Rama has failed to return, Sita begs Lakshmana to search for his brother. Lakshmana is torn. At first he refuses to break his vow, but when Sita accuses him of not loving Rama enough to rescue him from danger, Lakshmana agrees to seek him out. He uses his magical powers to draw a charmed circle around Sita, telling her that she will be safe as long as she never crosses outside the boundary. Any mortal or demon who tries to enter the circle will be instantly consumed in flames. With this, Lakshmana disappears into the forest.

Sita waits anxiously, and the next person she sees is a wandering monk who begs her for alms. He is a pitiful sight, and Sita is too softhearted. She steps outside the circle to put an offering in his begging bowl, and at that instant the monk is transformed, assuming his real identity as the ferocious demon Ravana. He scoops Sita up and abducts her to his island kingdom in the south, beginning yet another adventure in the saga.

My circle in the dirt was more powerful than the one Lakshmana drew; I never dared crawl outside it. But Mary's mysterious disappearances were for a mundane reason, as it turned out: a secret boyfriend she could only meet in the park when she took her little charges out.

I'm not sorry that she used a myth to train me. The anecdote has an exotic ring, and it fits into a pattern. Flash forward to 1987, at a decisive time when I was coming out of a personal crisis. My frustration with conventional medicine was turning into personal rebellion. A thriving private practice and my position as an attending physician at some prestigious hospitals were at stake. Boston medicine was willing to abandon me if I wanted to abandon it.

I had made my decision to bolt. At the time, people were glued to a sensational television series, *The Power of Myth*, where Bill Moyers was interviewing the eminent authority on world mythology, Joseph

Campbell. I was transfixed. It was like breathing air from a forgotten world. In India taxi drivers create mini shrines inside their cabs to invoke protection, complete with plastic effigies of Ganesha, a beloved god with an elephant's head and round belly. Their dashboards are plastered with photos of gurus, and long-haul trucks are emblazoned with a slogan invoking Lakshmi, goddess of prosperity: *Jai Mata Di* (Hail Mother Goddess in Punjabi). A new billionaire might place stone statues of various gods and goddesses in the foyer of his multistory mansion before having the interiors decorated by a Parisian designer. The living mythology of modern India provides local color but is also a symbol of deeply felt meaning.

Campbell was a born storyteller who could clothe legends in the fragrant romance they evoked long ago. I remembered that I was once wrapped in mythic ideas — and ideals — that had dropped away like an old skin. Romance wasn't really the point. Campbell held mythology out as a living presence, the underpinning of everyday life. Unwittingly a businessman waiting on a street corner for the light to change was a hero in disguise. His life had the potential to be a quest. Beneath the mundane details of his days, a vision was crying to be born.

I saw myself through Campbell's eyes — I think millions of other people did at the time. I was standing on the corner waiting for the light. Only no one had ever promised me that it would turn green. We were very close with the Rao family. Dr. Rajindra Rao had the first private X-ray machine in Jabalpur. His practice primarily screened people's lungs for tuberculosis, which was rampant at the time. He also made a team with my father, confirming with an X-ray what my father's acute diagnostic skills had detected in a patient. His wife, Mallika, was also a doctor and had become the leading gynecologist in Jabalpur. Their combined clinic made them quite prominent in the city. The Raos' daughter, Shobha, was nicknamed Ammu, the homey term used in South India for a little girl. Ammu was two years younger than Sanjiv. We accepted her as our sister. On the festival of *Rakhi,* a sister ties a braided bracelet around her brother's wrist, while her brother pledges to protect her. Growing up together, we performed the ritual with Ammu—and still do, with the occasional lapse (Ammu has a real brother, too, named Prasan, two years older). Today she lives outside Boston, following in her father's footsteps as a radiologist.

As the oldest, I was the leader of the pack, and I went so far as to assign each of us a military rank, with me as captain. (Looking back, I'm touched, with a twinge of guilt, at how trusting my troops were as they followed me, listening with rapt attention to my commands, which were more like iron whims.) We played every game together, and Ammu, a bit of a tomboy, even agreed to be part of the all-boy cricket team Sanjiv and I started in the neighborhood.

Ammu's father owned a prized possession that awed everyone he passed: a maroon Chevy Impala. The car was originally owned by a man who had made a fortune manufacturing *bidis,* the cheap cigarettes wrapped in the leaf of the ebony tree and tied at one end with a string. The poorest workingmen could afford bidis, and they were a constant smell in the streets. (Bidis remain a horrible health hazard, but the divine must have a sense of humor. Nisargadatta Maharaj, one of the most revered south Indian gurus, ran a bidi shop in Bombay, above which he gave sublime spiritual guidance.) Bidis had made the Impala's previous owner a multimillionaire, rich enough to import an American highway cruiser, before he tired of it.

One day, with a wedding to attend far away from Jabalpur, our two families, the Chopras and the Raos, piled into the Impala in a state of great excitement. There were eight of us, but room was made to squeeze in the Raos' jack-of-all-trades servant, who cooked for us at night and was presumed to be able to fix the car if it broke down en route. The trip from Jabalpur to Delhi was five hundred miles. We broke up the tedium by stopping off to tour the famous diamond mine in Panna. The mine is an open scar on the landscape, dug in stepwise fashion like an open-pit coal mine and filled with bright green waste water in the middle.

Dr. Rao had turned the driving over to my father. As we pulled out of town, a noisy black car spewing exhaust seemed to be following us. A turn onto the main road, and it stayed on our tail. Dacoits.

That's what my father presumed they were: local bandits. The dacoits must have suspected that anyone leaving the diamond mine in a big American car must be carrying diamonds. This was still turbulent post-independence India. Some regions were riddled with racial and religious violence. The clash between Hindus and Muslims that began in 1947 with the overnight partition of India and Pakistan had led to a vast murderous purge that claimed even Mahatma Gandhi to an assassin's bullet.

My father tried to lose the black sedan, but after a few minutes the tense situation had become a full-blown car chase. Our pursuers tried to run us into a ditch. My father gunned the engine to put some distance between us and them, but after a moment the black sedan caught up. It pulled alongside close enough that we could see three fierce men inside. But I don't remember being frightened. In fact, Sanjiv and I were thrilled.

A word about bandits and their peculiar status in India. Any attempt to make daily life orderly seems to fail there. If you send your best dress shirt to the dry cleaner's and there is a spot on one sleeve, they may helpfully cut both sleeves off (as happened to an outraged American friend a few years ago). Or they might use kerosene instead of dry-cleaning fluid, a smell that never quite goes away. You learn to put tape over the postage when you mail a letter, to discourage postal workers from stealing the stamps and discarding your letter. In a third-class hotel a family may tire of waiting for their dinner dishes to be taken away — presuming that a large family has been sleeping in one room in the same bed — so why not store the dirty crockery in a dresser drawer? The next guest may be a bit surprised to discover them there when he opens the drawer (this happened to another visiting friend), but not all that much. Behind the apparent chaos, every social distinction is known down to the finest detail.

The hidden order that rules India is a way to preserve everyday life. There are dividing lines everywhere. People are silently aware of caste, even now, decades after it became illegal to discriminate on the basis of caste. A person's name instantly reveals where he was born and usually the dharma, or family occupation, he follows. By the time you have heard a stranger's name, caught his accent, and assessed his dialect and vocabulary, perhaps a minute has passed, but in that minute was revealed a condensed autobiography—and with it a tightly bound package of prejudices. Modernism threw people together who never wanted to breathe the same air. They had to sit together in tight railway coaches, and no country packs its populace onto railways like India. The strict old rules, such as the one requiring a Brahmin from the priest caste to go home and bathe if the shadow of an untouchable crossed his path, were no longer practical. Was it really viable, under British rule, for a person born into an upper caste to throw out all the food in the house and clean it from top to bottom after a foreigner came to call?

India's messy dance between chaos and order is crystallized in the dacoit. Between the early Thirties and mid-Fifties, a notorious bandit named Man Singh far outdid any legendary American gangster like John Dillinger. In his whole career Dillinger was credited with robbing two dozen banks and four police stations, in the course of which he actually killed only one person, a policeman. Man Singh committed more than eleven hundred armed robberies and killed 185 people, not counting numerous kidnappings for ransom and shootouts with the law—he killed thirty-two policemen.

Singh was born in the Chambal Valley in the central state of Madhya Pradesh, in terrain crisscrossed with deep winding ravines and scrub forest—perfect hiding places. Singh occupied a secure social standing where he lived; he was never turned in despite the sizable reward on his head. He was a provider. His gang consisted of his extended family, more than a dozen brothers and nephews, and when he spoke in public, in brazen defiance of his outlaw status, Singh was humble and respectful. After he was gunned down in 1955 by Gurkha soldiers as he sat under a banyan tree with his son, a temple was erected in his honor. Dacoits worship at this shrine today, it is said, praying to be kept safe on their next robbery.

A complicated tale, as interwoven with contradictions as the whole society, or human nature. Outlaws in every culture are romanticized, but where else outside India do they have their own temple? Where else could the most famous female dacoit, Phoolan Devi, surrender to police with ten thousand onlookers cheering as she placed her rifle down before a picture of Gandhi? (After serving her prison sentence, the "Bandit Queen of India" was elected to Parliament, only to be gunned down in front of her house in New Delhi before she turned forty. My good friend, the director Shekhar Kapur, rose to international fame with his 1994 film, *Bandit Queen*. It contained a graphic scene of sexual assault on the young Phoolan Devi that one outraged critic called "the Indian rape trick," but this scene underscored why she became a kind of feminist martyr.)

We sigh about the shortcomings of human nature; we all make peace with our personal demons. In India the demons are celebrated as necessary. Creation is the play of light and dark, and both are divine — even Ravana, king of the demons, pleads for a way to become enlightened after he is defeated by Lord Rama. Lord Rama doesn't cast Ravana down to hell; he grants him his wish. In scripture there is the tale of a temple thief who reaches final liberation, or moksha, immediately after stealing an oil lamp. Spiritually, to be a criminal is a form of suffering, so this was the last gesture of atonement needed before Shiva, lord of spiritual seekers, was satisfied that the thief deserved enlightenment. The saint today was a sinner yesterday, playing out thousands of lifetimes of karma. The secret to hidden order is to enforce the rules of right and wrong while secretly knowing that they merge into the same thing in the end, stepping stones to eternal grace.

Arriving in India, a visitor has no choice but either/or. Either chaos is your enemy or your friend. Escape is impossible. Going crazy is an immediate prospect.

Back in the maroon Impala the dacoits following us grew more serious. They pulled up alongside and tried to push us off the road. Did my father now ruefully recall the warnings not to drive after dark on ill-made two-lane roads? He probably wasn't even rattled. He and Dr. Rao were both doctors: confident, educated men who were used to handling emergencies.

My mother and Mrs. Rao began praying for our safety. They knew that the worst of these rural bandits carried guns, which were highly unusual in India at that time. Sanjiv and I knew to keep our excitement to ourselves. Ammu took her cue from us. We raced down the road until we reached a turnoff to the next sizable town. At the last minute my father swerved sharply onto the dirt track that led off the main road. The dacoits were going too fast to make the turn. By the time they slowed down and backtracked, my father had found the local police station, and our pursuers took off. I have no idea how long the chase actually lasted; it exists in the continuous loop that memory makes out of our greatest thrills, worst traumas, and moments of unbearable suspense.

My brother and I shared a childhood that knitted us together while shaping two very different people. Our paths showed signs of diverging quite early on. I was always more interested in my studies than Sanjiv, while he excelled as an athlete. Perhaps because of that there was no sibling rivalry. Our personalities blended smoothly on the cricket team that we formed in Jabalpur.

At the height of empire there was immense stoic suffering among the British, who insisted in maintaining the customs from back home, most fatally in how they dressed. Thick wool uniforms on the parade ground made no sense in the Raj under a sun that made soldiers drop in their tracks. No adequate treatment for tropical diseases existed. Colonialists died of typhoid and typhus as frequently as the natives they looked down on as primitives and pagans. The only relief from hellish heat was to send the women and children up to the hill stations in the north, close to the foothills of the Himalayas. These cool oases were homesick duplicates of an English village: Victorian houses adorned with gingerbread trim for parrots and monkeys to perch on and screech through the night.

Such surreal anomalies persisted, as in the heavy flannels that Indian cricket players wore unself-consciously in the grueling sun. Sanjiv and I grew a passion for the game very early. After watching a match between a visiting team from the West Indies and our state team from Madhya Pradesh, I decided that we should organize a neighborhood team. I appointed myself captain and made Sanjiv vice captain. We recruited the children of servants and orderlies. (Did they look on us as no different from the British who used to order their parents about? If so, love of the game silenced their resentment.) We dug up a mountain of red sand behind our house to create a cricket pitch and played against other kids' teams in town.

Sports are living proof of paradise for boys that age, a taste of delightful freedom recollected in nostalgia, when sunshine was unending.

While I was the captain, our team depended on Sanjiv to win matches. In the game of cricket, a century (scoring one hundred runs in a single inning) is considered a significant achievement. Sanjiv once scored two hundred in an innings—a double century. He was held in awe by all of us.

I was a good athlete, too, just not on a par with my brother. But I was more reckless about taking risks to win. One incident in particular was my undoing. We were attending a private boys' school run by Irish Christian Brothers. (In the hopes of converting their students to Christianity, the Christian Brothers had developed a prestigious school system across India that ranked among the best in the country.) One particular brother had ordered me not to spin the ball outside the leg stump when I pitched, a throw similar to a curve ball in baseball that is a difficult thing to do correctly. If you didn't do it right, the cricketer at bat would hit it out of the park. Watching the match from a distance, my teacher shouted at me not to bowl outside the stump. But I was feeling cocky, and I refused to be intimidated. I knew that, if I did it right, I would get the batsman out.

The first two tries were a disaster: The cricketer hit it out of the park (which isn't the equivalent of a home run since he stays at bat). The shouted orders from the sidelines, which were growing more furious, only made me more determined. It was foolhardy to experiment in the middle of a match, but fortune smiled on me. The third time, I got him out. I'd proven that I could do what I had believed I could. Unfortunately my teacher didn't see it that way. During a break he took me to the dorm, ordered me to lower my pants, and caned me for refusing to take orders. In India an important remnant of British rule was absolute respect for authority, with a humiliating dose of corporal punishment if you flouted that authority. The lesson? Adhering to the rules is more important than the result. It was what made the system work.

I've already mentioned that a character trait was building invisibly inside me around authority. I saw myself trying to please authority but with a streak of resentment. I cannot say if being caned made the trait stronger or not. A rebel wasn't created overnight. The mixture of influences in the psyche is too subtle to tease apart.

But years later, when I was serving a residency in Boston, I preferred angry rebellion to the prospect of another dose of humiliation. As a young doctor in his twenties, a fellowship placed me with one of the leading endocrinologists in the country. My passion for study hadn't abated. I had already finished one two-year residency and passed the boards in internal medicine. At that time, in the early Seventies, a resident needed a good fellowship just to make ends meet, and I had a young family to support. But I wasn't happy in my work. My supervisor was overbearing, and all my time was spent in his laboratory, either injecting rats with iodine or dissecting them to see how the iodine had affected them.

Endocrinology, which is the study of the hormones secreted by the endocrine system, is a precise, technical specialty. I was more enthusiastic about seeing patients than toiling in the lab, but I was still fascinated by the detective work. Forty years later, the investigation of the three hormones secreted by the thyroid gland seems very basic, but at the time the fact that my supervisor was one of the pioneers in studying the Reverse T3 hormone was big news. We worked in an atmosphere of tense one-upmanship, competing with other research teams in the field — the thyroid was supposed to be our whole world.

I was an immigrant who had embraced Boston medicine for its prestige and potential, but associations with India swirled around me. A colleague from medical school back home, coincidentally named Inder Chopra, had played a major role in identifying Reverse

T3. And the rat is sacred to the god Ganesha. Not that a shred of the sacred remains when you have a dissecting scalpel in hand. I didn't miss its absence, back then.

My discontent came to a head during a routine staff meeting. My supervisor quizzed me on a technical detail in front of the group: "How many milligrams of iodine did Milne and Greer inject into the rats in their 1959 paper?" This referred to some seminal experimental work, but I answered offhandedly, because he didn't really want the information, only to put me on the spot.

"Maybe two-point-one milligrams. I'll look it up."

"This is something you should have in your head," he barked, irritated. Everyone in the room grew quiet.

I got up, walked over to him, and dumped a bulky file of papers on him.

"Now you have it in your head," I said, and walked out.

My supervisor followed me into the parking lot. I was agitated, fumbling to start my beat-up Volkswagen Beetle, the signature vehicle of struggling young professionals. He leaned in, speaking with studied control to disguise his anger.

"Don't," he warned. "You're throwing away your whole career. I can make that happen."

Which was quite true. The word would go out, and with his disapproval I had no future in endocrinology. But in my mind I wasn't walking away from a career. I was standing up to someone who had tried to humiliate me in front of the group. My impulsive rebellion was instinctive and yet very unlike me. At such a precipitous turning point, no one, I think, reaches inside to find a store of memories that build to that moment. We construct reasons for our behavior after the fact, adding to the story of our lives arbitrarily. But as erratic as our reasons may be as we tick them off in our heads, they are always self-serving. The ego plunges impulsively into a situation, after which the shadowy part of the psyche begins to rise to the surface, bringing with it those insecure things we call second thoughts: guilt, regret, reliving the past, self-recrimination, panic, alarm about the future. The ego has to regroup around these subtle but persistent attackers.

A process starts that no one has control over, negotiating between all the psychic forces that make demands upon us. Some people are self-reflective; they engage consciously in the whole process and meet it head on. Most people do the reverse. They try to distract themselves and manage to escape the underground war going on inside them — except for the inescapable late-night hours when sleep won't come and the shadows of the mind roam without check.

I belonged in the second camp. I managed to start the VW and left him standing there in the hospital parking lot, fuming and vindictive. Word did go out, and I faced the prospect of having no job except for any moonlighting work that might come my way, the lowest paying drudgery in Boston medicine. Pain would follow. I knew this less than five minutes down the road. It made me stop off at a bar before going home to break the devastating news to Rita.

What mystified me was the complete turnaround I had just made. Everything in my upbringing had instilled a respect for authority: the charmed circle, the duty of Rama to protect his younger brother, the caning after the cricket match. The hardest traits to change are the ones that have seeped into us so thoroughly they become a part of us. The fact that you have absorbed a trait doesn't make it normal, but even the most insidious aspects of the mind do feel normal; that's what makes them insidious.

In religion there's an old saw: No one is more dangerous to the faith than an apostate. Boston medicine was the true faith. I had no intention of renouncing it. If you had questioned me the day before I dumped a file on an eminent doctor's head, I would have sworn allegiance. Frankly I had no reason to change sides, not rationally. You don't walk away from a church when there is no other church to go to. But the only way to see if there are demons lurking outside the circle is to crawl over the boundary that protects you. This was the real start of a revelatory life. I can't take credit for any of the revelations, but a hidden force inside me was invisibly preparing the way.

4

Lucky Sari

Sanjiv

Chopra brothers with their childhood friends, Ammu Sequeira
and Prasan Rao, on their way to school, Jabalpur, 1956.

MY PATERNAL GRANDMOTHER was an uneducated, rather docile woman, but she was also very wise, and feisty when necessary. While she never graduated from high school, she taught us that education doesn't come just from books. My father often told Deepak and me a memorable story: One afternoon, when he was five years old, he was in the kitchen having lunch with his younger brother and his younger brother's best friend, Ilyas, a Muslim.

In their house, the kitchen sat right next to the prayer room. Unexpectedly a local priest, a pundit as they were called, dropped by to visit, as he often did. When this pundit saw Ilyas in the kitchen, he was outraged.

"You pretend to be very religious," he told my grandmother, "yet you have a Muslim boy sitting in your kitchen, right next to the Hindu gods and goddesses. God will never forgive you."

Deepak and I never heard my grandmother raise her voice, but apparently she did that time. At least that's the way our father told the story.

"How dare you talk to me like that," she said. "Ilyas is my son's friend, so he is like my son. What is all this Hindu-Muslim business? My God doesn't know about that. Get out of my house right now and take your God with you. And never, ever enter this house again." And she threw him out.

While my father taught us the value of education and made sure we attended the best possible British schools, it was the women in our family who taught us to acknowledge and appreciate our spiritual side and who showed us the meaning of respect and compassion. My paternal grandmother was half-Sikh and taught us the values of that religion. To explain Sikhism she would tell us stories of its founder, Guru Nanak.

One day Guru Nanak was taking a nap on a cart. A Muslim priest noticed his feet were pointing directly toward a mosque. He angrily shook him awake.

"How dare you," the priest scolded him. "You've fallen asleep with your feet pointing to Allah. Blasphemy!"

"Please forgive me, learned man," Guru Nanak responded gently. "I apologize for my sin. Please, point my feet to where Allah is not."

With stories like this one, our father's mother taught us the dangers of believing that one god, any particular god, is somehow superior to other gods, which is the basis of respect for all beliefs. It was her way of reminding Deepak and me to keep our minds open to the values of other people.

That was reinforced by my mother, of course, who lived her life believing that no one human being was better than another. She steadfastly refused to subscribe to the caste system. My mother simply had faith. There really isn't any other way of describing her, although this story comes pretty close. In 1957 my parents were living in Jabalpur, and independent India's first prime minister, Jawaharlal Nehru, was coming to town to reopen a weapons factory that would now be building Mercedes-Benz trucks for the army.

Most Americans are aware of the contributions of Gandhi, who led a great revolution by practicing passive resistance, but in India Nehru was equally beloved. Together they had led India out of British servitude. Nehru was an extraordinarily charismatic man and a brilliant leader who carefully plotted the path that has led to modern India. India today is a result of his vision. For many in India, he was as much George Washington as he was Martin Luther King Jr.

Weeks before his arrival in Jabalpur, people began making preparations for a momentous greeting. My mother worried constantly about which sari she would wear for this occasion. My father couldn't understand the fuss.

"What difference does it make?" he asked. "There will be millions of people in the streets. He's not going to notice your sari." But she insisted on buying a new sari anyway.

"He's going to notice me," she said. "He's going to acknowledge me." Of course that wasn't going to happen. Nehru didn't know my mother. But she had faith it would happen.

Nehru's parade route took him past our house on Narbada Road. At four thirty in the morning, we were all dressed up and standing in the street. My father was wearing his army uniform, all his medals shined. Deepak and I wore our school jackets and ties. And my mother was wearing her new sari. By 7:00 a.m., hundreds of thousands of people lined the road, and the police had erected barriers to hold them back. We waited a long time, but suddenly a small convoy came around the corner. The prime minister was standing in the back of a jeep, waving casually to everyone. The crowd was screaming, "Long live Nehru! Long live Nehru!"

As Nehru's jeep came slowly down the street the roar grew deafening. The people all around us were screaming, shouting, reaching out to touch him; he continued waving. But as his jeep passed in front of us, Nehru suddenly took the rose he always wore from his lapel and tossed it almost directly in front of my mother. She picked it up and looked at my father.

"What did I tell you?"

We went back into the house and placed that rose in a vase and then took everything else out of that room. For three weeks people came to our house from all over the city just to see the rose that Mr. Nehru had given to Mrs. Chopra. At the end of that time, she threw a party and gave everyone in attendance a rose petal. For some people it became a family heirloom to be handed down from generation to generation.

But the part that stays with me is that my mother never doubted for an instant that the prime minister was going to acknowledge her. As irrational as it seemed, she had faith.

There was at least one situation in which her faith went a little too far. My mother was a cricket fan. In 1959 the powerful Australian team came to India to play a weak Indian team. International cricket matches were extremely important in India. The whole country would come to a grinding halt — people would skip work, children would stay home from school, the traffic would disappear from the streets. Nobody gave India much of a chance to win this match. But in what is still known as the Miracle at Kanpur, an aging cricketer named Jasu Patel became a national legend by taking an extraordinary nine wickets out of ten. That would be like hitting four home runs — in one inning. My mother was sitting by the radio listening to the match on All India Radio. She happened to be wearing a favorite sari that day, as did many sports fans, because she was convinced that what she was wearing was good luck. So for the next forty years, every time India played an international cricket match she wore that sari. The fact that India lost the majority of those matches didn't bother her. When Deepak and I teased her about it, she was unperturbed.

"Say what you want. I'm still going to wear that sari." And so she did. Even the dry cleaner would know when an international cricket match was in the offing.

Our mother demonstrated her compassion every day with the patients who came to my father's medical office in our home. She would greet them at the door herself.

"How did you come?" she would ask.

The answers ranged from chauffeured car to a walk of many miles: "We heard of Dr. Chopra in our village. We came by bus so he can make the diagnosis."

Sometimes, rather than charging them anything she would give them twenty rupees for their return fare.

The story that best exemplifies the values that I was taught by my mother actually took place after Deepak and I had left home to become doctors ourselves. But her actions in this situation were no different than they had been at any time while we were growing up. Our parents were living in a house they had built in an area of Delhi called Defence Colony. About nine o'clock in the evening, their cook, Shanti, was placing food on the table when the doorbell rang. That wasn't at all unusual in and of itself — patients often came by the house at night.

Shanti went to answer the door, and a minute later my parents heard unusual sounds. Suddenly three young men pushed Shanti into the dining room, covered in blood from a cut on his head. All three of the intruders had knives, and one of them also had a gun. They started screaming at my parents, making all kinds of threats. My mother stood up to them.

"I know what you want," she said. "Money and jewelry. We'll give you whatever we have in the house. Your need seems to be greater than ours. Here you are." She took off the jewelry she was wearing and handed it to them.

"That's not enough," the leader yelled. He demanded the keys to the safe and forced them into the bedroom.

My mother handed him the keys and began helping him open it, when she realized one of the robbers was still beating Shanti. That was when she finally got angry.

"Stop that!" she screamed at him. "He has two young children. If you want to kill someone, kill my husband and me. We've had a good life and our children are well settled. But don't you dare beat this young man. He's done nothing to you and we're giving you what you want."

The thieves looked at one another, unsure what to do. They stopped beating Shanti. Suddenly the leader tossed the earrings my mother had given him onto the bed, then bent down and touched my mother's feet, a gesture of great respect for older people and a way of asking for their blessing.

"I forgive you," my mother said, "and I hope you mend your ways."

"You have been very kind," he said. "It doesn't seem right for us to take everything. Your face looks bare without your earrings." He turned to the other thieves. "And I recognize this man. He's the doctor who treated my father seven years ago. Let's go."

They tied up my parents and Shanti and locked them in a bathroom. Before leaving, however, the leader of the gang warned them not to identify them to the police, threatening to come back to harm them if they did. My mother gave him her word she would not.

My mother, who was then in her fifties, untied my father's ropes with her teeth and then called the police. The robbers were clumsy and left several clues, including their fingerprints, and were quickly arrested. But when my mother was told that to recover her jewelry she would have to pick the robbers out of a lineup, she refused, explaining that she had made a pledge and her word was more important to her than jewelry.

A few months later the leader escaped from prison and was killed in a fight with the police.

My mother also tended to our manners, teaching us proper behavior. These lessons I remember very well. She drilled into Deepak and me that when we were offered anything we were never to simply take it; we had to be offered something three times before accepting. Three times — she was very clear about that.

My favorite dessert was a sweet called *Rasgulla*. When I was five years old, my family was having dinner at my uncle's house, and my aunt offered me rasgulla. I remembered my lesson.

"No, thank you," I said. That was one.

"Come on," she said. "Don't you like sweets?"

"No, thank you," I repeated. "I'm okay." That's two.

But then, instead of offering it to me for a third time, she moved on to the next person. Wait a second.

"Auntie," I called out. "Can you please come back and offer it one more time?"

Growing up, Deepak and I had very different interests. Deepak was always more scholarly than I was; I was the better athlete. While he was reading newspapers and books and grappling with philosophical questions, I was playing cricket, soccer, field hockey, or table tennis, or I was running marathons, pole vaulting, and high jumping; if there was a competition I wanted to be part of it, even if it was just throwing darts. In fact, my best friend and I would often race each other — Deepak's job was to blow the whistle to start the race and to time us.

So while Deepak was winning academic honors, I was filling a trunk with athletic trophies. Deepak worried constantly that I wasn't studying enough or finishing my work. He would even complain to our mother: "Sanjiv hasn't done his homework and he won't come in the house." Let him play, she would say, let him play.

Like my brother, I have a strong visual memory, and in India we were taught by rote. A lot of schoolwork simply required learning to repeat what was on the page, and that was never difficult for me. I was always able to get my work done and get good grades. I had discipline; I was focused and organized. From a young age, I set goals and worked until I had accomplished them.

That said, my mind occasionally wandered at school. If our teachers caught us doing that, they would rap us on the knuckles with a ruler. They said they were disciplining us for our own good. Admittedly I was more than once the subject of their benevolence.

Of course, without television, computers, or video games we had few distractions. In fact, when I was ten years old I won an award in school, and the prize was a book about American television. I had never seen television but I loved that book. I just stared at the black-and-white photographs of this box with people in it for hours. It was amazing to me. I learned about television stars like Jack Benny and Milton Berle. While Deepak was reading about politics and philosophy, I became fascinated by this amazing device.

Growing up, Deepak did things the way they were supposed to be done. Perhaps this was because he was my older brother and thus felt a greater degree of responsibility. Me? I was always poking at things and breaking the rules. I was certainly more of a free spirit than my brother ever was.

But it was safe for me to be that way—I knew that Deepak was there looking out for me.

5

Miracles in Hiding

Deepak

Deepak self-portrait, 1961. He was fourteen years old when he won an essay competition for "The Nature of Time" at St. Columba's.

MIRACLES ARE SLIPPERY. We all want them to exist, but if they did, it would turn the ordinary world upside down. Imagine airplanes needing a miracle to stay aloft in the sky. Every passenger would be praying, not just the ones with an extreme fear of flying. A safe landing would display the grace of God; a disastrous crash the wrath of God. It's much safer to know that airplanes fly because of a principle in physics, Bernoulli's principle, which allows flowing air to lift a wing. Millions of people trust airplanes to work without understanding Bernoulli's principle, because they know that science is more reliable than faith. Miracles are flashy, but you wouldn't bet your life on one at the airport.

When I was growing up in India, this whole scheme of the rational and predictable hadn't yet taken hold. As wobbly as miracles are considered in the West, they were cherished in the East. A miracle didn't defy the laws of physics or make everything uncertain. It proved the existence of God (which no one doubted anyway). More than that, a miracle justified the entire world of my ancestors. In their reality God had a finger in every pie. That fact was deeply reassuring. God saw you. He cared for your existence, and the fact that miracles were so slippery — they always happened to someone you didn't know or someone who had been conveniently dead for several hundred years — only added to the glory of a divine mystery.

My father, as a Western-trained physician, was one of those who shredded the mystery. He was surrounded by people who clung to a miraculous reality. One of his brothers, a traveling salesman for field hockey equipment, was fond of visiting every holy man he could find. He firmly believed that simply sitting in the presence of a saint, as all holy men were commonly called, brought him closer to God. In my father's eyes this behavior was a holdover from the old, superstitious India that needed to disappear. By implication he wasn't just embarrassed when poor villagers revered him. They were displaying ignorance about modern medicine, something he spent his life trying to wipe out.

But there were still things to marvel at, even revere, in my father's rational scheme. One evening, when I was seven, he came home from work in a state of barely suppressed excitement. I think this was the first time I ever saw him break out of his normal reserve.

"Quickly, son. Wash your face, straighten your clothes. We leave in two minutes."

By the time I was ready, my father was straddling his bicycle outside.

"Come. Hurry!"

He tapped the handlebars, and I hopped on. We rushed into the twilight together, leaving my mother and four-year-old Sanjiv at home — he was too young for this adventure, whatever it was, and she had to take care of him. Daddy pedaled furiously through the balmy streets of Pune, refusing to tell me where we were going.

"You'll see. Just hold on."

Together his secrecy and excitement made my imagination run away with me, or would have if I didn't have to focus on not pitching off the handlebars as he veered around corners. We weaved through the same assortment of vehicles and animals you still find outside the main cities: cars, motorbikes, scooter rickshaws, other cyclists, and bullock carts. Only in my childhood, there were fewer cars and more carts. We raced through the city's bazaars, and in my mind I remember — adding to the romance of our adventure — that I begged Daddy to stop and let me watch a snake charmer by the side of the road. He was about to pit a cobra against a mongoose in a deadly fight.

But memory plays tricks after so many years. I was a seven-year-old boy on an adrenaline high who had seen more than his share of those fatal combats. It is unlikely that a snake charmer would have been performing after dark on those dimly lit streets.

The crowd that awaited us wasn't imaginary, though. It was just disappointing: a large group of properly dressed men sitting in an assembly hall. No wives or children. My father found two of the last remaining chairs and greeted a few of the other men. We were in the British army barracks where he worked. The hall was part of the small brick building known as the MI Room (short for military incidents), where the doctors treated every form of illness and injury.

My one remaining hope was that I had been hauled off into the night to witness a medical monstrosity. Instead, an English gentleman in a frock coat and spectacles mounted the stage to loud applause. He bowed slightly, then began to lecture with fuzzy slides projected on a makeshift screen, his voice proper and dull. The slides showed lots of white dots with halos around them.

My father was enraptured. I was an overstimulated seven-year-old. I quickly fell asleep leaning against my father's warm side.

Daddy was still exuberant when he woke me up and perched me back on the handlebars. We pedaled home slowly, his hand on my shoulder to steady me.

"Do you know who that was?" he asked. "He's Fleming, the man who discovered penicillin."

"Where is Penicillin?" It sounded farther away than Pondicherry or even London.

To which my father laughed. He told me the story of the little white dots and the lives saved because of the curative powers of common bread mold. For centuries, he explained, moldy loaves of bread had been thrown away without anyone suspecting that a miracle lay hidden inside the fuzzy green growth that made the bread unfit to eat. It was a boon to humanity that Sir Alexander Fleming had paused to look more closely instead of throwing out some petri dishes of bacteria that had been "ruined" by the same mold.

Everyone agrees that miracles lie hidden. A yogi meditates in a remote Himalayan cave; penicillin sat under our very noses. The question is: What brings the miracles to light? There seem to be only two choices. Either the grace of God reveals miracles, or the rational mind uncovers them by going deeper into the construct of the physical world. Strangely as I grew older, I seemed to belong to the small camp that rejected either/or. Couldn't a miracle be right under our noses, woven into the fabric of nature, and still be evidence of God?

Imagine a world where Sir Alexander Fleming shows slides of a levitating yogi with a halo around him. That would come very close to my ideal.

I never heard any complaints from my father about the superstition that was rife in his own family. He avoided the irrational with polite silence and was blind to anything that could not be explained by science. All around him, however, human nature took its course, falling in love with anything that was as irrational and inexplicable as possible. A special focus of our credulity — I was part of the irrational pack for a long time — was my uncle Tilak, who was five years younger than my father.

At the age of four Tilak began to have vivid memories of a past life. He described every aspect in detail, including where he had lived and the names of his family. Such an event is not uncommon in India. (In fact, decades later, researchers at the University of Virginia, beginning in 1989 under Dr. Ian Stevenson, would find that it isn't uncommon anywhere in the world. Hundreds of children, usually between the ages of two and eight, have been documented as having detailed recollections of a previous lifetime.) My father's family, who already considered Tilak an unusual child, decided to investigate his new memories. As a matter of course, this meant consulting an astrologer.

A neighborhood astrologer can be brought in to tell a young girl the most propitious day for her wedding or to predict whether a boy will travel abroad (a calamitous turn of events in traditional Indian society). But there is a special class of astrologers who specialize in past lives, known as Bhrigu readers. Here we can't go in for a penny without going in for a pound, because Bhrigu comes from the pure world of miracles. When you consult a Bhrigu reader, he doesn't draw up your astrology chart himself. Instead, he finds the exact chart that was *already* written for you centuries, even millennia, ago. In essence, an astrologer who lived at the time of Shakespeare or even Jesus, perhaps, knew that you were going to arrive for a Bhrigu reading on a certain day in the future, and to show his absolute mastery of time and fortune, prepared a chart to answer the very questions you came to ask.

How this art came to pass carries us into the epoch of myths. When the god Brahma created the world, he had seven wish-born sons, who sprang into existence from his mind. The world was conceived in wisdom, and these primal rishis, or seers, were sent to guide newborn humanity. One day the wisest of these early humans gathered together at a great religious festival. They soon fell into dispute over which of the three gods — Brahma, Vishnu, or Shiva — should be worshipped as the greatest. To settle the argument, Bhrigu was sent to ask the gods themselves.

First he arrived at the dwelling place of Brahma, his father. But when he asked his question, Brahma waved him away impatiently, saying, "I'm busy creating the world. I have no time for you."

Next Bhrigu went to the abode of Shiva, who was even more dismissive and arrogant. "I'm busy destroying creation as quickly as it is being made," he said. "I have no time for you."

At the third dwelling place, when he called on Vishnu, Bhrigu found the god sleeping on his side with his consort, Lakshmi, at his feet. Impulsively Bhrigu kicked Vishnu in the chest to wake him up. It was a hard kick that left an imprint still to be seen on images of the god. Vishnu sat up, rubbing his chest.

"Are you hurt, my dear Bhrigu, from kicking me?" Vishnu asked. "I am strong enough to sustain any wound, but you are not."

This show of compassion rather than arrogance immediately made Bhrigu decide that Vishnu, the god who sustains the cosmos, was more powerful than the gods who create and destroy it. But before he could leave, Lakshmi confronted him, indignant that anyone should injure her husband. On the spot she cursed Bhrigu such that he would forget his immortal knowledge. Not to be trifled with, Bhrigu cursed her back.

"You, Lakshmi, are the goddess of prosperity, but from this day forward you will never be able to stay with any man." Which is why no human can count on good fortune his entire life.

This myth comes with a tale that applies to the ability of astrologers to foretell the future. When he returned home, Bhrigu despaired of losing his knowledge. So his devoted son Shukra devised a secret plan. When his father went into deep samadhi, the state of meditation that reaches pure awareness, Shukra would whisper the name of one of his friends in Bhrigu's ear. At that moment Bhrigu would see and reveal that friend's entire span of births and deaths, which were secretly written down by Shukra. One after another the son received the charts of all his friends, and they went on to acquire deep knowledge, becoming the first astrologers in the line of Bhrigu. Their power to foretell the life of someone born far in the future had a divine source. (To most Indians the son Shukra is far better known than the father. His name refers to a brilliant light and became the Indian name of the planet Venus.)

My father's family needed to call upon that power to see if Tilak's memories of his past lifetime were correct. They traveled to the *sthan*, or seat, of Bhrigu in Hoshiarpur, in the far northeast corner of Punjab, where the charts were stored. There the readers confirmed that the boy was right: His chart gave the same village that he had seen and the same names of family members. The chart held some darker aspects, too. Tilak, it predicted, would wander between being a man and a woman. He would marry but never have children, and then he would die prematurely, in his fifties.

All of this happened when my father was only eight or nine, so he had only the vaguest memory of the trip to the Bhrigu readers. But when I was young I thought that Tilak was the strangest of my uncles. He had an effeminate body, with wide hips and a swinging gait; beneath his shirt one definitely saw breasts. Then it happened that he got married but had no children, and although they had been forewarned, my father's family was shocked to learn that poor Tilak had died suddenly from unknown causes. He was only in his midfifties.

I had my doubts about becoming a doctor, and I almost didn't. My father underwent a similar crisis when he was young. He came from a conservative religious family. From an early age he became accustomed, as so many Indians are, to having his parents make decisions for him. Sometimes the decisions were trivial. He wasn't allowed to go to the cinema, for instance, unless the film had a religious theme. But big decisions were also taken out of his hands. My grandmother took credit for fixing his course in life. Rather than fighting against his doubts, she said, "I agree. The course is long. I don't expect you want to work that hard anyway."

If this was intended to activate a young man's contrary streak, or a Chopra family trait for never doing what we're told, the tactic worked. After serving in World War I, my grandfather had taken his pension and retired to a piece of land outside Rawalpindi, the city in Pakistan now called Islamabad. The only medical school in a wide range was King Edward Medical College in Lahore. My father earned his degree there and became the breadwinner for his family until his younger brothers could finish college in Rawalpindi.

There was no question at any point that my father would take an interest in the traditional medicine of India, *Ayurveda,* even though in every part of the country it was Ayurvedic medicine that people relied upon. This brings us to a juncture that is still uncomfortable for an India rushing to overcome impoverishment and take a place at the world's banquet table. Does modernism demand the extinction of ancient ways? It's an exhausting dilemma. At the height of empire, Britain's confidence in itself was totally unnerving to the people being colonized. Since traditional India had been toppled with barely a few skirmishes, opening its gates to the East India Company without a struggle, that must prove that destiny favored the West. So the thinking went. God himself smiled on the invaders, which was enormously deflating for a society like India that was immersed in God.

The defeat of traditional culture spread with insidious thoroughness. The most honored spiritual texts, like the Bhagavad Gita, became neglected, not among ordinary people or the priests, but among the educated, forward-thinking classes who fell under the sway of the West. There was even a religious revival along Christian lines, where Hindus went to church thinking that if the Christians could conquer India, Jesus must have more *Shakti* — divine power — than the goddess Shakti herself. In these churches the chanting and rituals of Hinduism merged strangely with proper Victorian Anglican services.

By then the tide of modernism was unstoppable. Educated Indians were as convinced as the colonialists that tradition equaled ignorance and superstition. Most Westerners do not grasp what a shock it was when Gandhi, who had begun his career as a lawyer in South Africa, threw off his thick tweed suit and starched collars to dress in the traditional wrapped skirt, the *dhoti,* worn by common people. By a stroke of irony, when Gandhi's generation was growing up, they had so little traditional knowledge that they first read the Gita in English translations, and the India Congress Party, which eventually succeeded in liberating the country, was founded under the aegis of an Englishwoman named Annie Besant. It wasn't until foreigners fell in love with ancient India that permission was given for a select number of native Indians to look back over their shoulder.

They were filled with awe when they did, and a newfound sense of self-respect. But Gandhi's philosophy of turning back the clock entirely, as symbolized by the hand-driven spinning wheel he sat beside and spun on (the same wheel later became the central emblem of the national flag) was clearly hopeless idealism. To raise your station in life meant becoming Westernized, and my father's generation, while adoring Gandhi and freedom, didn't turn their sights backward.

Krishan Chopra would be selfless and generous to his patients. He would accept responsibility for the care of an entire community and not ask to be paid beyond his army salary. That much seems un-Western in the extreme. But there was no science in Ayurveda, and the village *vaidyas* handing out folk remedies and homespun advice were not real physicians in his eyes. Like prehistoric crocodiles floating lazily in the river and bellowing to their mates at night, the vaidyas were relics who survived because India measures change in epochs, not decades. (Did it irritate him that my grandmother on my mother's side had faith in homeopathic remedies or that she dressed our childhood cuts and scrapes with herbal compounds? If so, he remained quietly tolerant. On both sides my grandparents turned to anyone at hand, including vaidyas and faith healers, when they needed healing.)

My father was so devoted to the science that Fleming and the great microbe hunters represented that it didn't occur to me that rebellion might have motivated him, too. His father, whom everyone called Bau-ji, was a disciplined soldier and a disciplinarian inside his family. My grandmother bore him fourteen children, although only eight survived. He expected his offspring to walk, talk, eat, and act as he did. This must have been oppressive for my father. But Bau-ji also provided them with the opportunity for an education. Besides my father, my two Bombay uncles became successes, one as a prominent journalist, the other as a Bollywood movie director. (An uncle who is your father's younger brother is called *Chacha* in Hindi, and one of these men, Rattan Chacha, would later become as important an influence in my life as anyone after my father.)

My father reacted to his strict upbringing in a fortunate way for Sanjiv and me. We experienced a loving, open-minded father, unsuited by temperament to being a disciplinarian. When I was around eight, my brother and I got into a fight with some cousins. My mother found out and demanded an explanation. Hanging our heads, we defended ourselves by saying that the cousins had used a curse word.

"And then what?" she asked.

We cursed them back, we explained. She turned her face away, and her silence meant that something bad was in store for us. She told my father about the fight at the dinner table, but he didn't get angry.

"It's my fault," he said with obvious sorrow. "I should have taught you better." He laid down his fork and wiped his mouth with a napkin. "I won't have any dinner. I will fast to atone for my failings."

My father was sincere to the point of innocence all his life, so I know that this wasn't a ploy. But as psychological tactics go, it was devastating. Daddy rose from the table while Sanjiv and I pleaded with him to stay. But he ordered his plate cleared and wouldn't listen.

I learned very early how upsetting it is to betray your household god, all the more so if he is a gentle god.

The separate worlds we live in are artificially constructed. We live behind mental walls because we are convinced that we want to or have to. One simple proof is that no one ever walks away from India. To be apart from her is like being a child playing outside without seeing his mother watching from an upstairs window. In my case, Bhrigu must have been watching. I was sitting in my clinic office in La Jolla some years ago when I felt the urge to do something my mother taught me as a child. She would open the Bhagavad Gita at random and ponder the verse that her finger fell on. (I think some Christians do the same with the Bible, and like my mother, they probably try to divine a message intended especially for them.)

My finger landed on a famous verse in book ten, where Krishna describes his superlative qualities to the warrior Arjuna ("Among rivers I am the Ganges. Among mountains I am the Himalayas."), and where my finger touched down, "Among rishis, I am Bhrigu." At that moment the phone rang. It was my friend Professor Arvind Sharma calling from Canada. He had an acclaimed Bhrigu scholar visiting from India who was also a pundit — a Brahmin who kept the Bhrigu tradition alive. My name had flashed in Arvind's mind. Was I interested in a reading? A tingle went up my spine. But unfortunately there were scheduling conflicts, and it was impossible to meet the pundit. The pundit told me to recite some special mantras, and through the mail I received a small effigy of Bhrigu. I did make an effort to try the mantras, but a week or so later I returned to my normal meditation and forgot about the incident.

Some time later I found myself in Delhi with my parents, and I mentioned Tilak Chacha and his strange story. For whatever reason, my father acted as though he had only the vaguest memory of his brother. Someone else insisted I get the astrology reading I had missed. I was doubtful. Countless Indians consult astrologers on a regular basis, but not in my family, and if anything, my interest was less than that of my parents. But why did Bhrigu's name keep popping up? Did he have something to tell me? The best place to find out was still Hoshiarpur. It was too far away to drive, but one of my mother's brothers was a retired admiral in the Indian navy. He requisitioned a military helicopter, and within a few hours we were descending like an apparition out of the sky in Hoshiarpur, where my family had made a pilgrimage long ago. Villagers who had never seen a flying machine watched us with their mouths open.

We arrived at the sthan and were met by dignitaries who had somehow gotten wind of our visit. An elder gave a short speech. I was asked for a few words, and then they asked my father, who was eighty by then. He spoke more than a few words, but soon we arrived at the door of the sthan, where another group of dignitaries flanked us, insisting on performing some necessary prayers and offerings.

The helicopter pilot jiggled my elbow.

"You can't go in."

"Why not?"

It turned out that he wasn't authorized to fly the helicopter at night, and since evening was approaching we departed, with extreme reluctance. As soon as I could reach a telephone I called the pundit that Arvind Sharma had put me in touch with. He listened in silence while I recounted our frustrating trip.

"It doesn't matter," he finally said. "You didn't use the mantras anyway. Your chart told me you wouldn't."

When a circle is about to close, we often don't pay attention. I thought I was through with Bhrigu, but I wasn't yet. Sitting alone in my office, I had a brainstorm. Grabbing a cell phone, I called my father.

"Tilak," I said with some excitement. "He must have had Klinefelter's syndrome." It all fit medically—his effeminacy, the combination of woman's breasts and male sexual parts. Klinefelter's is a genetic rarity, the result of a male baby having an extra X chromosome. Normally a girl baby is born with two X chromosomes and a boy with an X and a Y. But Tilak, along with perhaps one embryo in a thousand, was born XXY. Some people with Klinefelter's syndrome grow up exhibiting few or no symptoms, but he had most of them, including low fertility and premature death.

After a pause, my father agreed. "It fits."

He was reluctant to say anything else about his ill-fated brother, but I pressed him. Did he think that Tilak had really known about a past life?

"I don't like to talk about things I cannot explain," Daddy replied.

Our talk drifted to other things, but there was a silent click as two worlds found a way to fit together. Science and mysticism, Bhrigu and Klinefelter's. They were each more comfortable claiming to be the only *real* reality. But India holds both in a wriggling embrace, and almost invisibly I had reached the point where I did, too.

6

Rama and Lakshmana

Sanjiv

Sanjiv, sixteen, on a holiday break while a premed
student at Delhi University, Pune, 1965.

MY MOTHER OFTEN TOLD DEEPAK and me the story of Lord Rama and his younger brother, Lakshmana. Deepak and I related them to our own relationship just as we were supposed to. Lakshmana is greatly respected in the Indian tradition for his loyalty to his older brother, even at the cost of his own happiness. In most of these stories Lakshmana is much more emotional than his brother, but after Rama's wife, Sita, is kidnapped, Rama becomes so angry he almost unleashes a weapon capable of causing tremendous devastation on the world. Lakshmana stops him, for once the voice of reason.

In our childhood, Deepak was certainly more responsible than I was, although at times he did take advantage of the fact that he was the leader. Deepak and I would play with our closest friends, Ammu and her older brother Prasan. We were so close that each year we celebrated Rakhi, a holiday when a sister ties a thread around her brother's wrist to celebrate their relationship and pray for his health. In addition to tying a ceremonial thread around Prasan's wrist, Ammu would tie a thread around my wrist and Deepak's wrist. So when Deepak ordered Ammu, Prasan, and me to run back and forth one hundred times while he timed us, that was exactly what we did, obeying happily. Deepak was older than us, so we believed he must know more than we did. If he told us to climb the tree in our backyard, we climbed that tree — and when Deepak told us to jump out of that tree, we jumped. Luckily no one got hurt.

We trusted each other. Deepak had enough faith in my abilities that when I was shooting my air rifle at a can sitting on a post, he stood behind the post and told me to continue.

I put down the gun. My aim was good but not perfect — I didn't want to take the chance. But Deepak insisted, telling me the story of

William Tell and his son. This put me in a difficult quandary: Do I fire the gun and risk seriously hurting my older brother, or do I disobey him?

I fired the gun and hit him in the chin.

I wanted to run into the house and get help, but Deepak, whose chin was bleeding, ordered me to stay put. He quickly made up a story about tripping on a barbed wire fence; he wanted us to lie to our parents to avoid a reprimand. That was a difficult thing for me to do, but as they always told us, he was Rama and I was Lakshmana. I proved my loyalty by going along with the story.

Over the next couple of days, Deepak developed a swelling on his chin. Our grandmother noticed this and brought it to my father's attention at dinner.

"You're the brilliant doctor," she said, "but I don't believe you've properly diagnosed your own son's condition. There's probably a piece of barbed wire in his chin. Take him for an X-ray tomorrow and check it out."

The next morning Deepak went with our father to the hospital. At home I paced the veranda nervously, watching for my brother and father's return. Every few minutes I would go inside and check with my mother.

"Did they call from the hospital yet?" She looked at me with suspicion.

"You seem awfully concerned." Just then the phone rang and my father told my mother that the X-ray showed an air rifle pellet lodged in Deepak's chin. A surgeon had been summoned to remove it. We were admonished to tell the truth but not punished.

Over the years Deepak developed a dimple in his chin. I think it makes him look dignified and noble, but it also reminds me of the episode every time I see him.

While Deepak and I were close, we were also very competitive. We were never truly rivals, but we did try to one-up each other. We would try to determine who could swim a hundred laps the fastest, who could play the fiercest game of table tennis or chess, who could outrace the other on a pair of roller skates, who had the strongest vocabulary. I wanted to beat him every single time, and Deepak felt the same. Even though I was his younger brother, I don't recall him ever letting me win. I guess we learned that competing to the best of your ability built character more than being allowed to win. And when it came to sports, I was often able to win despite the age difference.

Deepak eventually got even with me for shooting him. We were fighting with wooden swords one day, when Deepak accidentally cut me on my nose. I was left with a slight scar there, neither as noticeable nor as dignified as Deepak's dimple.

My family instilled great confidence in both Deepak and me, sometimes more than might have been warranted. We were surrounded by accomplished people: our father, the renowned doctor; our uncle, the heroic admiral; another uncle, the well-known and respected journalist; and so on. We were told, repeatedly, that we were capable of achieving whatever goals we set for ourselves. As a result, neither of us ever backed down from a challenge — that I can recall. For Deepak those challenges were usually academic; for me they were often physical. Kids fight, and Indian children are no exception.

For instance, when we were at school in Jabalpur, we all had to deal with a tough classmate everyone called Roger the Bully.

During our lunch break, we often played marbles. The players would put a certain number of marbles in the circle and then each one would try to knock as many as possible outside the perimeter with his striker marble, slightly larger than the rest.

One day one of the other kids came to school with some beautiful Chinese strikers. We made a deal: three of my ordinary marbles for one of his special Chinese ones. I was good at the game, and that day won the whole pot in less than twenty minutes, an impressive feat. I was feeling quite proud of myself, until I heard the voice of Roger the Bully behind me.

"Give me half."

This was a moment every young child fears, no matter where in the world they might be: the bully demanding his share. Everybody in the school was afraid of Roger, even Deepak. But I turned to look up at him.

"I'm not giving you any marbles," I blurted. "These are mine. Why should you have any?"

I have to admit that if these were ordinary marbles I might have given them up to avoid a conflict. Roger was a year older than me and at least three inches taller. But these Chinese marbles were beautiful. I had made a fair trade, won the marbles matches, and wanted to keep my entire winnings.

When I challenged Roger he immediately went into a boxing stance, like he was about to thrash me. So I stood up and decked him. I didn't stop to think about it — I just hit him right on the chin and knocked him on the ground.

The older boy looked up at me with fear in his eyes. And then, to the surprise of everyone in the yard, Roger the Bully burst into tears.

That incident was the end of Roger's bullying, and it turned me into something of a school hero. And surprisingly, Roger the Bully and I became friends.

We had been taught to stand up for ourselves from a very young age. Our parents always asked us how we felt about things that affected our family, and took our answers very seriously. They encouraged us to speak up, a lesson that both Deepak and I obviously learned. Once, when I was about four years old and in first grade, my father took me with him to the market to pick up a crate of Coca-Cola. At that time I had the habit of sucking my thumb; my parents had tried everything to get me to stop, with no luck. As we drove around a curve we saw a car on the side of the road with a flat tire.

"Do you know why that car has a flat tire?" my father asked.

"No."

"Because the son sitting next to me is sucking his thumb." I pulled my thumb out of my mouth and looked at him. As we drove along I thought about what he'd said and, in some strange way, understood the point my father was trying to make.

I was a somewhat precocious four-year-old, a quick learner, and our father had a habit that bothered me — for more than twenty years he had smoked two packs of cigarettes a day.

A little farther up the road, we came upon a huge truck lying on its side. Policemen and medical personnel were on the scene. I stared at the scene, illuminated by flashing ambulance lights, as we drove by.

"Dad, did you see that lorry?" I asked. "Do you know why it happened?"

My father smiled and asked me why.

"Because the father sitting next to me smokes cigarettes!"

In the years since, I have learned the bittersweet pleasure of having your child use the lessons you've taught against you. In this instance my father thought about it for several seconds and then rolled down the window of the blue Hillman car he was driving and flipped his cigarette into the street. I smiled smugly. Then he went further. He took out a Ronson lighter that had been a gift to him from a British officer. He looked at me and then tossed it out the window. Within a couple of weeks he had stopped smoking completely and never smoked again. Naturally I stopped sucking my thumb, too.

Our father wrote in his book, *Your Life Is in Your Hands,* that "parents must foster a warm and friendly relationship with their children, and encourage them to develop diverse interests." My parents did this successfully, and Deepak and I admired both greatly for it. We each carry with us elements of their characters, their core values and principles, which in turn we have tried to pass on to our own children.

Growing up in India as the children of a respected physician allowed us to enjoy many privileges. Once, after my father had treated a prince from an Indian state, we were invited to stay in his palace.

Deepak and I woke up early in the morning and went out to the palace balcony. I looked down into the courtyard and couldn't believe my eyes. I literally rubbed my eyes to be sure I wasn't dreaming. Down below was the most majestic animal I had ever seen: a beautiful pure-white tiger. This was, in fact, the first living white tiger seen in nature. Its name was Mohan. It had been captured by the prince as a cub and he had raised it himself.

That was the India of our childhood: beggars outside the high walls protecting the wealthy, the sounds of merchants hawking their

goods, while inside a white tiger sat placidly on a perfectly manicured lawn. But what Deepak and I learned was that we had been
given a great deal, and that in return it was our dharma to behave
responsibly, to respect other people, and to give back at every conceivable opportunity.

That, in essence, is the path that both of us have followed.

·················

7

Laus Deo

Deepak

Krishan Lal, thirty-four, and Pushpa Chopra, twenty-seven, in
Jammu, 1960. They were blissfully married for more than fifty years.

I CAN'T LET JESUS DOWN. I should love him. Everyone says he loves me. What will he do if I don't love him back?

Thoughts like these ran through my mind constantly as a teenager. To worry about God at that age is a common thing. But in India, worrying about Jesus isn't. My situation was unusual, however. The teachers in school, who were all Catholic missionaries, kept an eye on us, a gentle scrutiny, and there was always a subtle expectation. It would surface in odd ways. An Irish priest, someone who had become a friend, who had played sports with the boys on the cricket pitch, would take me aside. He would put a hand on my shoulder and smile to reassure me.

Nothing's wrong, lad, don't worry. We just need you for Christ. Can you do that for me?

Every native-born boy they took into that school knew that the recruitment pitch lay in store. I pushed that day off by not thinking about it. Unlike my devout mother and grandmother, I wasn't absolutely sure I knew the right God to pray to. Jesus had taken the British a long way. Was Shiva doing anything about it?

A Catholic private school was the elite option in India in the Fifties; if cricket flannels were an anomaly in the tropics, what about knee socks, a green blazer, and a school tie? Wherever we lived at the time, I threw on a uniform every morning before catching the six-thirty bus across Delhi, or walking up the hill past tea plantations in Shillong, or kissing my mother good-bye in Jabalpur. The religious aspect was never raised at home. My father was intent solely on giving his sons the best education. He had received a good one himself, but it took an act of noblesse oblige from Lord Mountbatten to grease the rails for him. Fortune had favored him extravagantly. My father didn't want to take any risks with us. Everyone knew that the best education came from Jesuit schools run by the Christian Brothers, so he enrolled us in one such school after another as we moved to each new post: St. Aloysius, St. Edmund's, St. Columba's. These weren't just saints' names. They were tickets for the first-class compartment that rolled toward our future.

In my whole life I can remember only two crushing humiliations. The second occurred in medical school, years later. The first took place in Shillong, one of the beautiful colonialist hill stations in the state of Assam. This was a landscape green and cool enough to make a sergeant major's wife shed a tear for Shropshire and Kent. The station sat at five thousand feet, the rumpled earth around it anticipating the leap to the Himalayas stretching away to the north. Every morning, I walked to a school on a hill, St. Edmund's, with fragrant tea plantations spreading a carpet of soft foliage as far as the eye could see.

The only serpent in this Eden was that St. Edmund's was a much harder school than the one I had attended previously in Jabalpur. Every month, the principal handed out report cards in a formal ceremony, the boys lined up in order of merit. The highest you could receive was a gold card, which only went to one or two boys. If you got one, the principal would shake your hand warmly and invite you for tea and a movie. For a blue card he might shake your hand and give you a friendly hug. A pink card would be handed over with a neutral expression. If you had sunk so low as to deserve a yellow card, the principal would look away disdainfully as he thrust it at you. It was a devastatingly effective way to indoctrinate the boys, and I couldn't bear the idea of getting anything less than a blue or gold card. I sweated to earn one, but after the first month, I suffered the agony of watching every other boy march up for his handshake until I was presented with a yellow card and that disdainful look.

To weep uncontrollably when you are eleven years old seems poignant from the distant perspective of an adult. At the time, though, it collapses your world. I thought the humiliation would stay with me for life, and the point isn't that I was wrong. Just *thinking* that I was forever scarred is what burned the humiliation in. I indulged in melodrama alone in my room. Jesus had stumbled on the way to Calvary, and now so had I. Before, I had blazed a trail of glory. Approval was the air I breathed, and of course it was impossible for me to see that my trail had been littered with vanity, greed, and fear. Aren't they the common coin in school when you consider the dark side?

The dark side of life may be universal, but it doesn't affect everyone the same. You may curse it for ruining your future or feel a kind of grudging gratitude — for lessons imparted or for greater dangers that were warded off. I'm sure that some of my classmates grew up deeply resenting the pressure that was put on them from Western Christian values. Years later, when I read George Orwell's essays, I came across a dismal opinion. Orwell wrote that the worst advertisement for Christianity is its adherents. This wasn't true when I was at school. I never personally experienced the abuse that has come to light among predatory priests, thankfully, though the practice of caning, which the missionaries brought with them from Ireland, has become rightfully disgraced.

We did have some intensely devout classmates, called the seminarians. They began studying for the priesthood at age twelve and lived at the seminary while attending school with the rest of us. A number were Christian from birth, since they came from Goa and had Portuguese surnames like Da Silva and Da Souza. I was puzzled by such devotion and asked one boy why he wanted to become a priest. His eyes widened.

"They fly you to Rome, and then the Pope makes you a priest. The Pope himself!"

So it was the travel? My dream was to fly to London and see the house on Baker Street where Sherlock Holmes lived. The seminarians were dreaming bigger — I was impressed.

Sprinkled into our school were also some Catholic converts; they came from poor families and attended on scholarship. Every day, the Catholic boys went to catechism class. The rest of us, the motley pagans, were given the choice to go along to catechism or to attend a class called Moral Science.

"Moral science" seems like a peculiar concept to me now. It was actually more like moral logic. The lessons were aimed at systematically proving why Christian morality was correct. If we understood logic, we'd know that the teachings of Jesus were universal and ir-refutable. I was already mesmerized by the story of the Passion in the New Testament, which couldn't be improved upon for blood and poetry. Primarily I loved Jesus as an action adventure hero. What could be more adventurous than fighting for God against the devil until your ruthless enemies nail you to a cross?

Moral science drove home the iniquity of masturbation and ho-mosexuality, both approached in a gingerly sidelong fashion. You left class certain that something was awful but not knowing exactly what it was. Those lessons had only a temporary effect. What stuck for life? An abiding trust that love is the basis of true morality. (I once read an apt definition of the law as a set of rules set up after love is gone.) Someone from a family that wasn't as loving as ours would have had a harder time absorbing this teaching. I recall a debate on the existence of God that I attended years later. On one side was a scientific atheist, who hammered away at God for an hour with a barrage of rational argument. He sat down to scattered applause, and his opponent, a comfortably stout, smiling Catholic priest, took the lectern.

"Why do I believe that God is real?" he asked. "Because my mother told me so, and I believed her." He sat down to thunderous applause.

St. Columba's adjoined a girls' school, the Convent of Jesus and Mary. Like ours, it was a day school, founded in 1919 by an order of French nuns. The two grounds were separated by a wall, and my friends and I would sometimes cross over. Girls attracted us, but Moral Science had let us down badly in the girl department. It hardly seems credible that adolescent males could quiver at the thought of holding hands with a girl for ten minutes under the gaze of a suspicious chaperone. Girls were a faraway dream to me and my friends. In all honesty, we crossed the wall just as much to see the grotto filled with flowers that had statues of the Virgin Mary for the devout to pray to.

We were very good boys, which needs no special pleading. We didn't reek of incense. Piety comes naturally to a certain side of an adolescent, filled with sentimental dreams and naïve idealism. Those are society's labels, not mine. What makes idealism naïve isn't that you grow out of it but that no one teaches you how to hang on to it.

The silent devotion of the Mary grotto at the convent felt beautiful to me. One day, looking on while people came and went to kneel in prayer, I had the overwhelming sensation of a divine presence. The statue of Mary was sending it to me without my praying for it, or even wishing. This was the first moment I had an inkling of what a famous phrase in Indian spirituality means: ocean of bliss. Many people have had a similar experience.

The secret is what to do after the presence leaves you. I wasn't concerned with that at sixteen. It just felt as though Mother Mary's love came over me. The air grew sweeter, and I felt safe and cared for. Because a well-loved child grows up with the same things, it might feel more intense to have them emanate in a holy place, but there is no epiphany. The contrast isn't strong enough, perhaps? I didn't shrug off my experience, which lingered for quite a while, but the road to Damascus didn't stretch out before me, either.

On rare occasions my uncle Sohan Lal came to town. He was a traveling salesman who sold field hockey equipment, a Western game that India excelled at. No doubt he took the job because he was mad for sports. But Sohan Lal felt a strong attraction to saints, as I've mentioned, constantly finding obscure *sadhus,* yogis, and holy men in general. As he traveled the country, he would seek out the local saint and sit at his feet. Sometimes he would listen to the wisdom imparted by the saint, but mostly Sohan Lal wanted *Darshan.* This is the blessing that comes simply from setting eyes on a saint (the root of darshan is "to see" or "to view"). One time, however, the blessing went much further.

As he recounted it, Sohan Lal was visiting one of the huge congregations of holy men known as a *Mela,* where tens of thousands of spectators crowd the banks of a holy river to see spiritual luminaries —a meet and greet with God, so to speak. Remarkable encounters often occur at these events, and one happened to Sohan Lal. He met a yogi sitting in lotus position under a canopy.

"I know that you are a fervent seeker of God," the yogi said. "Tell me what your heart desires at this very moment."

"At this very moment?" Sohan Lal replied, flustered. "I want some barfi."

Barfi is the most common kind of candy in northern India; it can be bought from street vendors for next to nothing. The yogi held up a fist, unfolded it, and handed my uncle a fresh piece of pistachio barfi, which he had apparently manifested out of thin air on the spot.

Whenever he recounted this incident—which all of us children believed without question—Sohan Lal would shake his head sadly.

"I could have asked for enlightenment or a million rupees at least. But what could I do? All I wanted at that moment was barfi."

The day did arrive for the recruitment pitch. At St. Columba's the older boys went to the poorest sections of Delhi to hand out milk to the children. We mixed powdered milk with water and delivered it in a big truck. The kids met us with smiles, and we played with them throughout. It was more fun than charity work.

One day Father Steinmeyer—Irish like all the rest despite his German name—asked me what I was reading. Without television, reading was a big part of my life. When I told him that I was immersed in P. G. Wodehouse, the good father frowned.

"Kid's stuff. I thought you were more grown up than that."

I hung my head. Even a gentle reproof from a teacher sank in. By the lights of a St. Columba's boy, I had a right to feel ashamed for being so frivolous. Indian education was primarily by rote. At sixteen I could recite whole scenes from Shakespeare, not just one or two speeches. I had memorized long stretches of Tennyson and other Romantic poets.

Father Steinmeyer looked over at the four boys who were on the milk truck that day—me, another Hindu boy, a Sindi, and a Parsi.

"Have you ever thought about taking Jesus as your lord and savior?" he asked quietly.

We all shrugged and said no in embarrassed mumbles. It was the simple truth. The priest said nothing more. He turned back to the impoverished waifs crowding around us holding out their cups for more. As a pitch to young converts, this one was barely halfhearted. The wily machinations of Jesuits remained a fable to me. A few days later Father Steinmeyer handed me some books that he said were more suited to a mature young man than Bertie Wooster and his man Jeeves. They turned out to be Catholic novels, and whatever impression they made, it is long forgotten.

Which brings me to an unflattering truth. Just because God is in the air doesn't mean that you are breathing deeply.

Inevitably I grew to admire the British. The schooling did it to me. I could recite the whole of Macbeth's speech, "Tomorrow and tomorrow and tomorrow / Creeps in this petty pace from day to day" before I knew any lines of Sanskrit—or had an inkling of the spiritual weariness that was killing Macbeth's soul. But if my education was a devil's bargain, both sides kept it. The Jesuits were playing for converts, yet they were also devoted to teaching; the boys were playing for a ticket to ride, but we seriously wanted to learn. A devil's bargain could be thought of as a gentleman's agreement. And we did our best to turn into proper gentlemen.

In 1962, my last year of high school, Sanjiv and I lived with an aunt and uncle in New Delhi. After we came home and threw off our school uniforms, we would run outside and blend into the neighborhood. The scene was a welter of tongues, a savory bubbling of English, Hindi, and Punjabi. Without a second thought, even though we knew Hindi just as well, my brother and I spoke only in English, and this marked us. English was the gentleman's language, not the tongue of an oppressor.

One strong force, however, tugged against everything that was making us pious and proper—my uncle Rattan Chacha, who took Sanjiv and me in when we attended St. Columba's. Rattan Chacha had risen to become an important journalist with a national reputation, and once he branched out into movie reviewing, his life became unspeakably glamorous in my eyes. I'd never seen anyone hold forth with a cigarette in one hand and a glass of Scotch in the other.

Rattan Chacha was well informed about world affairs and had the strongest rebellious streak in the Chopra clan. It was a trait he traded profitably in. He was widely known as a socialist and an unbeliever. As he put it, "I have left-wing opinions and right-wing tastes." It was the perfect combination for someone who burned his candle at both ends. (Heart disease scared Rattan Chacha in later years, so he gave up the cigarettes, though never the Scotch.)

Sending shock waves was his game. Rattan Chacha talked incessantly, which suited me very well. I wanted to be him. (When I asked my wife, Rita, about the first impression I made on her, she thought for a moment and replied, "I'd never met anyone who talked so much.") Entertaining and handsome, Rattan Chacha dominated any room he walked into, but he had the saving grace of wanting to hear my opinions. Brilliant talkers cannot live without an audience, and they learn soon enough to throw their listeners a scrap; they let someone else talk for half a minute now and then. But when I debated my uncle on a burning topic, he actually paid attention, and so it was sometimes more than a scrap.

Rattan Chacha and his wife, Karna — we called her Karna Auntie — occupied a second-floor apartment in New Delhi with two and a half bedrooms. Sanjiv and I shared a bed in the half bedroom, which was essentially a cramped cell with a window looking down on to a grubby courtyard where the neighbors made a clamor and hung their washing out to dry. We loved being there.

At the time, my father was posted to Kashmir, during the armed conflict with Pakistan. He treated the injured troops who were carried back from the front lines. My mother traveled back and forth to be with him and us. When she was absent, we inherited Lakshman Singh, the faithful servant who had come with her dowry.

I was fascinated by my uncle's worldliness. One time he went with us on a trip to one of the hill stations. It was Dalhousie, and even though the setting was beautiful, this wasn't one of the prestigious hill stations like Simla.

"I see how it got its name," Rattan Chacha quipped. "It's dull and lousy."

He took us boys to the movies once and saw an empty seat with a sweater thrown over it. Tossing the sweater onto another seat, Rattan Chacha sat us down. A moment later an irate man approached us.

"I left my sweater to mark this seat as mine," he complained. Rattan Chacha shrugged.

"If you threw your sweater over the Taj Mahal, would that make it yours, too?"

His mentor in brazenness was his boss, Feroze Gandhi, a prominent publisher of several newspapers in Lucknow who had also taken up politics. In person Feroze Gandhi was even more domineering and provocative than my uncle. It reputedly shocked Nehru, not yet prime minister, when his daughter Indira declared that she wanted to marry Feroze Gandhi after meeting him on a trip to London. He was a Parsi, member of the sect founded by the Persian prophet Zoroaster. The Nehrus were Brahmins from Kashmir. (If you move in conservative Kashmiri Brahmin circles, they still cluck in distress over the match, seventy years later.)

Over any objections the wedding went forward in 1942. The groom's reckless lifestyle eventually caught up with him, and Feroze Gandhi died of a heart attack just a few days before his forty-eighth birthday. As a widow Indira came into her own and rose to be prime minister, which was all but inevitable in India, where a few elite families connected to the independence movement were considered sacred; they controlled national politics for decades. (Only in the West is Indira's married name confused with Mahatma Gandhi's. Feroze wasn't related to him. Gandhi is well-known to be a common Parsi family name.)

Rattan Chacha had a cultivated side. He tried to teach me Urdu, a language he loved for its poetry. I should have been a natural, since Urdu, spoken all over northern India, shares a common basis with Hindi. It has all the utility of a lingua franca, a pidgin language that traders carry around wherever they go. Swahili serves the same purpose in Africa. I wasn't adept enough, though, and what stays with me is mostly the lore and romance that my uncle loved to dispense.

Urdu came to India with the drift of Islam as it moved eastward from its birthplace in Arabia. Like burrs and seeds that become attached to a camel's flanks, words stuck to Urdu from Turkey, Persia, and other lands where Muslim caravans unfolded their wares. The Mughal invasion of India in the sixteenth century rooted Urdu in Delhi, but to be clear, saying that India was conquered by the Mughals is like saying a feather pillow was conquered by a punch. You can't defeat someone who doesn't resist, especially an ancient people who have absorbed many empires. In school I memorized Shelley's poem "Ozymandias," which begins with the image of a mighty ruler brought low: "Two vast and trunkless legs of stone / Stand in the desert. Near them, on the sand, / Half sunk, a shattered visage lies . . ." India doesn't chop emperors off at the knees. There's more subtlety in pretending to be conquered, offering a smiling shrug to the iron fist, and then waiting until the day when the conqueror looks in the mirror and sees an Indian staring back. The notorious passivity that Westerners see is actually a subtle art of war.

Rattan Chacha did manage to teach me how to recite some verses in Urdu, which don't really have their full effect in English. My favorite comes from a poet who also happened to be an emperor, born with a parade banner of a name: Abu Zafar Sirajuddin Muhammad Bahadur Shah Zafar. He was the last Mughal ruler of India, dying in 1862, and in school we learned about him as Bahadur Shah Zafar, the descendant of Shah Jahan, who built the Taj Mahal. The British made a mockery of the Mughal royal line by the end. The East India Company maintained the charade that they were not the rulers of India but had merely signed commercial agreements with all the princes, rajas, maharajas, and shahs, who in reality were their puppets. To preserve their dignity, the royal families could act as though they still held power. Their greed made them ready to cede anything in return for a lifestyle so luxurious that it became ghastly — one sees faded photos of diamond-bedecked rajas posed with big-game rifles astride their Rolls-Royces, bragging about the two dead tigers draped over the fenders.

The decadence of the last Mughals barely called for a military presence to hold their territory in check. What a few garrisons of redcoats couldn't manage was handled by native soldiers, the sepoys. If Zafar stood on the highest turret of the Red Fort in Delhi, built by his illustrious ancestors, he could see the limits of his actual rule; everything beyond the city of Delhi had eroded away. As Bahadur Shah, he was a poignant and pathetic ruler who left affairs of state to others while collecting the pension the British had granted him and finding refuge in his real love: poetry.

I wish I still had in memory the verses by Zafar that Rattan Chacha loved so much. Most were melancholy and romantic, as suited Zafar's fate. He made the mistake of entertaining, only for a day, the fantasy of regaining power. In 1857 the sepoys mounted an armed rebellion against the British army, inflamed, it was said, by a rumor that pig fat was used to grease the paper that their bullets were wrapped in. Since the bullets were unwrapped by mouth, this was defilement to the sepoys, many of whom were Muslim. A sepoy regiment marched on Delhi and lured Bahadur Shah into an audience. He was dismayed by their insolence, but he gave in to temptation when the rebels swore to restore him to power. He aligned himself with them, and they killed fifty-two British prisoners, mostly terrified civilians found in hiding, by executing them under a pipal tree outside the palace. This act was meant to ensure that Bahadur Shah wouldn't back down.

The sepoy regiments had plenty of genuine grievances against the East India Company, but the British looked upon the rebellion as being caused by religious frenzy. The poor old emperor, nearly seventy, made his son military commander and tried to bring civil order to Delhi, the only place he could hope to control. The result was chaos. The sepoy regiments were totally disorganized and couldn't agree on one commander — it certainly wouldn't be the inept, inexperienced royal prince. After the rebellion was violently quashed and the British had mowed down many members of his family, Bahadur Shah surrendered in exchange for his life and was put on trial. One can see photographs of him reclining on a divan awaiting his fate, a bald man with a neat, pointed white beard. His wide eyes are mournful, but you can still see the spark of a Sufi, a mystic, in them. As a young man Zafar had wanted to be a holy man and dressed in the coarse woolen robes of a wandering Sufi before he assumed the throne.

Zafar's punishment was banishment to Rangoon, Burma, where he survived several more years. He thought he was lost in a dream. In his poetry, he describes himself as a ruined garden that was once luxurious. The saddest of his verses speaks about his downfall from ruler of an empire to a beggar who can't find two yards of earth for his grave. I can find only fragments of his poetry translated into English, but one couplet sounds like something Shakespeare could have put in Hamlet's mouth:

What is man, who is made of clay?
I see only a bubble on the water.

After he died, the last Mughal emperor was recognized as a major poet in Urdu. Some articles began to refer to him as a true Sufi, and a few as a saint. I am more ambivalent. When I learned Indian history in school, my sympathies went to the British, but when I heard the music of Bahadur Shah's verses, I was on the side of the poets.

This inability to choose one over the other seeped into my character. I was turning into a highly competitive person, someone who saw Indian history from the British perspective because they had been the winners for three hundred years. But the pathos of my own people couldn't be dismissed. The poets spoke for a silent witness inside me. It watched without interference. It made no demands for me to change. I wouldn't have paid attention if it had. I was running the course with victory in mind every time I rounded the next curve.

The silent witness was patient. Time never runs out when you have an infinite supply.

8

First on the Waiting List

Sanjiv

Sanjiv brings his classmate and future wife, Amita,
on a trip to Pune during a school break with his
mother, Pushpa, and brother, Deepak, 1967.

IN THE VILLAGE OF CHERRAPUNJI they thought we were gods. Cherrapunji is on the Indian border with Bangladesh. It is one of the rainiest places on earth; according to Guinness World Records, it holds records for the most rain in a year and the most in a single month. It is an extraordinary place with breathtakingly beautiful waterfalls. When I was twelve, my parents decided to take Deepak and me there on an excursion. We drove up the side of a mountain in our little Hillman car through what felt like an unending series of snakelike turns, up and up and up. Throughout our journey the rain never slowed. But just as we arrived at the village, the clouds parted and the sun came out. There were little children there who had rarely seen the sun in their lives, so when it came out just as we drove into the village, they assumed we were gods to have made that happen. Even some of the shopkeepers thought there might be some kind of divine connection. They smiled, invited us into their shops for tea and samosas, and refused to accept any payment.

I had that same feeling when I was a young boy, sitting on a train at the Jabalpur station and looking out of the window to see hundreds of people paying their respects to my father, many of them crying. Even though I didn't understand at that age what it meant to be a doctor, it was obviously something very special. It was at that moment that I thought perhaps I too would become a doctor. Many years later my wife, Amita, and I went on a pilgrimage to Gomukh to see with my own eyes the origin of the holy Ganges. While I was there one of the people I had traveled with, a renowned Indian physician named Dr. H. K. Chuttani, asked me a question.

"Sanjiv," he said, "if you had your life to live all over again, what profession would you choose? And where would you live?" I looked up at the mountain, at the sky, and then responded.

"Dr. Chuttani, it's very simple," I said. "I would be practicing hepatology in Boston, teaching, writing books, and being a good doctor. Exactly what I'm already doing." He considered that for a moment.

"The air is thin at this altitude," he replied. "I'll ask you again at sea level."

We met a week later at a cocktail party in Delhi. My answer hadn't changed. I am very fortunate to be able to do what I love to do. The practice of medicine was our family business. I watched my father deeply enjoy healing and caring for people. He seemed genuinely happy when he went to work every day, and even at a young age I understood that was something very important. For my father there was nothing more exciting or fulfilling than to solve the mysteries of the human body. To him everything began with the correct diagnosis. In the evenings at dinner he would often talk about his new patients and describe their symptoms and the course he intended to follow. For me it was a bit like a soap opera, and night after night I would carefully follow the progress of patients I would never actually meet. Although I knew absolutely nothing about them personally, they would take shape in my mind and I would begin to care about them.

My mother, who was a high school graduate with no formal medical training, learned quite a bit about medicine through my father and often asked insightful questions, which he always answered in great detail. She was always so inquisitive. Did you cure this? Did you fix everything? What will you do next? What have the tests shown? Sometimes, in fact, she would actually make the diagnosis herself.

At one dinner my father seemed unusually concerned about a patient.

"I am worried about this sister's daughter," he told us. "Sister" was the word they used to describe nurses at the time. He continued, "She's a single parent with a thirteen-year-old daughter." He looked directly at me and said, "You may have met her at one of the festivals."

My mother asked her usual question: "What are her symptoms?"

"She has a high fever and an enlarged lymph node," he said. "I'm hoping it's strep throat."

"I just hope it's not Hodgkin's disease," my mother said. My father considered that for a moment.

"You know, you're probably right." Indeed, my father later diagnosed the little girl as having Hodgkin's lymphoma. We followed her progress at dinner for several years, until, sadly, she passed away.

My father taught us that diagnosing a patient is an art that requires total focus. It's rarely obvious from one or two symptoms. He took great pride in his ability to make difficult, sometimes obscure diagnoses, a trait that both Deepak and I inherited. He used to tell the story of his final examination for membership in the Royal College of Physicians.

"These are professional patients," he said. "They are people with real illnesses, some of them rare, who are paid to present their symptoms to students taking examinations. When the patient saw he was being interrogated by an Indian doctor he became quite uncooperative. There was an attitude to his responses. After greeting him with the usual civilities I started taking a history. And he refused to give me a firm answer to any question. Do you cough when you're in the hospital? 'Maybe.' Are you sleeping well? 'Sometimes.' After answering each question he would turn to the professional patient in the next bed and ask, 'Mike, do I cough?' 'Mike, do I sleep well?' Mike would answer, 'Maybe' or 'Sometimes.' It was impossible to get a direct answer."

But as my father listened to this patient, he was also looking carefully for any unusual signs. He noticed that the patient's eyes were moving slightly from side to side, a condition known as nystagmus. He also noticed that there was something slightly off about his speech.

"Please say 'British artillery brigade,'" my father said.

The patient repeated the phrase, slurring the words slightly, a symptom known as scanning speech.

My father asked the patient to hold up a pen he had in his hand, and noticed that the patient had what is known as an intention tremor.

"How long," my father asked confidently, "have you been suffering from disseminated sclerosis?"

It was the classic triad of symptoms — scanning speech, intention tremor, and nystagmus — seen in patients with disseminated sclerosis, a condition better known in the United States as multiple sclerosis. The professional patient's face lit up.

"My goodness, Doctor," he exclaimed. "You are one of the very few who made the correct diagnosis." Impressed, he went on to tell my father all the questions they would ask during his final examination — and reminded him of the right answers. That information helped my father pass with honors, an extremely rare accomplishment for a young Indian doctor at that time.

Unlike my brother, I never really doubted that I would become a doctor, and a great diagnostician, like my father. In India there are medical schools teaching science-based medicine, Ayurvedic medicine, and *Unani,* another form of traditional medicine, and graduates of all of these are considered capable doctors. I, on the other hand, was only interested in what I called modern medicine, the science-based medicine practiced by my father. While I believed other forms of medicine had their place, I felt that Western medicine offered patients the most sensible and proven forms of treatment. To me that was real medicine and that was the type of medicine I intended to practice.

The educational system in India is different from that in the United States. In America a student attends college before applying to medical school. In India there is one year of premed after high school and then students go directly to medical school. After completing my year of premed at Delhi University, I applied to three medical schools. My father was teaching at the Armed Forces Medical College at Pune and my brother was attending the All India Institute of Medical Sciences in Delhi, so I applied to these two medical schools and also to Banaras Hindu University.

I had decent scores on my premed exams, and I was immediately accepted to Armed Forces Medical College and to Banaras Hindu University. But I really wanted to attend the All India Institute of Medical Sciences, which was (and remains) the most prestigious medical school in the country. Unfortunately it was also the most difficult to gain admission to. Only thirty-five students were accepted each year from as many as ten thousand applicants. The admissions council whittled down the initial pool to ninety applicants based on our scores, then called each of us in for an interview. During my interview with Dr. Keswani, the head of the anatomy department, he asked me why I didn't want to go to the college where my father was a legendary professor.

"He was assigned there by the military service," I explained. "He didn't have a choice. I have a choice, and I want to attend this grand institution. This is a modern school with many brilliant people like yourself on the faculty, and there is modern thinking about medicine here. Many of the faculty have also trained in America." America, I said specifically, not England. He felt that the postgraduate training in America was the best. Finally I added, just to be safe, "I also like the modern buildings and the fact that there are table tennis tables in the vestibule."

"You want to play table tennis and study architecture!" he retorted, smiling.

I like to tell people that I was at the top of the admissions list, but truthfully I was at the top of the waiting list: number thirty-six. Number one in the entire nation was a lovely young woman named Amita Desraj, who had intended to join the Foreign Services and eventually become an ambassador. But like Deepak, she too had changed her mind and decided to go into medicine.

Fortunately each year three to four students among the thirty-five granted admission to the prestigious All India Institute of Medical Sciences chose not to attend the school because they received scholarships from other medical schools. As a result I was admitted to the medical school of my choice.

Even then it took an act of Parliament for me to become a physician. At the time, to attend the All India Institute a student had to turn seventeen by August 1 of that year. In elementary school I had been promoted from first grade to third grade because the teachers and the principal thought I was bright, something colloquially called a double promotion. Since I would not be eligible for admission and would have to wait almost two years to enroll, my father mentioned the problem to one of his patients: the future president of

India, Fakhruddin Ali Ahmed. He requested that Parliament change the rule. Under the new regulations, I squeaked in by twenty-one days and became the youngest student admitted in the history of the medical school.

The school was not difficult for me. I had been raised in the world of medicine and was comfortable with the language and the tools. It all came relatively easily to me. Unlike American medical schools, in India we learned mostly by memorizing material. There was little analytical thinking, just memorization and recitation. In premed, we would stand in front of the class and recite the entire periodic table. It's still right there in my memory. We used all types of memory aids. A symptom of liver disease, we learned in medical school, is that your palms get very red. It's called palmar erythema. A second sign is that patients develop red spots on their body, usually on the upper torso, that look something like the legs of a spider. To remember that, we used a limerick, which I've never forgotten, coined by a Dr. Bean, from Boston:

> *An older Miss Muffet decided to rough it, and lived upon*
> *whiskey and gin*
> *Red hands and a spider developed outside her, such are*
> *the wages of sin.*

Deepak was two years ahead of me in medical school and had laid down a difficult path to emulate. My first year he would get very upset at me because instead of staying in my room and studying, I'd go to the movies or out with friends to coffee bars, returning very late. I also still cherished competing in sports. I was the best cricket player and the best table tennis player for a number of years and won many trophies. My brother, on more than one occasion, told our mother that he was proud of my athletic prowess but worried about my academic performance. My mother happened to be at a bank sometime later and ran into Dr. Keswani from the anatomy department. He went up to my mother and asked how her sons were doing.

"I have no worries about Deepak," she told him. "He's an academic, but I do worry about Sanjiv, who seems to be too fond of sports."

"Don't worry," Dr. Keswani said. "I'll take care of him."

The student in the room next to mine was always studying. No matter what time I woke in the morning or came in at night, the light in his room was on and he was hitting the books. He had made it clear he disapproved of my study habits, which annoyed me, so when we were both about to be tested about the abdomen in Dr. Keswani's anatomy course, I said, "I'd like to challenge you. I'll bet you I get a better score than you in the abdomen!"

He accepted my challenge. This time both of us studied very hard, and we tied with the third highest score in the written examination. Then an interesting thing happened during our oral examination. Dr. Keswani asked me twenty questions, and I answered every one of them correctly.

"I'm going to give you ten marks out of one hundred," he said. This was his misguided way of encouraging me to study even harder. I was dumbfounded and outraged.

In India we were taught that the person you showed the most respect for, even more than your parents, was your teacher. The teacher was always infallible. There were quite a few instances growing up when a teacher would say something that clearly wasn't correct, but rather than speak up we accepted that we must be wrong and the teacher, somehow, right. Sometimes we would discuss it later.

"What the teacher said couldn't be true, could it?" We would all agree that it wasn't, but nevertheless the teacher had been saying the same wrong thing to students year after year and no one had had the guts to tell him he was wrong.

But this time I did something students in India almost never do. When Dr. Keswani told me he was giving me only ten marks I spoke back.

"I'm not leaving," I said. The junior professors and demonstrators in the anatomy department looked at me like I had lost my mind. "I'm not leaving," I repeated. "I studied very hard. I know my abdomen. I got the third highest score on my written examination. Dr. Keswani, I have a favor to ask. Go ahead and please ask me more questions."

It was just like when I stood up to Roger the Bully. No one knew how to act. Dr. Keswani looked both amused and a little angry.

"Okay," he mumbled. He asked me another five questions, and I answered each one of them correctly. "Very good," he said. "I'm going to double your marks." With that, he gave me twenty on the exam.

I was furious when I walked out of that room, but there was nothing I could do. So I called Deepak to lay the blame on him for telling our mother about my lack of diligence. Then I called my mother and told her the result of her conversation in the bank. But in my class I became known as the student who had the courage to speak back to Dr. Keswani.

For me my last term was the most exciting because we were finally allowed to put our theoretical knowledge to use, treating real patients. The All India Institute was a teaching hospital with more than a thousand beds. But directly across the street was the government-run Safdarjung Hospital, which also had a thousand beds as well as an additional two hundred patients sleeping on the floor or on mattresses. The range of patients we saw at those hospitals was remarkable. When a patient was diagnosed with an unusual condition we would all excitedly make rounds with our teachers. We saw tropical diseases that are rarely seen in the United States, treated every form of tuberculosis, and saw patients with rabies and even leprosy. The actual practice of medicine was as exciting as I had imagined it would be.

Although my class was small, there was an effort made to have a lot of diversity in the group. There were more women than men and 30 percent of the seats were reserved for foreigners and people of the scheduled castes. In the Hindu caste system these are the people who had been referred to as the untouchables. For some of those people the school presented a great culture shock. One of the students from a scheduled caste, for example, came from a very small village. He was scandalized to see female classmates wearing skirts or frocks, any garment that showed their legs, as this was forbidden in his village. He spoke poor English and was very shy when we started, but by the time we graduated he had become proficient in English and we had become friends. And he no longer covered his eyes when a female classmate walked in wearing a skirt.

The person I became closest to, however, was Amita, the number one student in our class. I met her a few weeks after our first term started. There is a tradition at the Institute that the freshman class puts on a show for the other students. Amita loved music, and for that show she played the harmonica and convinced the whole class to sing along while she played. She also played the guitar and eventually organized a band at the school. I saw this as an opportunity to spend more time with her. Unfortunately I didn't sing well or play any instrument. So when Amita asked me what I could do, I said, "I can clap and I can whistle."

In reality I could clap.

I went to all the band practices, although mostly I just stood there. The name of this band was Mock Combo, and they played popular Western music, from Elvis Presley to the Beatles, as well as American country songs like "Red River Valley." We had no idea where Red River Valley was, just somewhere in the Old West.

Amita and I also bonded over table tennis. I was quite skilled at the game—but so was she. Table tennis, or Ping-Pong as Americans call it, is very popular in India. Amita's younger sister was going out with the junior national champion, so Amita had played a lot. In Amita's home they had set up a net across the center of the dining room table. To me this was impressive: She was both a lovely and intelligent young woman and an excellent table tennis player. I asked her to be my mixed-doubles partner in the medical school tournament. She agreed and we won the final decisively.

In India at that time young people didn't generally go out on dates. Instead, we went out as a group. Often Amita and I would go to dinner with her two sisters and even her mother, which was quite normal back then. But eventually I knew it was time for more. I approached Amita.

"I want to take you out for a date," I said. She asked me what I wanted to do. "Dinner and a movie." She asked me what movie I wanted to see. (She wasn't making this easy.) "It should be a surprise,"

I said. And so we went to see *Dr. Zhivago*, which I had already seen and loved.

Gradually we got to know each other. Amita loved India, so much that she had wanted to join the Foreign Service and travel the world educating people about our country and its values. In school she had studied economics, but after being persuaded to go into medicine, she took her premed courses.

Amita, I learned, was a much more spiritual person than I was. Her father had been an engineer for the Central Public Works Department, constructing roads and bridges, alternating between urban and remote areas of the country. As with my family, every two or three years the government would send them to another post. Although her father was a very practical man, every morning he would sit cross-legged in a lotus position on a deerskin rug, reading the Bhagavad Gita and meditating. He practiced a type of yogic meditation. Eventually Amita, too, would close her eyes and sit quietly in that lotus position. She didn't know what she was doing, she told me, but even from that tender age she yearned for spiritual experiences.

By the time we were ready to graduate we had decided to marry. While arranged marriages were still quite common in India, we had found each other and fallen in love. We prided ourselves on being modern Indians. I went to my parents and told them that we had decided to have a civil ceremony rather than the traditional large wedding.

My mother, obviously, was very disappointed.

"It's not for me," she said, "but for your grandfather. He'll be very sad that you're not following the ancient traditions."

"Don't worry, Mom," I said. "I'll talk to him." I spoke with my grandfather and promised him that we would do things right. Typically, in Indian weddings, several hundreds of people are invited to the reception. I told him that we were going to have a large reception at the fancy Delhi Gymkhana Club, one of India's oldest clubs, and that our marriage would be blessed by a priest. This was sufficient for him; he just wanted us to be happy.

Everything was set. But when Amita and I went to court to get a marriage license we were informed that we were too young. We learned that you had to be twenty-one to have a civil marriage in India. So I went back to my parents.

"We've changed our minds," I announced. "We're going to have a traditional Hindu wedding." In preparation my father and I sat down with the priest who would officiate. We wanted to be married on a certain date, so the priest looked at the star charts and told us that the date was not auspicious. My dad, being a modern physician, slipped the priest a couple of hundred rupees and asked him to take another look. The priest suddenly exclaimed that a planet was in a different position than he had originally thought and that the date my father had suggested was indeed very auspicious.

As the priest was leaving, I walked outside with him to his scooter. Hindu ceremonies can sometimes go on for hours; it's completely up to the officiant.

"Listen," I said. "Don't go on too long. If you keep the ceremony short, there's another bonus in it for you."

We had a lovely, brief, traditional Hindu marriage ceremony and set off to live a modern life. I had certainly gotten much more than I had bargained for out of medical school.

As I write this I'm reflecting on how fortunate I am to be married to Amita, a beautiful lady, a brilliant pediatrician, a very spiritual being, and a kindred soul for more than four decades.

9

Innocent Bystander

Deepak

Chopra brothers with their parents, lakeside, on a trip to
Mahabaleshwar, 1967.

I HAVEN'T MENTIONED HOW DEEPLY my father's patients affected me when I was growing up, largely because they didn't. A constant stream of sick people came through our house during the Jabalpur years. Many were desperate and broken, bewildered by their illness due to a complete ignorance of medicine. They made a pitiful sight, but my world was preoccupied with two obsessions that blocked them out: I was obsessed during school hours with study, and I unwound by obsessing over cricket the rest of the time. In Shillong, Sanjiv and I would run down the hill to a kiosk in the teeming bazaar that sold *Sport and Pastime* magazine. It had the latest news and pictures of our heroes in action. These we tore out to paste in our scrapbooks. Two early obsessions might have shaped my life but for the fact that a self is built from invisible bricks as well as the ones that show in the facade.

My father wanted me to become a doctor, but I don't remember his expressing disappointment when I set my sights on journalism instead. He didn't believe in interfering and put his faith in being a quiet influence. When he and my mother discussed his cases every evening, I wasn't coaxed to join in. His decisive move was much more subtle. One birthday my present was a set of popular novels. I wasn't aware that this was an act of insidious propaganda. But all three books featured doctors as their heroes, each hero deeply immersed in adventure, melodrama, and affairs of the heart. It was easy to believe that examining a pathology slide under the microscope was inches away from falling desperately in love or, second best, saving the world. (Since the plots are engraved in my memory, I'll mention that the three novels were *Of Human Bondage, Arrowsmith,* and *Magnificent Obsession.*) Reading fiction, it was possible to feel that medicine was romantic and sometimes tragic. At home my father was a constant presence, so it didn't occur to me that he had risen from nothing like Sinclair Lewis's Martin Arrowsmith and was as brilliantly skilled as Robert Merrick, the surgeon hero in *Magnificent Obsession.*

Something in me changed. The spell woven in those books lured me away from journalism, despite the fact that at sixteen I would eagerly have modeled my life on Rattan Chacha. My parents were overjoyed when I announced my decision to study medicine, but it posed a sizable practical problem. I was due to graduate from St. Columba's in December 1962 without any credits in biology, and without biology you couldn't get into medical school. The system had a loophole, however. I was on an educational track that mimicked English schooling so closely that our final exams, after finishing the grade known as 11 Standard, were O Levels set by Cambridge University. The exams were shipped over from England and then returned to Cambridge to be graded by hand. This cumbersome process took seven months before I would know if I had passed with honors.

In the meantime, from December to the following July, I was privately tutored in biology by a Bengali who came to the house every day and rushed me through the basics. I would then take a year of premed in Jabalpur at the college level. After that I could apply to medical school. When it came time to dissect a frog, my tutor and I went down to a pond and caught the frogs ourselves (this was India). He showed me a trick — sneak up on the frog from behind and with one swift motion pinch its spine, rendering it immobile.

Back home we pithed the specimen, which involved sticking a needle at the junction point between the skull and the spine. This paralyzed the frog while keeping it alive (it also blocked any pain). If you are suited to becoming a doctor, the first moment you open up a living creature is fascinating, as you set eyes on a beating heart and can view under a microscope the red blood corpuscles squeezing in single file through semitransparent capillaries. The squeamish quickly turn away. As the seven months wore on, I had to memorize hundreds of taxonomic facts, giving me general knowledge about classifying plants and animals in Latin that was totally useless to a doctor. But filling a storehouse of nickel knowledge served me in a

peculiar and satisfying way. In effect, I pithed my emotions by sticking a needle at the junction point where the brain meets the heart.

Medical training winnows out a portion of human nature, especially the emotions. This is deliberate. A doctor is a technician whose
task is to spot defects and injuries in the human body. He relates to
it as a garage mechanic relates to a damaged automobile. Both run
body shops. The more efficient the interaction between doctor and
patient, the better. Tears and distress are irrelevant, even if they are
all too human. In my father's practice, his patients had not grasped
how to play their part with efficiency. They were like car owners who
accost a mechanic with statements like "I love my Subaru so much,
it breaks my heart to see it like this" rather than "The steering feels
a little loose." My father was also inefficient. He empathized with his
patients' distress instead of blocking it out so that he could imperson-
ally assess which parts were broken — and there were literally thousands of parts to consider, down to the most microscopic detail. (In
fairness, my father always warned us not to form an emotional attachment with patients, advice he routinely ignored himself.)

I'm exaggerating the contrast because my inclination was toward
the scientific and impersonal from a very early stage. I was nothing
if not a professional student. I could memorize reams of facts. I saw,
too, that if you didn't want to be left behind, you woke up to the bald
fact that medicine *is* science. My father was just at the cusp of this
realization, which may seem strange since Louis Pasteur had established the germ theory of disease in the 1850s. But practice didn't
keep up with theory. In *The Youngest Science,* Lewis Thomas's memoir of three generations of doctors, he points out the futility of medicine well into the twentieth century.

A doctor's traditional role was to comfort far more than to heal.
He sat at his patient's bedside dispensing hope and a generous supply of patent medicines that were nostrums at best. At worst they
were vehicles for substances like laudanum, a narcotic so liberally
prescribed that it turned countless Victorian women, who believed
in taking a spoonful of tonic a day, into hopeless addicts. Childhood
illnesses like rheumatic fever left damage that lasted for life. Survival

depended on the patient's immune system, not on anything the doctor could do. As for adult afflictions like cancer, stroke, heart attacks, and infected wounds, these were invariably fatal. Lewis points out that his father, a skilled physician, didn't routinely cure anyone until the discovery of penicillin in 1928. The wholesale marketing of drugs like streptomycin, the first antibiotic to treat the scourge of tuberculosis, didn't come about until the late Forties (not early enough in widespread use to save the life of George Orwell, who died of TB in 1950, much less D. H. Lawrence, who succumbed to it in 1930. Both were in their forties).

My father joined the great wave of scientific medicine as it arrived in India, which was the main fact that I absorbed. But I missed something important — maybe the most important thing of all — that was wrapped up in a wartime anecdote. He rarely spoke about his experiences in World War II, and most people have forgotten, if they ever knew, that the Japanese did invade India, marching up from Burma into the far northeast state of Manipur. There the Battle of Kohima took place, a grueling three-month siege in 1944 that became a turning point in the war. Kohima was later called the Stalingrad of the war in Asia, after the deadly winter siege in Russia.

Serving as a medical officer, my father encountered suffering that he never wanted to talk about. In that he was like many veterans after they came home. But one patient stuck in his mind, a private who overnight became unable to speak. It was assumed that he had suffered a stroke; aphasia — the loss of speech — results when a specific region of the brain, Broca's area, has been damaged. My father examined the young soldier and agreed with the diagnosis. But one day some new facts emerged.

Apparently mail had managed to arrive at the front, and this soldier had received a distressing communication that his mother had died. He went to his sergeant to ask for a few days' leave from the front lines in order to grieve, but before he could finish his sentence, he was angrily dismissed — no shirkers were allowed in the heat of battle. Going over his sergeant's head, he went to the platoon commander with his request, then to the regimental command. But each time, as soon as he got out the words "I need leave, sir. My mother has — ", he was abruptly cut short.

A day later he lost the ability to speak.

My father went to the distraught soldier's tent and sat beside him. He had made a connection between the mother's death and the symptom of aphasia. It wasn't due to a stroke. The soldier wasn't allowed to finish his sentence, and this traumatized him into the belief that speaking was hopeless. Why not stop altogether? My father didn't reveal his thinking but simply asked the soldier if he wanted to talk about his mother. At that moment the aphasia disappeared in a flood of tearful words.

When he recounted this incident, my father wasn't trying to evoke pathos. He was fascinated as a diagnostician. I can't pride myself on being precocious, either. Listening to the story, I didn't suddenly discover the mind-body connection. The only effect on me was hidden, one of those invisible bricks that build a self. Besides, there was Linnaeus's system of classification to memorize after high school, and when genera and species got too boring, I'd play tennis for hours on end with a beautiful general's daughter named Deepika, the female equivalent of my name. (The games went no further. Our names meant light, but we struck no sparks.)

When the autumn of 1963 came, I started taking premed courses in Jabalpur. More rote memorization lay ahead, years of it. I had no awareness of inner turmoil. I saw nothing insidious about learning to block out emotion as I learned to be scientific. Compassion was an unintended casualty, like an innocent bystander in the throes of wartime.

At seventeen I had no idea who Elvis Presley was, or Cassius Clay. They became real, and instantly exciting, thanks to a rich boy who rode his bicycle with me to Robertson College every morning. Sunil Jain knew about events in America because his parents talked about them. He goaded me (unsuccessfully) to bet on whether Clay could beat a hulking bruiser like Sonny Liston, and listening to him discourse on the subject of Elvis was like listening to an Apollo astronaut describe the feel of moondust under his boots. We usually met to discuss these alien topics in his family's mansion in an exclusive part of Jabalpur.

The only person I knew who had actually set foot in America was one of the Irish Christian Brothers who taught at school. His main impression of New York City was that he had walked block after block without hearing a bird and that no crows perched overhead. One day he announced to the class that Marilyn Monroe had died. From there he launched into dark warnings about the debauched lifestyle that many Americans led and told us to avoid two curses, fame and alcohol, if we ever went there.

Sunil had many sisters but no brothers. The sisters hovered in the background, giggling and whispering with curiosity about me. Servants drifted in and out of Sunil's private rooms with spiced tea or garlic and onion soup. But wealth wasn't nearly as thrilling to me as "Jailhouse Rock." In retrospect I suspect that Sunil, worldly as he was, didn't know about the Beatles. They arrived in my world much later, in the luggage of visiting med students from the United States, along with surreptitious tiny packets of LSD. Well into medical school I was invited to parties where *Sgt. Pepper's Lonely Hearts Club Band* was played incessantly while boys and girls sat on chairs sipping Coke. The girls' braided hair was glossy and black, the air scented with the jasmine sweetness of a flower called *Raat Ki Rani,* queen of the night.

Sunil was as ambitious as I was to become a doctor. Premed lasted only a year. I lived in the front part of the Raos' house, in the same compound where Mrs. Rao ran a maternity clinic with fifty beds. This place felt like home but also like the future I was meant for. The leading lights of the town went to her husband for X-rays and to her to have their babies. Sunil's family was unfamiliar but enticing: They were Jains by religion — the same as their family name — and therefore strict vegetarians. My lasting image is of studying with him late into the night, and of a large swing under the mango trees where birdcalls were mixed with the sound of giggling girls somewhere in the shrubbery. It was also at their house that a servant ran in gasping with the news that President Kennedy had been assassinated.

Every Indian knew that First Lady Jacqueline Kennedy was a great friend of Nehru's. (Whatever their relationship may have been, she took up yoga seriously enough that, without public notice, she invited a yoga instructor to her house for daily private lessons for many years.) Under Sunil's influence I had learned to look beyond London — the center of the universe for almost every Indian — across the ocean to America. But even if that hadn't happened, the Kennedy assassination would have seemed like an event of global importance, a blow that struck at the hearts of the young and hopeful.

I graduated from premed with the right credentials and the grades to apply to a major medical school. I was still seventeen, and since India followed the English model of going very young into medical training, I would barely be eighteen when I began to dissect my first cadaver. None of this seemed daunting to think about, but the process of choosing a medical school was confusing. I was accepted at the highly regarded Maulana Azad Medical College in Delhi, and I'm sure I could have been happy there. A more distant prospect was getting into the All India Institute of Medical Sciences, also in Delhi. Since it had thousands of applicants but accepted only thirty-five new students a year, the Institute ran its own battery of tests, with no weight given to your college grades. Besides a science exam, there was an English test (one of my strengths, fortunately) and a psychological interview that included, no doubt because of the Americans, a Rorschach inkblot test, the only one I have ever encountered.

The Americans came into it because the Institute was supported by the Rockefeller Foundation. It was actually built, however, by New Zealand government money in 1956 after the original plans, drawn up by Prime Minister Nehru for a medical school in Calcutta, were killed by a powerful Bengali minister. (Nehru's other project in modern education, the Indian Institute of Technology, was also born in 1956, on the site of an abandoned detention camp in Kharagpur. It became more famous than the medical equivalent. Getting into IIT for training as an engineer turned into a life-and-death matter for upwardly mobile families. When asked what she would do if her son didn't get in to IIT, one mother sighed and said, "There's always Harvard and Stanford.")

To my surprise I was accepted into the All India Institute and went on to receive a first-class medical education, which was highlighted by rotating visits from British and American professors from the top schools in those countries. But I must jump ahead. I said before that I was humiliated and crushed only twice in my life. The first time occurred when I got the yellow report card in Shillong. The second, which was far worse, occurred at the end of medical school.

Besides passing the regular course work, there was an oral exam for new graduates at the very end. This wasn't a formality; it spelled the difference between passing and failing. Each student was presented with a case to diagnose. The patient would have a rare or exotic disease which we would have to discover through doing a physical examination and asking questions — no blood work or laboratory tests were permitted. If we made the correct diagnosis, we then had to prescribe a course of treatment from memory.

For the sake of impartiality, an examiner from our school was joined by an outside examiner brought in from another medical school. If the aim was fairness, the result was intense rivalry. The outside examiners were sarcastic and belittling in their attempts to make us look bad. Even putting bowls of sweetmeats in front of them, which was supposed to soften their dispositions, didn't ease tensions. My outside examiner, unfortunately, was a fierce senior professor known for his brutality. But I was good at questioning patients and had confidence in my recall of obscure medical facts.

"What is your diagnosis of this patient?" the outside examiner barked as soon as I entered the room. I was taken aback. The professor from my school intervened.

"Wouldn't you like to hear his findings first?" This was the usual routine, since it was important to know how we had arrived at our diagnosis. The outside examiner brushed the question aside.

"Your diagnosis," he demanded.

"Friedreich's ataxia, sir," I replied.

The professor from my school broke out in a relieved smile, but the outside examiner laughed harshly.

"Who tipped you off?"

The man stubbornly refused to believe that I hadn't been coached. My face turned red. I felt dizzy on my feet. Friedreich's ataxia is a neurological disorder; it is inherited, and typical symptoms like difficulty walking and speaking are shared by other nervous disorders. I managed to find the presence of mind to protest that I hadn't cheated, but in a loud voice the outside examiner declared that the one thing he couldn't abide was a liar. I had failed the exam. After considerable begging, not just from me but from my professor, he relented enough to allow me to take the exam over. But the failing mark would stand.

The second time around was ridiculously easy by comparison. My patient showed all the common signs of rheumatic fever. I passed without honors when I had gone into that room the first time expecting to receive the highest honors. My blood runs cold at the memory, which proves the power of humiliation even when it isn't deserved. Another invisible brick hidden away for the future.

In medical school you cut up bodies. Everyone knows this, and some people are in awe, because they imagine that a wave of sick revulsion would keep them from slicing through a person's skin to reach in and lift out the liver or gallbladder. Actually there is very little revulsion. In the first place you aren't dissecting a person. All the juice — blood, saliva, spinal fluid, semen, mucous secretions, and the rest — have been drained out, replaced with preservative. The standard one is formalin, a solution of formaldehyde and water, and its smell is very difficult to remove once it has gotten on you. I understand this intimately because we didn't wear gloves while working with cadavers.

My dissecting partner was named Aruna, an attractive girl who was also a quick study. We were too focused on following the wandering course of the vagus nerve or peeling back the cornea after popping an eyeball out of its socket to behave like two normal eighteen-year-olds. But the smell of formalin on our hands, which we neurotically spent hours trying to scrub away, made us unfit to date anyone else, now that I consider it.

Medicine has been called a priesthood, and most of that initiation takes place in the dissecting room, because even without revulsion, cutting open a body is a momentous event. Everything sacred is violated. The heart is no longer the seat of the soul but a bundle of tough, fibrous muscle. If Pallas Athena sprang fully grown from the brow of Zeus, her feet must have been mired in the oatmeal-textured gray mush of the brain. A cold wave of objectivity settles over you, as it must.

For Aruna and me, our whole intent was on gross anatomy, a mechanical process of slicing, sawing, and peeling away. We didn't follow pictures but rather the detailed written descriptions in our textbook. These were amazingly lucid, and once you reached your desired goal, that part of the body would never be forgotten, even if it was one of the three tiny bones in the middle ear, which are one-tenth of an inch long and so flexible that they quiver at the sound of a mosquito's wings. Surgery is an act of deliberate violence that becomes moral because the surgeon is doing good. Chopping up a cadaver is just as violent, and it becomes moral because there's no one home. The ghost has fled the machine.

Morality is half of it, which no one even mentions when it comes down to wielding a scalpel. More critical is to make the violence normal. I didn't completely succeed at this. On my first day in surgery three of us were assigned to assist a tall, bearded Sikh performing kidney surgery. He was an imposing figure wearing a turban crisscrossed with green surgical tape. My assigned task consisted of holding a retractor in position, without moving throughout the entire procedure — this could have been as long as three hours. I don't actually know, because I was booted out of the operating room.

My troubles began as I moved closer to the patient to take one of the retractors that were holding back skin and connective tissue so that the surgeon could see what he was doing. He was leaning over the exposed kidney, and I came too close, accidentally brushing the sleeve of his gown with a gloved finger. Without saying a word or even looking in my direction, he walked out. Through a small window in the door we watched as he removed his gown, scrubbed his arms and hands, and put on a new pair of sterile gloves. This took five agonizing minutes. Then he returned, still without saying a word, and carefully retraced the steps to get back to where he had left off.

Somehow, in another attempt to get close enough to watch, my hand brushed the sleeve of his gown again.

"You, stand over there," he snapped, pointing to a spot well away from the table. "Don't touch me again." Glaring at me, he stalked out of the room and repeated the entire cleaning procedure a second time, for what seemed like half an hour. I was terribly embarrassed, standing silently and all but motionless behind him when he returned. Clearly I couldn't be trusted to do anything except observe. But even that proved to be too much. I focused for a few minutes on the surgeon's back—the only thing I could really see—but then my eyes began to wander. I noticed a black rubber disk on the floor. I couldn't guess what its purpose was, and without thinking I moved my foot and stepped on it.

Sparks flew from the surgeon's hands. I had stepped on the electrical connection to the special knife used to cauterize blood vessels, shorting it out and giving him a jolt. He put down his instruments and turned to face me.

"You are not a surgery student," he said in a flat, deadly tone. "You are a bull in my china shop."

When he told me that I didn't need to come back, it wasn't necessary to add "ever, ever again." We both knew he was right. For the rest of medical school I never participated in another surgery. So it seems ludicrous that I passed the course. But I did, thanks to the constant presence of memorization. I sat with my surgical textbooks and learned by rote a skill I could no more have practiced than an actor pretending to be a surgeon on television. But I became an excellent theoretical surgeon. I learned all the techniques and memorized every surgical instrument and its uses. Since our exams required us only to answer questions on paper, not to actually operate, I went into the finals without the slightest anxiety about not passing.

Why do so few doctors have a Buddha moment? Being filled with compassion is the essence of Buddha nature, as it is called. Legend has it that when he was a privileged prince named Siddhartha, the future Buddha sneaked out of the palace one night and set eyes on a sick man, an old man, and a corpse. This glimpse of human suffering made him renounce his right to the throne, and the sight of a fourth man, a wandering monk, told Siddhartha how to seek the solution to suffering.

I don't think I'm being accusatory when I say that modern medical training practically ensures that compassion won't be unnecessary. The first sight of a massive gunshot wound in the emergency room is a terrible, upsetting experience. The second is slightly better. By the hundredth, however, you are drained of shock and pity for the most part. Repetition dulls your response, but that is only superficial. What really happens is adaptation, one of the wonders of the human nervous system. Anything can be normalized once the brain is trained to accept it. Entering a burning building, riding on the back of a killer whale at Sea World, hauling snow crabs out of the raging Arctic Sea — they all progress with astonishing quickness from "You want me to do what?" to "It's the job."

Adaptation is a two-edged sword. It allowed me to fit into the specialized world of medicine by suppressing the parts of myself that weren't needed. At moments I could still step back and be more human, could hold the hand of a dying woman with real pity or shake my head sorrowfully, after I came to America, at the sight of a ghetto child who had been caught in the gunfire between two gangs in New Jersey. Adaptation doesn't completely hard wire your brain.

Unless you want it to. In the cold light of day, isn't compassion a hindrance when you only have ten minutes to save the life of a gunshot victim? This logic is good enough for the practice of emergency medicine. When I was a young doctor, it satisfied me. But there's a flaw in the logic. What if compassion is a form of healing? If that seems too far-fetched, say that compassion is a window through which we can see a different world, where a completely different way to heal becomes possible. In that world there are ancient kinds of traditional medicine. There are shamans and healers. There is energy work, herbal remedies, sacred rituals and prayers. In my training, however, no such world existed — or should be condoned. The window must remain sealed, and it was for me for many years.

10

Real Doctors

Sanjiv

Deepak and Sanjiv on their first ski trip to Vermont, 1973.

TWO YEARS AFTER DEEPAK concluded his medical training, Amita and I did our posting in the village of Kurali.
As part of our one-year internship we had to spend three
months in a village diagnosing and treating the poor and uninsured.
It was called the social-medicine rotation. Kurali was only about
forty miles outside Delhi, but it was entirely rural. The town, where
the electricity would go off several times a day, had a bicycle shop, a
tea store, a few other shops, and a small school with a principal and a
teacher. We lived in one room, more of a hut, which was often lit by
candles. But that lack of modern amenities did not concern us at all.
For the first time we were actually practicing medicine. Being only
twenty years old and having the trust of these villagers was a very
powerful feeling. At times it made us feel like we were much older,
and much wiser, than in fact we were.

It was a challenging situation. We'd spent four years learning how
to use the tools of the modern physician, and we were expected to
practice medicine without any of them. Deepak had warned us what
to expect, so we were not surprised to discover that the dispensary
had only a limited number of drugs and almost no medical equipment. We didn't even have an X-ray machine. It was hands-on medicine at the most basic level.

We did have two registrars in medicine who supervised the interns
assigned to the three villages in our area. They were brimming with
knowledge and experience. We thought they were so wise. At night
we would sit with them over dinner and talk about medicine. We
were very busy, seeing as many as one hundred and fifty patients a
day. Most of my work was stitching up wounds, setting broken bones,
and giving out tetanus shots. Amita treated almost all of our female
patients and the majority of the children. In India many women will

not go to a male physician, so she treated the entire range of women's conditions.

It was hard work, but I loved every minute of it. I was doing what I had wanted to do my whole life. And on occasion I was able to make a real difference in a patient's life. One gentleman came to see me with very vague symptoms. He had lost some weight, he had a slight fever and a very brassy cough, and he was often tired. Even at that young age I loved the challenge of diagnosing a difficult case, applying the lessons learned in the classroom to a real-life patient. I put my stethoscope on his back and asked him to breathe in and out. His heartbeat seemed unusually loud, so I asked him to count "one, two, three" in a whisper. I could hear it loudly through my stethoscope. This sign is called a whispering pectoriloquy. It often indicates that the patient has a tumor abutting the airway, conducting the sound. I couldn't be certain, but I suspected he had lymphoma.

I told the registrar my patient needed an X-ray. We had a van that made the trip to Delhi several times a week. He was sent to the All India Institute and, sure enough, he had a mass in his chest. It was biopsied and it came back positive for Hodgkin's lymphoma. He was treated with radiation and did well for several years.

I had saved a life. It was an extraordinary feeling. I was lauded by the registrar for making that diagnosis based only on a small physical finding. For a few days I was a local hero.

There were conditions we treated in that village that I would never see again in my entire career. A young boy who had been bitten by a dog was brought to the clinic by his mother. In that situation the greatest fear is rabies. One of the symptoms of rabies is hydrophobia. I don't know why this happens, but if you put water in front of someone with rabies it terrifies them. It always seemed strange to me, but that's what we had been taught. So I filled a pitcher with water and put it in front of his face—and he started screaming. He jerked violently to get away from it. His face was contorted with fear. It was a remarkable but sad sight, but it made it easy for me to diagnose his illness. The young boy died. His face and expression are indelibly imprinted in my memory.

While there were no Ayurvedic hospitals or clinics in this area, there were practitioners of this ancient medicine who worked from their homes. Most of the people who lived in Kurali respected both forms of medicine. Sometimes patients came to see us after Ayurvedic treatment had failed to cure their problem, and sometimes they went to a local practitioner after our treatment.

Our days were filled with treating patients, but at night we were free to do whatever we wanted. Amita and I were newlyweds living in the country, away from our families. After the pressure of medical school, in some ways this was an idyllic situation. We often got together with our classmates posted in the nearby villages. We didn't have a car, so Amita would sit on the crossbar on the front of a bicycle and I would pedal the four or five miles through the fields to the next village. We would drink beer and dance to modern Western music like Elvis Presley and the Beatles. Then we'd get back on the bike and ride home under a sky filled with bright stars, bathed in perfect silence.

At this time India was fighting a war against Pakistan and we were used to having blackout drills. There were nights we were riding on those dark roads when air raid sirens went off, followed by the sound of a plane overhead. Those beautiful skies were suddenly threatening. We looked up, afraid that it might be Pakistani bombers. Only later did we learn that my uncle Admiral N. N. Nanand would play a pivotal role in India's eventual victory.

There was one ride home I remember well. We had been celebrating in another village and our classmates served us pakoras, a popular type of fritter made with chicken, potatoes, or cauliflower. They tasted delicious, but our classmate had neglected to tell us that he'd baked *Bhang*, a product of the hemp plant similar to marijuana, into the fritters. I had never tried any type of drug before and I was powerfully affected. It was not a feeling I liked and I was really angry when I found out what he'd done. I cursed him, vowing to take vengeance, then drank a pot of coffee to get sober as quickly as possible. But then we had to ride bicycles back to our village. There were nights I'd ridden home after drinking a few beers, but this was the longest ride of my life. That was the last time I ever experienced a recreational drug.

When our posting in the village ended we had changed considerably. Amita and I had arrived in Kurali as young medical school graduates with no practical experience. We left months later having treated thousands of patients, flush with confidence in our abilities and clinical acumen. We were ready to be real doctors, not just kids with a medical degree.

11

Godfather Land

Deepak

Chopra family grabbing a moment with
Hillary Rodham Clinton, June 2007.

I RODE TO MY WEDDING on horseback, with people dancing in the streets. All the relatives on my father's side wore flower garlands and joyful faces. I was ecstatic, too, and in the back of my mind I uttered a small grateful prayer for having learned to ride a pony growing up; there was only a slim chance the groom would fall off his mount when he arrived at the bride's house to greet her. The traditional procession of the groom to meet the bride is called a *Baraat*. Sometimes the horse is white; mine was brown, and to tell the truth it was a placid animal, being a veteran of weddings all its life, not races.

We were moving through Defence Colony to a house not far from our own. A hired brass band tooted all the way. Rita must have heard it in the distance as her aunts and cousins finished fussing over the gold and jewels that an Indian bride is decked out with — these are usually heirlooms passed down from both families. I adjusted my turban and straightened up in the saddle as our dancing procession rounded the last corner to her house. The pundits who would perform the ceremony awaited, and a place had been made in the back for the sacred fire.

When you throw in the finery draped over the horse (and me), the flower garlands that the two families put over each other before embracing, and the Christmas lights twinkling in the bride's house, a Westerner might smirk at the gaudiness of this affair. (Because a close aunt of Rita's had just died, there were no twinkling lights in the house, actually.) But I was playing maharaja for a day, and Rita, as my maharani, looked radiant. There wasn't a speck of gaudiness. This was splendor.

We had arrived at this moment in February 1970 after a romance that had lasted two years, during which our physical contact amounted to less than what occurs on many first dates in America.

Our families had known each other for years, since before I was born. Her father's surname was also Chopra, and both couples were married on the same day, by chance. The two fathers had the armed services in common, since Rita's father had served in the air force, both British and Indian. Secretly the two mothers had hoped to make a match, but Rita and I weren't told. Arranged marriages were common — and still are — but we were left to make our own choices. There was no prejudice in our minds against parents deciding that a certain match would be good for both sides. I knew of happy marriages that had been arranged, and so did Rita. Her older sister's was one. But we fell in love by a sinuous path because, as wildly romantic as Indians can be, practicalities aren't ignored. The word "suitable" is used a lot.

Although we had been aware of each other from early childhood, it took very sad circumstances for us to move closer. I was still in medical school. I came through the hospital wards on rounds one day to see a very sick woman with Rita sitting by her bedside. This was her aunt, I learned, who had been admitted with a serious lung condition that turned out to be untreatable. It took a year before she passed away in the hospital, going through stages of degeneration that robbed her of speech and eventually of breath. Rita came regularly to visit during that year, and we began to talk.

The heart was discreetly given space to grow. We talked but didn't touch. She brought up the Beatles, who were no longer alien to me. They had followed a guru to India in 1968. The Beatles stayed only briefly, in Rishikesh far to the north, where many spiritual luminaries had their ashrams, but once the world saw photos of them with Maharishi Mahesh Yogi, it made him instantly famous. The West suddenly turned its gaze on India; the country had been put on the map. Maharishi wore white robes and a long beard, already turning from gray to white. There was always a rose in his hand. He had laughing eyes and a radiant smile. When he greeted someone, he held his hands together in the gesture of *Namaste,* with a faint bow of the head, and murmured *"Jai Guru Dev,"* a salutation to his own teacher. (The phrase entered into the lyrics of a Beatles song, "Across the Universe," and one reads in various accounts that their stay in India was very productive. Music was more on their minds than enlightenment.) None of this felt exotic to me — for one thing, I had visited yogis with my uncle — but the hint of charisma around Maharishi made me remember those wire-service photographs.

As infrequently as Rita and I had met in the past, one encounter sticks out. I was at St. Columba's, waiting for the bus in front of the girls' convent school. It began pouring rain, and a car pulled up. Rita's mother called out, offering me a lift, and as I gratefully climbed into the backseat, I found Rita beside me. It was a romantic shock for teenagers to sit so close. I didn't forget it. This encounter, along with one other, was enough to start whispers of a romance. I was half of the two-man debating team that my medical school sponsored, and we happened to stage a debate at Lady Shri Ram College, the women's college in Delhi where Rita was studying English literature. Rita showed up and, more to the point, she sat in the front row, right at my feet. I'm sure I was nervous and that I tried to stick out my chest. Debating had gotten me noticed. Not just by Rita. A man came up after our team won a contest and told me that I had a good voice for radio. That had crossed my mind, but very soon I was reading the late-night news for an overseas broadcast that reached Indians in other countries, especially in Africa.

It was heartbreaking for Rita to watch as her aunt got worse and no one could help. (This was the aunt who died just before our wedding, adding the only note of somberness to the day.) I found myself discovering reasons to be on the ward when I knew Rita would be there. At that time private telephones were very difficult to get in India. There was a two-year waiting list, and even then getting one often meant paying a hefty bribe. So the only opportunity we had to be together was when Rita visited the hospital.

We didn't date, but because our families had known each other for so long, we were permitted to socialize. Two years and several turning points passed before the wedding. I graduated without distinction from medical school thanks to the debacle with the outside examiner. With my father's encouragement I decided to go to America for my advanced training; London had been the place to go when he was young, but no longer. The Americans went from triumph to triumph in medical research.

India didn't want its best graduates to flee to the West, so it had banned the test that the United States required before foreign-trained doctors could enter the country. I had to fly to Ceylon to take this exam, which was only minimal. Once I arrived in America, I would still have to pass the same state medical boards as any native-born doctor. While I was in Ceylon I was walking through the bazaar, and a beautiful necklace caught my fancy. I brought it home with me, and when I saw Rita I gave it to her and asked her to marry me. She said yes and burst into tears. When we told our mothers, they were so excited that they kept frantically trying to call each other and getting busy signals for several hours.

With the help of an American foundation that supplied foreign doctors for community hospitals and even paid their airfare, I landed an internship in Plainfield, New Jersey, at Muhlenberg Hospital. It was a private facility, very well equipped, with four hundred beds. Newly married, our trip to America was also our honeymoon, with eight dollars for travel expenses, all that the Indian government allowed citizens to take out of the country. Fortunately my uncle Narendra, who was an admiral in the Indian navy, had been a naval cadet in England. He still had the equivalent of a hundred dollars stashed overseas, which he gave us as a belated wedding present. The number one hundred is propitious, which added to the kind gesture.

After landing at JFK, Rita and I found ourselves checking into a motel somewhere in the wilds of New Jersey. We were exhausted but too excited to sleep. I flipped from channel to channel, fascinated with color TV, which neither of us had ever seen. I landed on coverage of tennis from Wimbledon, which was interrupted by a local news bulletin. During an attempted robbery, two people had been shot. The victims were being wheeled on stretchers into an emergency room. My stomach churned, and I half collapsed onto the bed.

"My God," I exclaimed. "They're taking them to my hospital."

For the first time in my medical career I felt frightened. I had no preparation to deal with patients in an immediate life-and-death situation. I'd never even seen a gunshot wound. I perched on the edge of the bed staring at the phone, afraid that I'd be called into the ER. Thankfully the phone didn't ring.

I began working the next night. I was in charge of the entire ER on the overnight shift. On strict instruction I was not to wake up the chief resident unless it was absolutely necessary. Even then he would not look fondly on being called by a nervous intern in the middle of the night. I was determined not to let that happen. Everything was under control, because it had to be.

Our time in Plainfield lasted a year, beginning in July 1970. When I walked into the ER for my first shift, the doctors who showed me my locker and gave me a tour of the acute care facilities were not Americans. There was one German, but the rest had Asian faces like mine, from India, Pakistan, the Philippines, and Korea. The nurses, who included some in training at the adjacent nursing school, were local girls, often with Italian last names. What had brought so many foreign doctors together was the Vietnam War. A severe doctor shortage had arisen as the army drained away medical school graduates while other young men, who might have wanted to become doctors, were drafted to fight.

For all my nervousness, there was no one to treat on my first shift. This wasn't like an inner-city ER with its constant flow of patients from the streets. Toward the end of a listless night, one of the duty nurses appeared, saying that I was needed for an expiration. I'd never heard the term before, but I didn't want to embarrass myself, so I didn't ask. She led me down an abandoned corridor into a hospital room where the patient was lying in bed, staring with fixed eyes at the ceiling. Ah, that's what expiration meant.

"What do you expect me to do?" I asked. "He's dead."

"A doctor has to pronounce before we can move him," she said.

This nurse must have introduced a good many foreign doctors to American lingo. I checked the body for a pulse; there wasn't one. I hadn't brought a medical flashlight to examine the man's eyes; if his pupils didn't react to light, it was one of the critical signs of death.

"I forgot my torch," I said. "Do you have one?"

"We want you to pronounce him, not cremate him!"

That an Indian would use the British term for a flashlight wasn't part of her experience, apparently. There was nothing more I could do, so I started to leave, but the nurse stopped me. The man's relatives, who were gathered in the waiting room, needed to be told. It was my responsibility to deliver the news. In India this wouldn't be anyone's job since the patient's family is always in the room with him.

Reluctantly I went where I was told to go. Maybe eight people were in the waiting room. They got to their feet when I walked in, wearing silent, solemn expressions. I started to speak when I realized that I didn't know the dead man's name. His relatives waited expectantly, and I found the only words that came to mind.

"I'm sorry, but we've had an expiration."

Some of the family burst out crying. One man pumped my hand, profusely thanking me for everything I'd done. I nodded, trying to preserve my dignity, and fled. A feeling of complete helplessness lingered, and I thought, how strange to be in a country where a sick man is connected to a battery of machines and disconnected from his family, whom he needs the most.

Acute care became a public crusade in Plainfield after a serious train wreck with multiple victims. This was just at the beginning of trauma medicine as a specialty—another field where America was far in the lead—and I learned to work at a furious pace. The local crime rate was high by my standards, even in the suburbs. Guns were easy to obtain, and every Friday night saw the arrival of at least two or three ambulances with young males, generally black or Italian, who had taken a bullet in the chest. The time pressure was intense.

I prided myself on turning into a doctor machine as the victims rolled in. With an assist from an ER nurse, our team tried to keep the victims from passing out and to extract a story from them about what had happened. Getting a useful medical history was practically impossible. Meanwhile I, the newbie doctor, examined their wounds, took their vital signs, hooked them up to a cardiac monitor, IV drip, and oxygen tube, probed for critical damage to the major arteries, heart sac, and spleen (locations of quick fatalities if we didn't get there first), made sure that the patient wasn't bleeding out internally, started transfusing saline solution and the first pints of blood if needed, removed the bullet, closed the wound, called for a surgical consult if the damage was especially horrendous, and filled out my notes as the groaning, half-conscious patient was wheeled off to his next stop in the wards. There was a likelihood that these same young males would show up down the road with another gunshot wound, but we worked at a life-and-death pace without thinking about that.

It wasn't all trauma associated with violence. I found myself treating the sudden medical emergencies of everyday life: drunks who had fallen down and gashed their heads, children with high fevers, a woman who began hemorrhaging as she was trying to perform a self-abortion, a professional man having a heart attack. Often an incident implied a story that the person was too embarrassed to reveal. One of the other interns saved a collection of X-rays to pull out at the height of doctor-and-nurse parties. The X-rays revealed some of the amazing and wonderful things people lost in unlikely orifices.

The breaks between emergencies were a dead time. I had been reading Mario Puzo's *The Godfather,* and asked one of the local nurses about the rumors that the Mafia had a sizable influence in that area of New Jersey and that it even had a financial stake in our hospital. She gave me a smile I couldn't read.

"Let's just say that if my father knew I was dating a Korean doctor, they'd have something to pull out of the river tomorrow."

After two months I felt totally in charge when a night's calm broke into organized frenzy for half an hour. I don't know if my cockiness was out of bounds for my surroundings. I was so exhausted pulling long shifts, driving my red VW Bug home at dawn in a state of terminal bleariness, that I couldn't think of what was coming next for me. Then one night an ambulance brought in a young man who was dead on arrival, and I called the county medical examiner. It was after midnight.

"I don't have to come in," the medical examiner told me on the phone. "Just sign off on cause of death."

"There's a problem," I said. "I don't see anything wrong with him — no wounds, no obvious marks."

"Right. So put down heart attack."

I was taken aback. The DOA was just a kid, maybe twenty-three at most. Virtually no one that age dies of a heart attack.

"Don't you want to do an autopsy?" I asked. I had already told the medical examiner how young the dead man was. Maybe he had been poisoned or was the victim of a dangerous disease that might be contagious. What about the risk to his family and friends? I thought.

The voice at the other end grew sharper. "Who do you think you are? Put down heart attack."

There was a moment's tense silence, and then I refused. The next morning I was called on the carpet by one of the attending physicians who was my supervisor.

"Whatever the medical examiner tells you to do, you do it" was the clear message I received. It was a matter of obeying the rules, not finding out the truth. The dead man was poor; no trouble would be made over how he died. But my insolence couldn't be dismissed that easily. Our attending physicians were all Americans. They typically didn't consider anyone trained in Asia to be a real doctor. Even the single American intern on staff, who had gone to medical school in Bologna, Italy, was suspect. The more tactful attendings tried to conceal their prejudices, but the implication was never far away.

My supervisor began talking more pointedly. He reminded me that I needed this job, what with a young wife at home and a baby on the way. I knew what was good for me, didn't I? We wouldn't want anything to go wrong. (Troubling images from *The Godfather* flickered in my head.) Toward the end, however, his tone softened. He put his hand on my shoulder.

"Hey, if you do a really good job here, who knows? Maybe you can get to Boston."

I doubt his sincerity looking back, but his words started the wheels turning in my head. Boston medicine was the holy grail for a young, ambitious doctor. My debating partner in medical school, a Muslim named Abul Abbas, was a brilliant student. We had become best friends, and his brilliance carried him directly from India to an internship at Peter Bent Brigham Hospital, one of the most prestigious hospitals affiliated with Harvard. Abul Abbas kept in touch, regularly calling me with enviable tales about the paradise that was Boston and urging me to get there as quickly as possible.

It didn't take long. When my year's internship in New Jersey was completed, I secured a residency at a good place in Boston, thanks to Abul's help. For the next two years I'd be working at the Lahey Clinic. It was a private hospital, which Abul called the Mayo Clinic of the East, with ties to Harvard even though it wasn't an affiliated hospital like Brigham. Rita and I settled in the predominantly black section of Jamaica Plain, which had disturbingly high crime but also the only rents cheap enough for a struggling resident. What lay ahead was the hardest work of my life, harder than I could have imagined, even though I considered myself tireless — you had to be, if you wanted to keep playing the hero.

To augment my thousand dollars a month from Lahey, which mostly went toward the rent, I moonlighted at a suburban ER for four dollars an hour, which meant that I might go three or four days without sleep. Medical training in America was brutal. Our long shifts were supposed to make us think on our feet and to make the right decisions under stress. Because it was still in my character to obey authority without question, I didn't ask how much good it did a patient if his doctor was semicomatose and mumbling his way through giving orders to the charge nurse. Exhaustion was no excuse. Anxiety about making the slightest mistake was a powerful incentive.

One day near the end of my two-year residency — I was now at the Boston VA Hospital, a vastly more frenetic and stressful environment than the posh private clinic I'd grown accustomed to — I went on my morning rounds. When I was an intern I couldn't make a move without an attending physician's permission, but residents can practice medicine independently once they get a state medical license. I had done that after my first six months in Massachusetts, adding hours of study to the grueling pace of work.

That morning I arrived at the bed of a patient who had suffered a heart attack the day before. I scanned the chart and called over one of the nurses.

"Do you recognize this handwriting?" I asked, pointing to the patient's chart. She gave me an odd look.

"It's yours, isn't it?"

I thought about it for a moment. "Yeah."

According to the chart, I had resuscitated the man with CPR after his heart attack, intubated him, opened his chest, and put in a pacemaker.

It wasn't that I hadn't recognized my own handwriting; I simply couldn't remember doing all those things or even having been there in the first place. This was very upsetting, but I couldn't let on. With a reassuring smile, I got away from the nurse and only revealed my dismay to another resident, who had been pulling the same exhausting shifts. He shrugged.

"Don't sweat it, man. That's the whole point. If you survive the craziness, you can do the right thing in your sleep."

When my parents heard that Rita was pregnant, they were overjoyed, but I had other, less welcome news. She would be flying back to India to have the baby. My father was bewildered that a doctor who had made it to hallowed Boston couldn't afford to have his baby there. But when we moved to Massachusetts, Rita's pregnancy was deemed a preexisting condition. Insurance wouldn't cover it, but for $450 — less than half the cost of paying for the delivery — we could buy Rita an Air India ticket to Delhi and back. I wasn't willing to borrow money from my parents, and so when Rita was in her ninth month, barely a week from going into labor, I drove down to New York and saw her off at JFK. It was a difficult moment. I kept staring out the window until the plane was out of sight. Ultrasound exams for pregnant women were not in wide use then, but we had gotten one, and the doctor who ran the test was reasonably sure that it would be a girl.

I had had a bad scare earlier. When Rita went for a routine blood test, the pathologist called me up and said that her red blood cells looked abnormal, showing signs of anemia. This was not ordinary anemia but a genetic condition called thalassemia, and if Rita had inherited it, so would our baby. I knew that children with thalassemia often died before reaching adulthood. I tried to control a sense of panic. The nearest medical library was in New York City — we hadn't left yet for Boston — where I drove with the intention of immersing myself in reference books until I knew everything about this looming threat.

Rita's red blood cells looked somewhat abnormal, but that didn't mean that she or the baby was in danger. Thalassemia is caused by a recessive gene, and it takes both parents to be carriers for the full-blown disorder to appear. Even then, the chance of a baby being infected was 25 percent. I began to calm down. Statistics indicated that only 3 to 8 percent of Indians from our region had thalassemia. Since Rita had grown up normally, without slow development, bone deformation, or any other signs of thalassemia, our baby was safe. Rita probably had thalassemia as a trait in her genes but not the disease itself. The trait doesn't need treatment since it causes no harm.

Once the threat receded, my curiosity was aroused. The Greek word for the sea is "*thalassa*," and this gave thalassemia its name — it affects people of the Mediterranean (a separate strain exists in West Africa and other pockets around the world). How did a Mediterranean disease make it to India? The best guess is that it followed Alexander the Great on his long march of conquest to the East. In the summer of 325 BCE he stood on the banks of the Indus River as the most powerful man in the world. He had taken eight years and marched his army from Macedonia three thousand miles to get there. Legend has it that he sat on the banks of the Indus and wept because there was no more world to conquer. (The truth is that his troops probably revolted and demanded that he turn back.)

A massive cultural change was underway. The West would seep into India in many waves, one invasion after another. Alexander would take Indians back home with him: astrologers, yogis, Ayurvedic physicians. The physicians added to Western medicine, it is surmised, since Greece was the cradle of ancient and medieval medicine in Europe. The astrologers and yogis were said to astonish the young emperor with their knowledge. Alexander had only two more years to live before he died just shy of thirty-three in the royal palace in Babylon, still planning more military campaigns. He had his sights set on Arabia. Whether he was poisoned or died from a mysterious malady is debatable, but it's almost a certainty that his army and a caravan of camp followers trailed thalassemia behind them. The rates for the disease are highest where they went, declining steadily as the army got farther away from the Mediterranean and mixed their genes with other peoples. Rita's family came from the part of northwest India, later Pakistan, that lay directly in Alexander's path. She carried history in her blood, which somehow made me feel a shiver of wonder.

After the birth took place at Moolchand, my father's hospital, he phoned me to tell me that everything had gone smoothly. We had a baby girl. Rita was to stay in Delhi six weeks to ensure a full recovery before she and Mallika — whose name means flower — met me again at JFK. We drove back to Jamaica Plain, with an excited new father clutching the wheel and creating a road hazard since he couldn't keep his eyes off his baby.

Our block in Jamaica Plain had seen an invasion of Indian doctors, all living in a row of dilapidated two-story brick houses. A shared culture and low rents bound us into a tight community. I was happy that Rita was saved from the aching loneliness of a resident's wife who rarely spent time with her harassed husband. It also helped that we had the resilience of young people. (I disagree with Oscar Wilde's famous quip that youth is wasted on the young. I couldn't have survived without it.)

It comes as second nature to new immigrants to stay out of sight. Attracting attention feels like making yourself into a target. In this regard I was very different from the norm; I secretly envied one of our neighbors when he decided to show off his raise at work by buying a new Mustang. It made the desired impression. The wives agreed that it was a beautiful car; the husbands fumed in silence, knowing that their own cars had dropped two notches in pride. But we lived in an area notorious for car thefts. The Mustang was stolen, not once but several times a month.

My task was to drive the owner to the police station after his Mustang was found. It inevitably was. The thieves would take it for a joy ride, and a few times the hubcaps were missing. After the fifth time in a month that I drove my neighbor to the impoundment lot, I'd had enough. He was already in a black mood, but I took a deep breath and said that I wasn't doing this anymore. One last ride, and that was it. Which turned out to be prophetic: When we arrived at the facility, his car had been stolen from there. That was its destiny.

We tried to ignore how tenuous our personal safety was. One night I was driving home from the Lahey Clinic, which was then on Mass Ave., and at a stop I was too tired to move quickly when the light turned green. The car behind me honked, and my reaction must have been too slow for the driver, because he leaned out his window and started screaming. We exchanged rude hand gestures — I had learned that much in America — and I drove away. But in the rearview mirror I saw that he was following me. This was just a suspicion at first, but when I had made it all the way to Jamaica Plain, it became a certainty.

I pulled up to our apartment, ready for a confrontation. My pursuer stopped in the middle of the street, got out, and approached my car. My blood froze. The man had pulled out a handgun and was brandishing it wildly. With no time to think, I started flashing my headlights in his eyes and madly honking the horn. It was early in the morning. Suddenly windows flew open up and down the block. In each one, an Indian head stared down at the street.

My would-be assailant stopped and looked around. He was close enough that I heard him mutter something before he got back into his car and sped off.

"It's your lucky day, s—thead." Actually I was lucky to be from India at that moment. My welcome to America was complete.

12
First Impressions

Sanjiv

Deepak and Sanjiv's parents visit Sanjiv's apartment in Boston, 1973.

I FOLLOWED DEEPAK'S PATH to the West to complete my medical education. Our father's generation had gone to England to complete their training, but there they had encountered a British ceiling. Indian doctors in England were allowed to rise to only a certain level, and when they returned to India they were behind their classmates in seniority and only rarely caught up. As a military physician my father was not subject to the same challenges. In medical school Amita and I saw almost everyone ahead of us graduating and heading for the United States. When people asked us what our plans were when we finished medical school, America was the obvious answer. It was sort of automatic: Graduate, pass the exam, and off you go to the United States.

For Amita and I there was an added consideration. During our studies Amita had given birth to our daughter, Ratika Priya Chopra, a beautiful little girl. We knew that our internship was going to be very difficult and time-consuming. We were both going to be on call at the hospital every third night and every third weekend. When we were scheduled to leave for America, Priya, as we called her, was more than a year old. We could either give up the opportunity to study in America or allow her to stay with her loving grandparents. My parents adored her. Although Deepak was older than me and had married a month before Amita and me, Priya was their first grandchild. We agreed on the sensible path. Priya would stay at home with my parents and join us in America as soon as possible.

Deepak had gone to America two years before we were eligible to go. Because long-distance phone calls from America to India were so prohibitively expensive — as much as forty-five dollars for three minutes — we rarely heard from him. On occasion he would call our parents to reassure them that he was fine. We did see Rita when she

147

returned home to give birth, but she didn't tell us much about living in America.

Much of what I knew about America came from *Archie* and *Peanuts* comic books. Through these I knew that Americans liked hamburgers and milkshakes, and that kids in convertibles went to these hamburger joints. At school we were taught a subject called general knowledge. Just as we were taught math and science, we were taught the general knowledge that any educated person should have. It was in that class that I won the book about television, which I read and reread long before I actually saw any. But in GK we also studied America and Canada and, truthfully, my impression was that Canada was a better country. My impression of America was that the people who lived there worked very hard and were very rich. A book I read about Canada described beautiful farms, young people playing ice hockey, and people who were always friendly. Maybe they didn't have as many cars or TV sets as Americans did, but the way they lived seemed more peaceful and less of a rat race. It just didn't seem to me from afar that Americans were very happy people. Even at a young age I thought it would be fun to go to Canada, but I had no real thought of actually going anywhere. I considered myself very Indian. I was proud of the fact that I was receiving a wonderful education in the best schools in an exciting, independent country. India was changing and I expected to play my role in that change.

I did learn some things about America. I knew about Pat Boone and John Wayne. I loved Elvis Presley from his movies *Jailhouse Rock* and *Kid Galahad.* We were taught a little about slavery, and that segregation still existed. Abraham Lincoln was compared to Gandhi. We learned about a woman named Rosa Parks who refused to sit in the back of the bus. When we talked about this in school some of my classmates asked why Americans were racists, and we had to remind them that we were, too: We had a caste system. And we certainly knew about President Kennedy. The educated people of India were enchanted by JFK. One of the first American movies I ever saw was *PT 109,* the story of JFK saving his crew during World War II. I remember being on a bus on a Saturday going to school for a cricket match when someone listening to a transistor radio told us that five Indian generals had died in a helicopter crash on the border with Pakistan and there was speculation that it was sabotage. We were worried that this crash might lead to fighting with Pakistan, and everybody was quiet and depressed. A few minutes later that same person heard on his transistor radio that President Kennedy had been assassinated. People immediately started crying, including me. The match was called off and we went home. India came to a halt, and just like the rest of the world we listened to the news coming from America.

While in medical school Amita and I accepted the fact that we would go to the United States for as long as five years to finish our training in our respective specialties. I planned to spend three years doing internal medicine, two years in my specialty, gastroenterology, and then return to India and perhaps join my father and Deepak in a practice. Amita intended to study pediatrics, the favorite choice of women physicians in India.

Amita knew even less about America than I did. In her family, whenever there was any talk about going abroad it was always about Europe and England. Our institutions were British, our schools were British. We were Indian first, but Great Britain was clearly in our heritage. Her very first impression of America came from a girl who had come to India from there when Amita was in the seventh grade. Amita had never heard such a strange accent and asked the girl where she was from.

"She said the USA," Amita remembered. "I had never heard of that. I asked her how USA could be the name of a country, it was just capital letters. Then she told me it stood for the United States of America. Although I had seen maps of North and South America when we were studying geography, I didn't quite understand that America was a country until several years later."

Like most Indians, her strongest impressions about America came from music and movies, especially movies like *Cleopatra* and *Come September*. She loved Elizabeth Taylor, Doris Day, and Sophia Loren. (Sophia Loren may have been Italian, but the movies Amita saw were made in Hollywood.) While the music from *Come September* may not have been so popular in the USA, for years it seemed like every band in Delhi played it at every wedding reception until everyone was tired of hearing it.

While Deepak traveled to Ceylon to take the Educational Council for Foreign Medical Graduates (ECFMG) examination, Amita and I went to Hong Kong. Although we considered ourselves relatively sophisticated, our eyes began to open to the world during that trip. There were two experiences that struck me: First, we went to a movie that started at midnight! We'd never done that in India. And then, when we came out of the theater we were both hungry and at two thirty in the morning there were merchants and vendors on the street. One of them was selling fish and chips, which he put in a newspaper cone and handed to me. It was all part of an adventure, delicious fish and chips in a newspaper at two thirty in the morning.

The next evening, we were walking down a main street and Chinese, Malaysian, Japanese, and English prostitutes were all lined up. They were calling to me in four languages. If I had ever seen call girls in India I was too young to understand what they were selling. I was twenty years old and walking with my new wife, but they still asked if I wanted to go with them.

"I'm married," I told them. "This is my wife."

"That's okay," one said. "She can come, too!"

We weren't in Delhi anymore.

After we'd passed the ECFMG exam Deepak advised us that the Ventnor Foundation that had sent him abroad would ensure that we would be matched to the same hospital where he had done his internship. We applied and were sent to Muhlenberg hospital in New Jersey. Once again I was following my brother. We were each given eight dollars for the trip, and Deepak sent us another hundred suggesting we would need it as our itinerary called for us to stop in Rome, Paris, and London.

Our trip did not begin well. As we walked down a street in Rome, Amita slipped and broke the strap on the brand-new sandals she had bought in India. We didn't think this was much of a problem until we walked into a shoe shop. The least-expensive sandals in that shop were about seven thousand lira, the equivalent of a hundred U.S. dollars.

Amita started to cry. I asked her why.

"If shoes are this expensive abroad, I don't think we're going to be able to survive on the salaries we're earning. Maybe we should stop and go back to India."

I reassured her that we would be fine, although secretly I, too, was apprehensive. That was a lot of money for a pair of sandals.

In London we stayed in a lovely cottage with an associate of Amita's sister who was working there as a senior officer for the Indian Administrative Service. It certainly seemed like an impressive position to us. One night he told us that he had bought tickets for us to attend one of the most popular plays in London. We were thrilled. We had both read about the British theater and we wanted to see a show.

"What's it called?" I asked.

"*Oh! Calcutta!*" he said.

From the name, we assumed this was something we would enjoy. We assumed it was simply a British play about our country. He left us at the theater and said he would meet us afterward. We had wonderful seats in the second row. When the play started and naked actors walked onstage, Amita and I were absolutely astounded. I mean, our jaws dropped open. Modesty was central in Indian culture, and we had all been taught how important it was to maintain our privacy. Even two young people touching each other in public was considered by many to be inappropriate. Here, actors and actresses were performing completely naked. In India it would have been scandalous; in London it was entertainment.

I remember the experience vividly. Toward the end, one naked actor turned to another and asked why the play was called *Oh! Calcutta!*

"By jolly, it couldn't have been called *Oh! Bangkok!*"

Amita and I would have lots to learn about living in the West.

After landing in Boston and spending a few days with Deepak and Rita, we went to New Jersey. Our real introduction to America began at Muhlenberg hospital. They gave us a good orientation, instructing us in how to shop in a grocery store and how to open and use a bank account. My mother had been concerned about how we would handle the money we earned. She told us that tradition called for us to give our first month's salary to Deepak, just as we had given whatever we earned to our parents when we were in India. That made perfect sense to us, but when we tried to give our checks to Deepak he wouldn't take them. He insisted that it was time for us to learn how to handle our own finances.

The hospital issued us each a black doctor's bag with a stethoscope, a hammer, and an ophthalmoscope. But it was the uniforms that created our first problem. I was given white trousers and a smock-type shirt, which suited me fine. But the female doctors at the hospital were issued skirts and smocks. In India, Amita typically wore a two-piece *Salwar Kameez,* a sort of tunic over pants, quite comfortable. When she wanted to look older—so she could get into the movie theater, for example—she would wear a sari. When she was being measured for her uniform she asked if she could wear pants. No, she was told—female doctors wear skirts. She didn't like it, but there was nothing she could do about it. She asked them to make it as long as possible. The larger problem was that she had to wear panty hose.

Women in India didn't wear panty hose. I'm not even sure panty hose were widely available in India; there would have been little need there, since proper women didn't display their legs. Amita had trouble getting used to the way they gripped her waist, and every day she would get two or three runs in them and have to throw them out. She got so frustrated and angry; she would wear a new pair every day and every day she would snag them or rip them. She complained that she was spending most of her salary buying panty hose. One of the most useful things she learned at Muhlenberg hospital was that, as soon as she saw a run, she should put a small amount of colorless nail polish at the end to stop it.

My first day in the hospital I was introduced to the other interns and members of the staff. Around me there were physicians from

England, Hungary, Italy, Australia, the Philippines, Pakistan, and India. Some of them had risen to become the chief of a division or a department. There was no unspoken barrier holding them down. I'd heard America was a land of opportunity, but here was the proof standing all around me.

During that orientation we were also told how the hospital worked. They told us it was very important to call the operator to tell her we were leaving when we finished our shift so we wouldn't be paged.

One night as I came to work, a fellow intern, also from India, was finishing his shift and asked if he could borrow a dime. I gave him one and watched as he went to the pay phone and deposited it, then dialed once. After a moment I heard him speak.

"Hello, operator? This is Dr. Rao. I'm now leaving the hospital." Then he hung up.

Now I was the expert.

"You're supposed to call the hospital operator, not the New Jersey operator!"

Truthfully Amita and I weren't that sophisticated, either. After we had finished working our second or third night, I suggested that she call Deepak and Rita in Boston to tell them we were fine.

"Good idea," she agreed, and then picked up the pay phone and told the hospital operator, "I'd like to make a PP call to my brother-in-law Dr. Deepak Chopra in Boston." Amita couldn't understand why the operator started laughing. In India, a PP call meant person-to-person but, as we discovered, it has a very different meaning here.

Everything about America surprised us. Of course we were enchanted by television. I was mesmerized by the beautiful young women and handsome young men singing on *The Lawrence Welk Show*. My favorite show was *Sanford and Son,* starring comedian Redd Foxx. On one episode I remember well there was a holdup and a white cop and a black cop came to investigate. They asked Sanford to describe the robbers, which he did. Then the white officer asked him, "Was he colored?"

Sanford looked right at him. "Yeah. He was white."

We rolled around laughing and went on to repeat the line over and over to the other foreign doctors at the hospital. Everyone thought it was amazing that you could make a joke like that here.

One of our most memorable experiences took place only two days after we had settled in Plainfield. When we were staying in Boston with Deepak, we had seen Rita go into the grocery store Stop & Shop while we waited in the car. At Muhlenberg we were each given a two-hundred-dollar advance, so we decided to use some of it for food shopping. We knew we could buy food at a Stop & Shop. We walked about half a mile to downtown Plainfield looking for one. As we walked we saw a young woman coming out of a parking lot with a baby in one arm and a toddler holding her other hand.

"Can you tell me where the Stop and Shop is?" I asked politely.

"Is that a grocery store?" she asked.

"Yes, it is. We were just in Boston and we went to it."

She nodded. "There's no Stop and Shop here, but there is a Pathmark. That's where I'm going now. Why don't you come with me?"

So we jumped in her Oldsmobile station wagon and she drove us there. It was several miles from our apartment, but we didn't even consider how we would get back to our apartment with our groceries. This was the first large American supermarket we had been inside. We had never seen anything like it. It had an amazing variety of canned foods and cheeses, pet food, flowers, milk and cottage cheese, sardines, dozens of varieties of Baskin-Robbins ice cream. There was shelf after shelf of items, and with our advances we could buy much more than we wanted. We were mesmerized. We could have walked up and down those aisles for hours.

When we were finished, we took our bags and went outside, expecting to walk home. We were young, we thought. We could do it. But the lady who had driven us there was waiting in her Oldsmobile.

"I saw you buying a lot of groceries and I was concerned how you'd get back. So I thought I'd drop you off."

We spoke on the way home and explained that we were interns at the hospital and had just arrived. As she dropped us off she asked, "Are you free on the Fourth of July?"

"What's so special about the Fourth of July?"

"It's Independence Day, a national holiday." We were free, as it turned out, and she picked us up and brought us to her home for a family barbecue, where we met her family. We ate hot dogs and cheeseburgers and chicken off the grill. We played horseshoes. That was the first time in my life I'd eaten food like this. I enjoyed the hot dog, but didn't care that much for the cheeseburger. We spent the day with these wonderful, gracious people who truly appreciated the gifts that America offered. The woman's name was Mary and her husband, Andy, was a Hungarian who had escaped from behind the Iron Curtain. On his first attempt he had been shot in the leg, but as soon as he recovered he tried again and was successful. He had joined the American military and become a Green Beret. Being welcomed to America by people like this, people who had risked their lives to get here while we had taken an exam, really made us look at this country differently. What was it about America that was so different from our home?

Everything, as it turned out. At the barbecue our hosts suggested we buy a car.

Buy a car? When we reminded her we had just arrived and had no money, she said something that began to describe America to us.

"You don't need to have money in this country. You're both interns and have a guaranteed salary."

She explained the concept of credit to us. Buy without money? Who ever heard of such a thing? But a few days later Mary drove us to the Volkswagen dealership in Plainfield. In 1972 there was only one car in America that sold for less than two thousand dollars: the Volkswagen Beetle. We got carried away and bought the Super Beetle, which had an AM/FM radio, not just AM, and cost twenty-one hundred dollars. Then we bought a color TV. We had been in America for less than two weeks and we were already in debt—but we felt rich.

I was fascinated by the things that Americans took for granted, especially McDonald's. It seemed like there were golden arches on every corner. We were amazed. At that time McDonald's used to advertise on its signs OVER EIGHT MILLION SOLD. Then they said OVER NINE MILLION SOLD. Amita and I watched with amazement as the number grew and grew. What is it this week? How many hamburgers did they sell last month? On our budget we would eat at McDonald's regularly, and I always had the cheeseburger and fries.

There were some things that required making an adjustment. We loved diners. Diners are a totally unique American experience. There was a diner on Route 22, the Scotchplain Diner, where we ate often, especially when we were coming back from driving our new Beetle into New York City. One night we were leaving the diner when we were pulled over by a policeman. I was a careful driver, so I couldn't imagine what I'd done wrong. We'd just left the diner and I knew I hadn't been speeding. I knew I'd signaled when I'd merged into traffic. I just couldn't figure out why he had stopped me.

"Were you drinking beer?" he asked me.

"Nothing at all. Just Coke."

"You sure you didn't have a few beers?"

"I haven't," I insisted.

"Do you realize you were driving on the wrong side of the road?"

Oh. That. I handed him my license.

"Officer, I'm very sorry, but I grew up in India and we drive on the left side. During the day there are cues. When I see a car coming I know I'm on the wrong side. But I just came out of the diner and there were no cars . . ."

He was understanding. Not only did he not give me a ticket, but he also offered to escort us home. While we told him that wasn't necessary, we were impressed. Look at them here, we said to each other. They're very efficient, but they're kind as well.

We also had to get accustomed to the weather. India, like much of the world, doesn't really experience four seasons. There was little air-conditioning. In the summer we would holiday in what are called hill stations, colonial British outposts at high altitudes, to escape the heat. While I had seen snowcapped mountains in India, neither Amita nor

I had ever been in a snowstorm, and we certainly had never experienced the cold of a New Jersey winter. The first time it snowed in the winter of 1972 we stood outside like young children, catching the snowflakes, feeling them land on our hands, faces, and tongues. It was an absolutely enchanting and magical experience. Figuring out how to deal with the bitter cold came later. But we have never lost our appreciation for the beauty of snow. We live in a suburb now, away from the hustle and bustle of the city, and at night, in the depths of winter, moonlight glints off the snow-covered trees. We still remember that first amazing snowfall.

We couldn't get enough of American culture. Many years later, as I was welcoming new interns to Beth Israel Deaconess Medical Center in Boston, one of them told me he was from New Jersey.

"When my wife and I came to the United States in 1972," I said, "we were interns at a small hospital affiliated with Rutgers. We have the fondest memories of New Jersey. Every weekend, we would go to see a Broadway show, or go to Chinatown for dinner, or visit the museums . . ." I went on to tell him all about our life.

"Dr. Chopra, can I ask you a question?"

"Of course."

"How come all your fondest memories of New Jersey have nothing to do with New Jersey?"

"You're a bright intern," I replied. "You'll do well." Then I added, "Princeton is charming."

As someone who had played sports in India, I was immediately interested in learning about the games played in America, especially baseball. One evening I was driving along Route 22 when I noticed a batting cage. I thought, That looks just like cricket. It'll be easy. I got into the cage and the machine pitched the ball and I swung at it — and missed. And missed again and again. Then I realized that a cricket bat is a flat surface and a baseball bat is a cylinder. Hitting the baseball was more difficult than I had imagined. But I practiced and eventually got pretty good at it.

One day Amita and I went to a picnic where they were playing a game of softball. When I was asked if I had ever played baseball I replied that I hadn't, but I'd played a lot of cricket and the essentials of the two games, hitting and catching, were similar. As a competitive person, I wanted to show off my skills, so I got up to bat. This was a bigger ball, thrown softly, and I slammed it. By watching other players I knew what to do: I ran directly to first base — carrying my bat with me as we do in cricket. No, they told me, throw your bat away. I had learned the first rule of baseball. It turned out the only similarities between baseball and cricket were that you hit the ball with a bat. Everything else was different.

As my team got ready to go into the field, a friend offered me a glove. A glove? I smiled and explained that wouldn't be necessary.

"Cricket players don't use gloves. We learn as young players to catch the ball with two hands and retract your hands at the instant you catch the ball, which absorbs most of the impact."

"Doesn't it hurt?"

"No," I said. My message was clear: Cricket players are tough. We don't need big gloves to field. In the end, I fielded very well and everyone was impressed.

But more than anything we could buy, or enjoy, more than the glamour of a Broadway show or the experience of eating at a diner and dropping coins in the jukebox on the table, what immediately impressed both Amita and me about America was the generosity and openness of the American people. The first place we experienced this was in the hospital. A few days after we arrived Dr. Eddie Palmer, a world-famous liver specialist, came to Muhlenberg to teach.

I was in awe. I sat down in the front row to take notes. Sitting a few seats away from me was a medical student who propped his feet up on a chair. I noticed that and thought it was odd. In India that would have been considered extremely disrespectful. No one would have done it. But I also noticed that no one said anything to him about it.

Dr. Palmer gave a marvelous talk, and I dutifully made my notes. At the end of the speech this medical student asked Dr. Palmer a question and was given a detailed answer. When Dr. Palmer finished, the student looked at him skeptically.

"I don't buy it."

This is amazing, I thought. A medical student challenging a legend? A student speaking back to his teacher? Where was the cane? This never happened in India, never. We were taught to respect our teachers, even when we know they're wrong. What was even more surprising to me was that Dr. Palmer didn't seem to mind. He simply responded to the comment. I knew right then that there was something fundamentally different about the American spirit that was considerably more profound than how many millions of hamburgers McDonald's sold.

Amita had a very similar experience. At the end of her first day at Muhlenberg hospital her professor, Dr. Paul Winokur, met with the new interns. When he asked her if she had finished seeing all of her patients she said, "Yes, sir."

There was a moment of silence, the other interns looking at Amita. Dr. Winokur smiled.

"Dr. Chopra," he said, "I haven't been called 'sir' since I was in the army."

What else, she wondered, would be appropriate? He was a teacher and he was older than she was. The level of familiarity that students had with their teachers surprised her. Some of them even addressed Dr. Winokur by his first name, Paul. He's your professor, she thought. How can you be so disrespectful? But Dr. Winokur didn't seem to mind it. In fact, he didn't even seem to notice.

That same night she saw another first-year resident put his feet up on the conference table and lean back in his chair. What audacity, she thought. Doesn't he understand how insulting that is? But no one objected to that, either.

It wasn't that we disapproved; we just didn't know how to deal with this casual attitude. We had no frame of reference for it. Our scale of right and wrong was being challenged. While it seemed disrespectful to us, the people who should have felt disrespected didn't object. It took us time to get used to this openness, but we did see the advantages of it. We began to understand that people in America were much less formal — and had their own ways of demonstrating respect.

We were also surprised, and pleased, that Americans showed great respect for working people. In India labor was so cheap that people who did menial work were not respected. We were products of a caste system, and even though it was breaking down, its shadows still existed. We thought it was admirable that Americans seemed to treat everybody equally, that there was little sense of superiority, of class. The doctors in the hospital treated the maintenance workers with as much respect as they treated the other doctors. All those things that were ingrained in us, that young people must follow the wishes of older people and that you are not permitted to speak your mind, it simply took us time to accept that this was not disrespectful at all, but simply the way people dealt with one another in America.

While most of the Americans we met were very friendly and welcoming, we discovered quickly that few of them knew much about the world beyond America's borders. Perhaps this comes from the fact that America is separated from Europe and Asia by the great oceans. In India it was imperative that we learned everything possible about the people we shared a continent with, as well as the countries of Europe. For so long India was a member of the British Commonwealth and we were impacted by all of England's battles. Our fate depended on the outcome, so we learned about it.

Many Americans knew little about India. When we told people we were Indian it was as though they expected to see us wearing a feathered headdress. They had no concept of how large, diverse, modern, and prosperous a country India was. At the hospital the majority of the interns were from different parts of India. When we were in the faculty lounge we spoke to one another only in English. When I was asked why we didn't speak in our native tongue, I explained that we didn't have one.

"There are a lot of different languages spoken in India. Not just different dialects but completely different languages. Mine is Punjabi, for example, and his is Bengali. I wouldn't have any idea what he was saying. English is the only language we have in common." There were even some people who were surprised that we didn't speak "Indian."

There were things that we had difficulty understanding. We'd come from a country where beggars lived in the street and survived on meager handouts of food and a few coins. When we went to a restaurant, or a diner, we were surprised not just by the size of the portions that were served but also how much of it was wasted. We would watch as the waiters carried away plates with one-quarter or more of the food back to the kitchen to be discarded. It was saddening to us to see that waste, knowing the difference that food would have made in so many lives. It took us some time to get used to the reality that Americans were often casual about the abundance here and perhaps didn't appreciate how different it was in other parts of the world.

I was also uncomfortable about the number of guns in the United States. While we had seen the gunslingers in American Westerns, we hadn't really expected guns to be so common. I couldn't think of a single relative, friend, or even a friend of a friend in India who possessed a gun, unless they were hunters. People don't possess guns to protect themselves there. Instead, they hire guards and install alarm systems. I don't know, for example, if my parents had kept guns in the house, how the robbery might have turned out. Not well, I suspect. So while I understood the meaning and the importance of the constitutional right to bear arms, I was still surprised at the gun culture of America.

What made us most comfortable when we first arrived was the discovery that modern medicine was practiced pretty much the same way in America as we had learned in India. Our education had prepared us remarkably well, although there was always that degree of doubt. One night a few weeks after I had started my internship at Muhlenberg I was doing a neurology elective. I was working with Dr. Greenberg, a neurologist who had trained at the Massachusetts General Hospital in Boston, and a man I held in great esteem. He informed me that he had just received a consult, a patient who was very weak. It was suspected that he was suffering from a serious neurological disorder known as myasthenia gravis, in which the patient eventually loses control of his muscles and often needs to be on a ventilator. He asked me to join him in seeing this patient.

The patient had just been admitted, so we hadn't yet received any lab results. Taking a detailed history, I learned that the man was having profuse, watery diarrhea. He was going to the bathroom ten, even twenty, times a day.

"Okay, then," I said, remembering my father's admonition that every patient has a story to tell, if only the doctor is willing to ask the proper questions. "What happens if you don't eat?"

It made no difference, he said. There were a few days that he'd lost his appetite and had eaten nothing at all — but the bowel movements continued. I made a diagnosis of secretory diarrhea, which doesn't abate even when the patient is fasting, and wondered if perhaps a tumor might be the cause of his distress. The GI tract is normally an absorptive organ, but a tumor can transform it into a secretory organ, one that just pours out fluid. Some forms of secretory diarrhea can lead to a condition called hypokalemia, a critically low potassium level, so I wanted to know his serum potassium level. We ordered the labs and when the results came back, his serum potassium was dramatically and dangerously low.

The patient turned out to have a villous adenoma, a tumor, in his rectum. If an adenoma is large, it can be malignant and spread. So the diagnosis changed very quickly from myasthenia gravis to villous adenoma with secretory diarrhea and hypokalemia. The hypokalemia had been causing his profound weakness. Dr. Greenberg was impressed and at lunchtime in the hospital cafeteria he complimented me in front of the other interns and some of the attending doctors.

It was a very smart diagnosis for a young intern and I enjoyed a great feeling of fulfillment. My father had taught me that medicine is not only a science but also an art, and every doctor will make many wrong diagnoses throughout his professional career. So when you do make the right diagnosis, it's important to remain humble. I knew that, but inside I was elated. I had made the correct diagnosis and avoided many unnecessary, expensive tests. Any question I might have had about my ability to meet American medical standards was answered to my satisfaction. I could be confident in the quality of my training. By our degrees, Amita and I were doctors — but by our training and our passion, we would become very good doctors.

13

....

State of the Art

Deepak

Champions of Action – Delos Living™ and Clinton Global Initiative, committed to creating a peaceful, just, sustainable, and healthy world. Morad Fareed, President Bill Clinton, Deepak Chopra, Steve Bing, Terry McAuliffe, Jason McLennan, and will.i.am, September 2012.

BUYING YOUR FIRST TELEVISION ON credit seems trivial, but it was enveloped in culture shock for Rita and me. Until we found a Little India in Jamaica Plain, loneliness was never far away for my wife. Just the physical sensation of being by herself in a room made her despondent. Houses are full of family in India and full of the noises that families make. The silence of a small apartment in New Jersey was oppressive, relieved only when Rita came to have lunch with me in the hospital cafeteria, which she did every day. It hurt me to see her sitting by herself in a corner, patiently waiting until I could break free. Even now I can conjure up the image and the feeling.

The solution we hit upon was to buy a TV set, and so with some trepidation we went to a local department store to price one. The salesman was chilly at first, no doubt thinking that Third World immigrants couldn't afford to buy anything, but once he heard that I worked at the hospital, his eyes lit up. Minutes later we were being offered a revolving line of credit, which we accepted in a kind of daze. At the local Volkswagen dealership the attitude was even more liberal: "The doctor wants a car? Give him a car!" There was only the vaguest sense on my part that credit meant debt, but it was a relief to turn on the TV all day so that Rita could fill the apartment with sound. It wasn't family, but it kept a frightening silence at bay.

Clearly we didn't pose a problem of culture shock to the Americans we met. They cared very little about India. We had exchanged British disdain for American blankness. Curiosity seemed to end once we were asked if cobras crawled under our beds and whether we rode elephants. The world was coming to America, which may have been why Americans felt so little need to know about anywhere else.

A doctor at Muhlenberg who owned a two-seater prop plane heard that Rita was pregnant. In a flush of generosity he offered to fly her to

India so that she wouldn't have to buy a commercial ticket. I pointed out that India was halfway around the world.

"My mistake," he said. "I thought it was in South America."

When you arrive in a new country already speaking the language, outfitted with a job and an education, the process of adaptation occurs quickly, on the surface anyway. Rita and I weren't aware of being changed very deeply. The lack of smells was odd. In India rooms are cooled by running water through a hay filter; the fragrant, evaporation-cooled air is then blown into the room. American air-conditioning was antiseptic and odorless. If the temperature went down to seventy-five degrees, we threw on our sweaters, which occasioned odd glances. We must have looked like seniors, or invalids.

When they come to this country, Asians seem peculiarly adept at throwing off as much of their home culture as they need to. Rita's father had become a business consultant after leaving the Indian air force. On his first trip to New York City his hosts insisted on taking him to the Rainbow Room at the top of Rockefeller Center. When the menu arrived, they pressed him to order a steak and he obliged. It was only when the food arrived that he realized steak comes from a cow. When we asked him how he managed to eat an animal held sacred in India, he shrugged.

"I struggled with my conscience, but then I thought, 'This meat came from an American cow. If no one here thinks cows are holy, theirs must not be.'"

Building a self doesn't stop at twenty-three, my age when I arrived here. Some unconscious shifts were occurring inside, almost all of them caused by the practice of medicine. An obvious influence was the impersonal nature of how we related to our patients. It was much more than what I had faced in India. As distant as I felt meeting sick people for fifteen minutes and running through a short litany about what was wrong with them and what I could do about it, behind my back I had gained a reputation for being warm. This mystified me. Perhaps it had to do with my showing a little personal interest in a patient, if only for fifteen minutes, rather than pretending to be interested. I was never good at putting up a front.

Later on, however, I suspected that there was simply a difference in emotional temperature between the two cultures. Indians love to get excited, and we exaggerate the horror of a crisis and the sentimentality of love. The extravagant excess of Bollywood movies, where a boy and girl exchanging a flirtatious glance makes the earth rumble, looks reasonably normal to an Indian audience. American audiences learn to enjoy it, if they ever do, from a sense of the preposterous. As for the emotional temperature of Americans, that varied, depending, it seemed, on how British their family roots were and how much money they made. My sympathy was with the poor, and almost immediately I gravitated to the Democrats because everyone told me they were friendlier to immigrants. (Years later, on a golf course in Jackson Hole, Wyoming, an oil man told me that I should consider getting close to the second Bush administration. He amazed me by saying, "We have our eyes on you, you know." The conversation came to an abrupt end when he informed me that there was only one precondition: I had to accept Jesus as my lord and savior. The Christian Brothers were much subtler.)

At the hospital I was shocked to hear other doctors refer offhandedly to "gorks" and "gomers." Gork refers to a patient who has suffered a severe head injury and lapsed into a coma from which he may never recover; the letters stand for "God only really knows." A gomer (for "get out of my emergency room") is a patient who is too far gone mentally or too close to death to be treated in the hospital, with the implication that he is a waste, taking up a perfectly good bed. A family wrestling with the painful decision to take someone off life support would be shattered to hear the doctor say, "Cut the gomer loose." I heard it almost every day in the residents' lounge in Boston.

It wasn't my position to tut-tut over anyone else's behavior only to wonder how much I was blending into the scene. Going to the VA hospital threw me into a rougher environment after I left Lahey for my second year of residency. You survived by being thick-skinned. Nearly everyone on staff handled the pressure by smoking. Our attendings usually preferred to puff on a pipe, which looked professorial, while the rest of us dragged on cigarettes. Doctors regularly smoked while making their rounds through the wards. One of the attendings who did this when he came for grand rounds was an eminent gastroenterologist and the editor of *The New England Journal of Medicine.* No one would have questioned him if they'd even dared to think about it. He died of esophageal cancer before he turned seventy.

Of course we disapproved of our patients smoking and warned them about the dangers. On break I'd look out a window to see a lung cancer patient, who had just been given the terrible news of his diagnosis, walking across the street to a convenience store to pick up a carton of Lucky Strikes.

Feeling immune to getting sick is a common trait among doctors. It's a psychological defense mechanism, an extension of inflated egos (once you start making big money, why not assume that you are invulnerable?), and a fairly realistic notion at the same time, since exposure to so many disease organisms results in a stronger immune system. (One of the things that made AIDS such a baffling mystery in the beginning was that the first patients to show up in the early Eighties were mostly young men with good immune response. By a twist of fate, HIV attacked them first, since their increased white cells were perfect hosts for the retrovirus. At the very outset, many doctors jumped to the wrong conclusion that the disease must be specifically targeting these men because they were active homosexuals.) In India medical care was typically free. In America the money I would make one day signified a state of grace.

These things weren't lost on me, but they were peripheral to the state-of-the-art medicine I was learning. Ten years after gaping at Rattan Chacha, I had become the guy holding forth with a glass of Scotch in one hand and a cigarette in the other, generally on Fridays when the staff got together at the end of the week to unwind. Yet America was just a window of opportunity to me at that time. I would return home after I had finished my residency in internal medicine. When my family tearfully saw me off at the Delhi airport they could console themselves with that.

I called home to keep in touch as often as I could. My parents had a telephone, fortunately, but I was reluctant to burden them with the expense of a person-to-person call. We used the dodge of having my father pick up the phone, refuse the call, and then immediately phone me back station to station. If Sanjiv was on the line, it felt like we were as close as ever.

I had dropped cricket when I went to med school, but Sanjiv kept playing. In fact, it was hard to keep up cricket madness in America, where the sport was unknown, and it drifted out of my sight. As his big brother, I felt obligated to tell Sanjiv that his grades weren't high enough in medical school. Was he studying hard? It worried me. No matter how much I did this, I never gave it a second thought that my goading and badgering might be a source of considerable irritation.

The oddest aspect of my assimilation centered around the birth of our daughter, Mallika. Rita was pregnant and getting ready for the flight to India to give birth. A friend took me aside to inform me that if she was born abroad, our baby couldn't grow up to be president of the United States. In 1970 this was hardly a realistic cause for concern, but it troubled me. I could see my little girl setting her heart on holding the highest office in the land. Could I be the one to dash her hopes? It took some hard convincing and hours of soul searching before I put this problem aside.

The one aspect of American life that I utterly failed at was sports. I made a few attempts to bond with other males. I told them that field hockey was one sport where India had high Olympic hopes. My enthusiasm was cut short when I was informed that in the U.S. field hockey is a girls' game. The only hockey that counted was played on ice, and it was a teeth-bashing contact sport. I wasn't keen on anything that happens on ice. Bringing up soccer was met with a blank stare. I had no idea that America was the only place where the game wasn't an obsession; suburban kids had barely started playing it. When I wouldn't relent and learn the complicated rules of baseball and football (at least I quickly stopped calling it American football to keep it straight from soccer), my attempts at boding on the sports front crashed.

Anyway, it was clear from their reactions that everyone felt a bit embarrassed for me.

When Sanjiv followed me to medical school two years later, my parents could say to themselves that they had fulfilled one of their key aims in life. It wasn't that their sons would be secure financially, or even that good parenting had led to happy children. The issue, which is peculiar to Indian life, was dharma. As a child I don't remember my mother being disgruntled very often, but if ever she became irritated with my father, he would settle matters with a single phrase: "It's my dharma." This had the magical effect of quieting her complaints, answering her doubts, and even bringing a look of contentment to my mother's face. If her husband was following his dharma, everything would be all right.

Dharma is multilayered. It's your work, the proper course of your life, and your duty. As taught for thousands of years, dharma is the invisible law that holds life itself together, whether it's a person's life or the life of the universe. A highway robber is a lawbreaker and an outcast from society, but in the back of an Indian's mind, if a dacoit is teaching his son how to be a dacoit, they are following their dharma, even up to the point where the police shoot them down. It's unthinkable not to have a place in the natural order.

Dharma can be simplistic and crass. In the secular life that most educated Indians live, God is smiling on you if you are rich. Money confers a halo. Driving a Mercedes tells people on the street that the universe is on your side. In the scheme of things, poor people go to a temple with their troubles; rich people hire Brahmans as private gurus to offer soothing flattery.

In America it came as something of a relief to leave all of that behind. In the first years, if I gave two thoughts about dharma, I can't remember it. Most of the other young doctors were single. I mixed in with them during extracurricular hours. Late Friday when we drank and smoked together was the shank of the evening for them. I got out quickly to go home to my family, just as things were revving up. In good conscience, though, I could tick all the boxes of dharma, just as my father had done all his life.

A little boy in the West can take comfort in the image of Jesus, with a lamb in his lap, gathering a flock of adoring children around him. A little boy in India takes comfort in the image of Lord Krishna holding up a mountain with one finger. As the fable goes, a village was being threatened by torrential rainstorms, and to protect it, Krishna plucked up Mount Govardhan and held it over the village until the danger had passed. Often the image shows the joyful villagers using sticks to help Krishna hold up the mountain, the lesson being that God doesn't need our help, but that we should do our part anyway. For Jesus to say, "Suffer the little children to come unto me" is kind. Krishna is more about keeping you safe.

When you go where your dharma leads, you are following a thread that will never break. Almost every choice a person makes in life must obey dharma, and if it doesn't, bad things will follow. These can be everyday misfortunes or crushing calamities. Bad doesn't just mean difficult or unpleasant, it means that you have lost your way. Since dharma is all but meaningless in the West, it's worth considering whether India has found some kind of secret key or is simply following an old, worn-out belief.

Invisible laws are not reliable, so dharma has been outlined in specific rules that each generation imparts to the next. The whole scheme can become incredibly complex and suffocating. If a high-caste Brahmin followed every minute ritual laid down in Hindu scriptures, there would be no time left in the day to actually live. For practical purposes, though, the rules are loose. My father was in his dharma if he honorably pursued his profession; his sons took up the family dharma by becoming doctors in his footsteps. If my mother frowned occasionally because he gave too much money away, dharma saved him because general goodness is part of the law. Viewed with nothing else than these things in mind, dharma keeps people on the right track, the track of virtue. But having divine approval for how you live each day isn't so different from devoutly following the Koran or the prescriptions of the Talmud that dictate good behavior for orthodox Jews.

The peculiarly Indian twist is that dharma is ingrained in human nature: It's instinctive. You can feel when you have stepped off the path. Self-awareness comes into play, and then the word "invisible" is inescapable. At every stage of my life I was building a self with invisible bricks. By definition I couldn't see them, and yet if I looked in the mirror decades later and beheld a middle-aged man who was rigid, proud, selfish, obsessive, or anything else undesirable, the flaw would be the result of a process that took years to develop. I would have only myself to blame, my own lack of awareness. Dharma sends its signals every day. The smallest bad thing is actually a disguised message to the inner self. The self cannot be understood without thinking of a coral reef rising from the ocean floor, one tiny bit at a time.

The paradox of building a self is that the process never stops for a moment; you can never decide what you're making. There is no master plan and no architect. All you can do is be self-aware. Let's say that seeing dozens of patients a day during my years in practice made me callous. An especially annoying patient might push me too far. Every physician sees repeaters who bring the same minor complaint to the doctor again and again. After the third visit in a month, a part of you wants to say, "You have the medical equivalent of a hangnail. Go home and quit bothering me. One of us needs a life."

If I ever caught myself actually saying these words, I might glimpse the truth: I've grown callous. But people are remarkably protected against self-awareness. It's far more likely that the process of growing callous would escape my attention, and if anyone else pointed it out, I would react with blame and resentment. We don't see the invisible bricks of the self, and there is barely a faint click as they fall into place.

Dharma recognizes that people have a stake in not knowing themselves. In an ideal world everyone would ask "Who am I?" every day, and since "I" is constantly shifting, each new day would bring a new answer. India has existed too long to wait until the ideal life arrives. The rules of dharma tell you how to build a self that will be approved by God automatically. Every traditional society has some version of this, but in India there is a force running through each individual, which is the same force that upholds creation. As in the Krishna fable, if you drop your stick, you aren't doing your part to keep the mountain up. (In Sanskrit the word "dharma" can be traced back to the verb "dhar," meaning to hold or support. Dhar is even older than Sanskrit, which makes it one of the oldest words — and concepts — in human language.)

To an outsider it may look as though dharma is oppressive in its insistence on following tradition, and there's no doubt that in India a son who lives in the house where he grew up, goes to the school his family has always attended, and works at the profession of his father and grandfather will win social approval. The groove seems mindless if you haven't grown up in the system. But turn the picture around, and following the American dream seems wildly reckless. American sons can't wait to move out of the house, find work that is anything but what their fathers do, and move to a city where life is better than where they grew up.

I can accuse myself of not having enough self-awareness those first years in Boston. I ignored the signals that were coming my way. So I was about to be shocked by the instability of happiness. No one told me about the risk of teetering between two worlds. The dream was coming true on the American side. How can you fail at your dharma when you are breaking your back trying to fulfill it?

A woman in her thirties goes to the psychiatrist. She's a new patient, so he starts to take a medical history. Although in general good health, the woman is more than fifty pounds overweight. She is married with five children, a stay-at-home mom. She reveals that her husband is currently out of work. The psychiatrist writes it all down.

"So, what did you come in for today?" he asks.

"I feel kind of depressed," the woman replies, "and I can't figure out why."

This isn't a wry joke that one doctor tells another. It actually happened to a psychiatrist in training that I knew. In a way, it mirrors a truth: It's not up to the patient to know why she feels bad, even if the reasons are staring her in the face. Today the punch line would be "I'm fat, I have five kids at home, and my husband just lost his job. Do you have a pill for that?"

It was a surprise for me to see how many patients in America believed in a pill for everything. The notion that your lifestyle can make you vulnerable to illness hadn't taken hold, and the solution — change your lifestyle if you want to get better — was even more tenuous. At the Lahey Clinic I was low on the totem pole, and the patients I examined were well to do and often very influential. A labor leader who could sway the votes of millions of workers came to Lahey grossly obese, wheezing with every breath, and abusing alcohol and tobacco from the moment he woke up in the morning to the moment he lay down at night.

What was my duty to this patient? I was given very clear instructions: "Be gentle, and whatever you do, don't tell him the truth."

Today such a code borders on the unethical. Back then, discretion was considered more ethical than anything else. Cancer patients were routinely not told their diagnosis. It wasn't a patient's right to know, and many were afraid of knowing. (It still isn't in many countries. One reads that Emperor Hirohito of Japan, who died of duodenal cancer in 1989, wasn't told his diagnosis even up to the end, despite the fact that he had been operated on as early as the fall of 1987.) I have come to feel that it borders on the unethical not to tell patients about the impact of their lifestyle choices.

I was far from feeling this way when I was a young doctor, though. What made you a hero was spotting the right diagnosis and not much more. The *Physician's Desk Reference* told you what to prescribe. When you handed a prescription to the patient, there was such a look of relief and respect that you grew to believe it was deserved — the drugs you dispensed out of a handbook were the symbol of your wisdom. On the medical pecking order surgeons stood at the top because they had skills that went far beyond writing a prescription (when they chat, surgeons say things like "Did you see that melanoma I saved today?") while psychiatrists were at the bottom because they had almost no drugs they could prescribe beyond a small array of tranquilizers — antidepressants hadn't yet come into their own. We didn't disguise our scorn for a doctor who spent his whole day listening to patients talk about their problems and then did nothing better for them than talk back.

These casual prejudices were deeply embedded in the profession. It took a crooked path for me to find my way out. The first steps were unwitting, more or less. I had begun to feel a genuine calling toward endocrinology. When my two-year residency ended I passed the boards in internal medicine and could have gone straight into general practice. But it was more prestigious to specialize. Rita and I had decided by this time not to return to India. Our parents took the news as best they could. My father, at least, understood that I wanted to progress in my career.

The most prestige attached to getting a research fellowship, and I was fortunate. I was offered one in an endocrinology program at a hospital affiliated with Tufts University that took only two or three new fellows a year. It was headed by a world-famous researcher in the field. My time would be divided between laboratory work, which would lead to publishing research papers, and seeing patients in the clinic.

Nothing about this was unusual for a young doctor on the rise. I was fascinated by being in the lab, and there was no way to foresee the blowup that would end my fellowship and almost my whole career. What mattered was the subtle interplay of hormones in the body, which is what endocrine research is all about. The field had miles to go before a complete understanding would be reached. The next turn in the road would lead me to studying the hormones secreted by the brain, not just the thyroid or adrenal glands. The brain, of course, is only a step away from the mind.

It wasn't a step I was willing to take yet. No one around me believed that the mind was a serious medical subject; science couldn't prove that the mind existed. Psychiatrists, it was widely said, wound up there because they weren't good enough to practice hard medicine. The human brain is soft in texture to the point of mushiness, but it called for hard medicine nonetheless. Human beings are beset by many mental woes. It amazed me that so many Americans, given their prosperous and easy lives, were under such a cloud of malaise. Mysteriously, to an Indian doctor, every day was filled with people complaining of depression and free-floating anxiety. It was vital to find an answer, which must lie in the brain. Somewhere in that chemical labyrinth lay the secret of happiness.

There was a kink in this logic that took me a decade to find. This is where the unwitting part comes in. At random I was given a clue about the mind-body connection. I was working full-time at a suburban emergency room in Everett after my Tufts fellowship came to a crashing end in the confrontation with my enraged adviser. One evening, a beefy Irish fireman came into the ER complaining of severe chest pains. When I examined him I could find nothing that indicated a heart problem. After I gave him the good news, saying that it was probably a muscle contraction around the sternum, the man didn't look relieved. With a scowl he told me I was wrong. He knew he was having a heart attack. What's more, he insisted that I write it up as a heart attack so that he could retire with a disability pension. When I told him I couldn't do that, he stormed out looking angry and depressed.

Several nights later the fireman returned, complaining of even worse chest pains. The doctor on call examined him and also found nothing wrong with his heart.

When I came in I inquired with the attending physician.

"He's malingering," he said. "It's a scam to get a better pension." After doing a second exam and finding no cardiac irregularities myself, I tended to agree.

Over the next few months the fireman returned to the hospital regularly. I tried to overcome my skepticism; I listened to the patient's detailed description of his symptoms and sent him for an echocardiogram, which came back normal, then for angiography to determine if his coronary arteries were blocked. Every test came back negative, but he couldn't be shaken from his belief that he had heart disease. For whatever reason, he could no longer function as a firefighter, so I reluctantly agreed to recommend that he be retired on disability.

His case came under departmental review several weeks later. Often this is a perfunctory hearing, but as the recommending physician I had to appear to defend my recommendation. I explained my reasons as best I could, but when I was flatly asked by the medical officer if I had detected any abnormality in the structure or function of my patient's heart, I admitted that I hadn't. Application for disability retirement was denied.

Two nights later I was called down to the ER. My patient was back. I shook my head in frustration when I heard it was him, but stepping into the treatment room, I saw that he was stretched out on a gurney with an oxygen mask and cardiac monitor hooked to him. He had suffered a massive heart attack, which had severely damaged the heart muscle. He had barely enough strength to open his eyes. He recognized me as I approached the gurney.

"Now do you believe me?" he mumbled bitterly. And then he died.

What had happened was beyond comprehension. Some patients take bad news very hard. They decline rapidly despite every medical measure, and when they succumb, the doctor will say, "He died of his diagnosis." But who dies from good news? By all normal standards this man had a healthy heart. I spent considerable time thinking about his case, and I finally reached the conclusion that he was the victim of fatal beliefs. Irrationally convinced that his heart was damaged, he had triggered a chain of disastrous physiological responses.

That was as far as the trail led. Medical science couldn't follow the tracks that went from a mere belief to a massive event in the body. Some potent forces must have been involved; as yet they were elusive. But now I had firsthand experience of the mind-body connection, even though my training told me to dismiss it. Soon I became fascinated by the role that the brain plays in the endocrine system, while at the same time refusing to take the mind into account. They were the same thing to begin with. That was standard knowledge imparted in medical school. If thoughts left invisible traces, brain chemistry didn't. The only reasonable choice was to follow the footprints you could actually see.

14

A Giant in Medicine

Sanjiv

Sanjiv weds Amita during their final year of medical
school in New Delhi, India, 1970.

IN MEDICAL SCHOOL I WAS taught how to be a doctor, but when I became an intern the most amazing and sometimes frightening thing was that people entrusted me with their lives. It was an awesome responsibility. My patients and their loved ones knew nothing about me, except for the fact that I was wearing a white coat, had a stethoscope strung around my neck, and a badge that read DR. CHOPRA. But that was sufficient for them; I was a doctor, their doctor. It is an amazing display of faith. They willingly divulged the most private information about their lives, often things they wouldn't have told their family members or closest friends. They weren't speaking to me, to Sanjiv Chopra. They were speaking to their doctor.

At Muhlenberg hospital, Amita and I worked very difficult hours. There was never enough time to do everything that needed to be done, but like all interns throughout history we somehow struggled through. I began working on the wards, presenting patients to the attending physician. After taking a detailed history and conducting an examination of each patient, I would formulate my diagnosis and prepare to explain and, if necessary, defend it. Attendings learn quickly which interns to rely on. Two months into my internship the chief of medicine, Dr. Paul Johnson, gave me an unusual promotion, allowing me to fill in as a resident at a Rutgers-affiliated hospital for a month. I'd thought I had exhausted all the hours in the day, but I learned there was no respite. Every third weekend, for example, I worked steadily from early Saturday morning through late Monday night. One time I had twenty-two admissions, making rounds in the coronary and intensive care units and the wards, seeing patients, writing orders and daily progress notes. Every few minutes my beeper would go off and the emergency room physician would call me with another admission. I had barely sat down after admitting the previous patient before the beeper would go off again.

I remember a patient with his leg in a cast who came into the emergency room complaining that he was having difficulty breathing. He had a history of asthma and had run out of his medication.

"I'm having a flare-up of my asthma," he said. I was concerned, however, that he might have a pulmonary embolism caused by a blood clot in his immobile leg that had dislodged to his lung. This is a potentially fatal condition. A scan confirmed my suspicion, and we started the treatment that likely saved his life. Working with patients who trust your skill and judgment was thrilling to me. It meant that I couldn't be wrong, especially if there was a life-threatening situation. As an intern there is a built-in safety net, a hierarchy: The intern can call the junior resident, who has an extra year of experience, to ask for advice. He or she, in turn, can call the senior resident, who can call the attending of record. By the time I had completed my year at Muhlenberg I was quite confident in my ability to diagnose patients with all kinds of illnesses.

Amita and I followed Deepak's path to Boston, knowing it was a mecca of medicine in America, the big leagues. I accepted a position as a junior resident at Carney Hospital in Dorchester. The hospital was affiliated with Tufts University. Amita did her residency in pediatrics at St. Elizabeth's Hospital. Not long after I had started working as a junior resident at Carney, I was summoned by an intern. One of his patients had a headache, a high fever, abdominal discomfort, and diarrhea.

"I need your help," he said. "I'm trying to do a lumbar puncture and I'm having difficulty getting into the lumbar space to get the spinal fluid out. Can you give me a hand?"

I walked into the room, took a quick but focused history, and examined the patient. I then reviewed his laboratory studies and made a diagnosis.

"He doesn't need a lumbar puncture," I said. "He's got enteric fever."

The intern was quite surprised. "Why do you think so?"

While enteric fever, or typhoid, was rare in the United States, I had seen quite a few cases in India. This was precisely the type of patient I loved, a mystery to be solved by the application of proven science.

"The patient complained of diarrhea," I explained. "He's got an enlarged spleen and a high fever, and despite that high fever his pulse rate isn't that high. Normally for every degree a patient's temperature goes up, his or her pulse should go up ten beats per minute. His heartbeat hasn't gone up anywhere near that much. This is a condition called relative bradycardia. He's also got a type of rash known as rose spots, and a low white blood cell count. This is a classic case of typhoid."

This intern shook his head in bewilderment. "But he was seen by Lou Weinstein." Dr. Louis Weinstein was a world-famous infectious disease consultant; he was considered the god of infectious diseases. I was a junior resident. I didn't blame the intern for doubting me.

I told the intern to run some tests and do a stool culture. Meanwhile I called the patient's attending with my diagnosis. He requested that I call Dr. Weinstein.

"Hello, Dr. Weinstein? I'm Dr. Chopra, a junior resident in medicine." Once I'd reached him in his office I told Dr. Weinstein that I had examined this patient, reviewed all his laboratory tests, and concluded that he had typhoid fever.

In India I would not have felt comfortable challenging a man of such distinction, but Louis Weinstein's ego was not a factor at all. There was a period of silence, then he asked me pleasantly where I had trained. I told him I had graduated from the All India Institute of Medical Sciences in New Delhi.

"That's a pretty good school. Did you see a lot of cases of typhoid there?"

"Dozens," I said. "We had wards filled with patients with infectious diseases, and many of them had typhoid." I told him what tests I had requested, then said I wanted to begin treatment with an antibiotic. He agreed. The next day the test results confirmed my diagnosis. The story of the junior resident who had correctly diagnosed what was a rare case of typhoid fever in Boston spread rapidly throughout the hospital. My reputation was assured at Carney. I was the guy who had trumped Lou Weinstein.

A few years later I applied for a fellowship at the Jamaica Plain VA hospital — where Deepak was already chief resident. Deepak had chosen endocrinology, but the specialty I chose was gastroenterology, the study of the digestive system, and its subspecialty, hepatology, focusing on the liver. Even when I was in medical school I was fascinated by the liver. The liver is an amazing machine. It's the largest organ in the human body and, for me, it has always been the most interesting; it does about five thousand different jobs. It handles so many complex, different functions. I would say to my cardiology colleagues, "You know, the only reason for the heart to exist is so it can pump oxygenated blood to the liver."

The head of the Division of Gastroenterology at the VA hospital was a legendary clinician and scholar, Dr. Elihu Schimmel, who said to me during my interview for a gastroenterology fellowship, "Sanjiv, if you have the same genes as Deepak, you're in."

That year was the only time in our lives that Deepak and I worked at the same hospital. As it turns out, there was actually a third Dr. Chopra at the Jamaica Plain hospital, a kidney expert. The staff would continually get us confused. Imagine: Three Indian physicians with the same last name. Sometimes an intern would walk up to me and say, "So, Dr. Chopra, you think this patient has hyperparathyroidism?" and I would have to tell him, "I think you need to talk to my brother, he's the endocrinology fellow." Or they would ask Deepak, "Dr. Chopra, when are you going to do a liver biopsy on our patient?" To which he would reply, "I think you need to talk to my brother."

But while we were at the same hospital, we never worked together unless we happened to be consulting on the same patient. At times when we were together in the doctors' lounge or at home we would discuss our most interesting and challenging cases, as we probably would have done with any other colleague, but that was the extent of it.

With each year of training I was gaining confidence in my ability to diagnose even the most challenging disorders. But very soon after

I arrived at Jamaica Plain, I received a very good lesson about how much I still had to learn when it came to the practice of medicine. The first week of my gastroenterology fellowship I was presenting a patient to Dr. Schimmel. I'd taken my time to prepare this presentation, knowing how important it was to get off to a good start. Before presenting the patient I put up a type of abdomen X-ray called a KUB or flat plate. I flicked on the X-ray view-box light and before I could switch it off, literally in seconds, Dr. Schimmel said, "Stop." I stopped. He stared at the X-ray for about thirty seconds.

"Sanjiv, this patient is a chronic smoker and an alcoholic. He has diabetes. He also had polio as a child. He needs to have his gallbladder removed."

I was stunned.

"Eli," I began (by that time I had grown accustomed to, if not entirely comfortable with, the informality of addressing senior attendings at American hospitals by their first names). "Which one of the other fellows presented this patient to you?"

"None of them," he replied.

"Then how can you fathom all of that from one X-ray?"

He explained: "His diaphragm's flattened and his lungs are hyperinflated. That's a sign of his being a smoker, emphysema of the lungs. I can see pancreatic calcification, so he's got chronic pancreatitis from alcohol. He has aseptic necrosis of the head of the femur and kyphoscoliosis, which can be a result of polio in childhood."

There were six of us in that room listening to him, enthralled and mesmerized. Nobody said a word and I'm sure we were all thinking the same thing: We are watching a virtuoso performance.

Dr. Schimmel continued, "Now, here there's a little rim of calcification on the wall of his gallbladder. When you see this it's called porcelain gallbladder, and up to sixty percent of such patients develop gallbladder cancer, so he needs his gallbladder taken out. Questions?"

I had one. "How can you tell he has diabetes?"

"Good, yeah," he answered. "He has a calcification of the vas deferens. If you see that in a developing country like India it's tuberculosis, but in the West it's diabetes." In a few seconds Dr. Schimmel had demonstrated his mastery as an astute clinician. For me it was an extraordinary application of medical science to a real patient. It showed me what was possible.

Of course further testing proved Dr. Schimmel was absolutely right. Dead-on. That day has been imprinted in memory forever. People without a medical background can't truly appreciate the difficulty of what he did. I've often told this story to colleagues in medicine over the last three decades and they are inevitably awestruck.

I knew I was in a spot of tremendous learning and I developed a close relationship with Dr. Schimmel. He was to become an inspirational mentor who has shaped the way I think. It has been my good fortune to have worked with physicians like Eli Schimmel. In America physicians become chairmen of major academic departments because they have earned it, whereas in many places in the world seniority and nepotism can be more important than merit. From Eli Schimmel I learned the right approach to medicine and I've taken that with me throughout my career. I was also privileged and fortunate that the following year I was chosen to do a hepatology fellowship with Dr. Raymond Koff, one of the world's most respected hepatologists.

Once, one of the other gastroenterology fellows was presenting a patient with an intestinal bleed to the fellows, medical students, and several faculty members. He related the history, explained the physical examination, and said, "The patient required four units of blood. So we—"

"Stop," Dr. Schimmel interrupted. The fellow stopped immediately. "How do you know he required four units of blood? Maybe he actually required three, or five. What you mean to say is that he was transfused with four units of blood. Just give me the facts, please."

Of course he was absolutely correct. The practice of medicine deals with observation and recall of facts. So from that day forward that was the way I started to think, talk, and write.

Several months later I had the opportunity to demonstrate to him how successful his lesson had been and, perhaps, to prove that I was a worthy pupil. One of the GI fellows was presenting a patient when Eli said, "So, lack of hydrochloric acid in the stomach stimulates the release of the hormone gastrin —"

This time I interrupted him. In India, of course, I would never have dared to do something like that. In America this back-and-forth was the way we learned medicine on the wards. I guess I had become Americanized by this point.

"Eli, that's not true," I said. "Lack of hydrochloric acid is permissive for the release of gastrin." Then I began a discussion of the topic.

When I had finished, Dr. Schimmel turned to the group and smiled. "Sanjiv, your thinking is so much more elegant than mine."

I was truly humbled. A nice compliment from one of the giants of medicine.

There was so much richness about living in America that Amita and I decided to apply for green cards to stay here, if not permanently, then at least for several years. So we discarded our original plan, which was to finish our educations here and return to India.

Only immigrants to America know the world of the green card, the card originally issued by the Immigration and Naturalization Service that makes a person a legal resident, meaning they have almost all of the rights, except voting, that American citizens enjoy. Without a green card you can't legally stay in America.

Getting a green card turns out to be a big industry. It requires a good lawyer and it can be both time-consuming and expensive. But when an immigrant finally gets it, it's like being handed gold. It means your life is changed forever.

Amita and I both applied for our green cards as we finished our internships at Muhlenberg hospital. Time passed and we didn't hear anything, we didn't receive any notices, so we assumed our applications were being processed, until we received a letter from Immigration more than a year later. "This is your third and final notice," it read. "If you don't appear for an interview on this date we will discontinue your file."

Third notice? We hadn't received any notice at all. But still, we were excited. We thought this meant we were going to be given our green cards.

We went for our hearing without an attorney. It never occurred to us that this was anything but a formality. This was America, the country that welcomed immigrants. The hearing officer was named Mr. Pickering.

"So," he began, "you've applied for immigration?"

"We have," I said. "That's why we're here."

He turned to Amita. "Now let me ask you independently." He looked at me and told me not to answer for her, then asked, "You've applied for immigration?"

"Yes, I have," she said.

Then he turned back to me. "And you, Dr. Sanjiv Chopra, you got your visa to come here on the explicit terms that you would train here for five years and then go back. So now you've both applied for immigration. You've proven you are liars and dishonest. You'll be receiving a notice within two weeks explaining that you have to leave the country within a month."

We were dumbfounded.

"What are you saying? I have accepted a fellowship at St. Elizabeth's Hospital and Amita is going to be chief resident in pediatrics at Boston City Hospital. We've signed contracts. We can't leave."

He shrugged. "I don't give a damn. Dismissed."

We were devastated. What about our plans? We probably didn't understand it at that time, but we had just entered a world familiar to so many immigrants, a world in which you feel powerless against the government, where every time you get a letter from the Immigration Service your heart starts beating faster. At first we had no idea what to do. How do you fight the government of the United States?

We had come to the States with the intention of going home when we had completed our studies. We hadn't lied about that, this wasn't simply some story to get us into the country. It was only after we were settled here that we began to even consider the possibility of staying. Our reaction was probably typical. When we made our decision to stay here we were somewhat ambivalent about it. We knew what we would be giving up at home, we knew we would miss many things about India, especially the closeness with our family, but we felt we could have a better life here. After we were told that we weren't going to be allowed to stay, staying here became the most important thing in our lives. Any doubts we might have had disappeared.

Amita called her program director at Boston City Hospital, Dr. Joel Alpert. She had completed her residency there, and he had picked her to be the first foreigner and the first woman to be chief resident of the in-patient service. It was quite an honor.

"I know somebody at Immigration," he told us. "I'll make sure you don't get that letter."

Then we were told we needed an immigration lawyer. The man who was recommended to us was Mr. O'Neal. We were told that his fees were sky-high but that he was very good. He fights for you. We met with him. He was a large, imposing figure.

"You're fine," he reassured us. "I'll come with you for the next interview. Don't worry about it. By the time we're done I'll have Pickering picking up peanut shells on Boylston Street."

He went to the next meeting with us. He reassured us that the meeting had gone very well. We were asked many questions, which we answered honestly. He sat behind us, didn't utter a word, but smiled confidently. Over the next few weeks we lived in a state of perpetual worry—until finally we got the word that we were approved for permanent residency. We were permitted to stay in the United States!

And while for many people the cost is thousands of dollars, O'Neal told us, "I didn't have to do much. Your credentials were impeccable. My fee is four hundred dollars." Four hundred dollars to be allowed to stay in America? That was certainly the best bargain of our lives.

We were so pleased to get our green cards that we didn't immediately consider taking the next step, becoming American citizens. This was decades before the great immigration debates had begun in America, and, at least for educated Indians, becoming a citizen was not difficult.

I had first considered the possibility of becoming an American citizen the year we arrived, while we were at Muhlenberg, and truthfully didn't see any obvious reason to do it. I'd spoken with Deepak about it, but he hadn't made his own decision about that yet, either. We were living in America and we had retained our Indian citizenship; in some ways that was the best arrangement for us. We had always been proud to be Indian citizens. But several years later, we were well settled here and I was working as the assistant chief of medicine at the West Roxbury VA Medical Center. The chairman of the department, Arthur Sasahara, asked me my immigration status.

"I have a green card," I said.

He shook his head. "You've got to become a U.S. citizen."

"Why?"

"We're part of the federal government," he explained. "If there's a crunch and we have to lay off employees, the first people to go are going to be temporary employees. Technically you are a temporary employee because you're not a citizen. So please go and apply for your citizenship."

This was a step I hadn't considered necessary. Although by this time I had no intention of returning to India to live, I still felt loyalty. India was my country, the country that had paid for my medical education. My parents were there. My childhood memories were there. My family had written our history on scrolls in a city there.

Many of the Indian friends we'd made in medicine had applied for their American citizenship. It wasn't an active topic of conversation in the Indian community in Boston, as it was considered very much a personal decision. But now there was a reason for me to take this step. To claim I was doing so because I believed strongly in the principles and values of America wouldn't be true. That belief grew stronger over the years as I traveled to dozens of countries around the world. While I did believe that this is a wonderful, unique country, I also retained a love for India. India, even with all its problems, is a wonderful country. And I have to admit that there were at least some pangs of guilt. The Indian government had given me this amazing education; I had fabulous teachers and role models in medical school. Then one day we had packed our bags and left. The way I rationalized it was that by becoming successful in America I could probably do more good for India than if I had stayed there. While in many ways that has turned out to be true, both for myself and Deepak, I can't say that I didn't feel some trepidation about my decision.

When I discussed this with Amita she had already made up her mind: She flatly refused. "I'm Indian," she said. "I won't give away my Indian citizenship."

In Amita's mind there was still a good chance that we would go back to India someday, and she was not ready to give up that dream. Amita has always been passionate about India and most things Indian, especially our great culture, even more so than I am.

This was a very difficult decision for us, and admittedly Amita and I had arguments about it. In that regard I'm sure we were no different than immigrants from any part of the world. This is an enormous commitment, and couples have split up over it. But for me the opportunity to do what I needed to do was here. I was adamant about it and told her flatly, "Amita, I'm not going back. And you know our kids wouldn't want to live there. They were brought up here. They're Americans."

I reminded her that some of our Indian doctor friends had returned home and it hadn't worked out at all for them. Almost inevitably they came back to the United States. While it was possible to go to India and establish a private practice there, and we could have worked with my father if we wanted to be in academic medicine, which I loved, there was less opportunity. Those classmates of ours who stayed in India had progressed inside the system, and there was little room left for people who were returning, no matter what credentials they had or how much experience they had acquired. The Indian government had created the category of "pool officer" for doctors who returned, which meant you weren't an associate professor or even an assistant professor. It was an untenable position. There was a legendary professor of pathology at the Mayo Clinic who had returned to India — but like so many other people who tried to make the journey, after a while he gave up trying to be successful within their system and came back to the United States.

Amita refused to apply for her citizenship, but I went ahead with it. When I went for my interview the official examined my application.

"So you're a doctor, huh? What kind?"

"A very good one," I told him. We both laughed, and I continued, "I'm sorry, I don't mean to be so facetious. I'm a gastroenterologist, specializing in hepatology. Liver disease."

Most Americans don't know exactly what "gastroenterologist" means, except that it has something to do with the stomach. But I had gotten an official who understood all too well.

"A gastroenterologist?" he said. "My daughter has Crohn's disease." For the next half hour we discussed Crohn's disease, the best treatments, and some of the exciting advances in the field. He asked me a single question — "Which president abolished slavery?" — and then said these exact words: "Welcome to America."

The official ceremony was held in Faneuil Hall in Boston, where several of America's founding fathers had made speeches before the Revolutionary War. You can feel the history surrounding you when you're there, and there couldn't be a more appropriate place to be sworn in as an American citizen.

There were approximately two hundred and fifty people there with me, and it was obvious they had come from all over the world. Many different races were represented and a few people were even wearing their native dress. The judge arrived late, but when he started the ceremony he asked, "So how many children are here?" Quite a few hands were raised. He asked them to stand up. "How many of you are going back to school after this ceremony?" Every single child raised their hand. That's when he said, "I hereby prohibit you from going to school today. Today is a very special day in your lives. You've become a United States citizen. This is a day to celebrate. I'm ordering your parents to go celebrate with you." Then he swore us all in.

The children cheered. I was so moved by the entire ceremony, where we were, what was said, the joy on all of those faces. This is amazing, I thought, America is a beautiful place.

Amita resisted for some time after that. It wasn't that she felt any less happy to be in America, but her love was still India. Her mind changed when we took our three children on vacation to Spain. We visited several cities before deciding to go to the Rock of Gibraltar. We drove all the way there. Because Gibraltar is still a British possession, we had to show our passports. The immigration official looked at Amita's and Priya's Indian passports and said, "I'm sorry, I can't let you in. You've got a single entry into Spain and you've already entered. Coming back from Gibraltar would be a second entry; you can go but you can't come back." So the two of them had to wait in Spain while my other two children and I went to see the Rock of Gibraltar.

The next time we returned from abroad, Amita had to stand in the foreign nationals' line to go through Immigration. That line is always considerably longer than the line for U.S. citizens, as the officials look extra carefully at visitors coming into the country. She found it vexing and finally said, "Okay, I'll become a U.S. citizen, but I'm doing it as a matter of convenience." She also went to Faneuil Hall to be sworn in. That whole experience, taking the oath in front of the American flag, sitting on long benches with immigrants from many, many different countries, really affected her. Some of her emotional ties had been severed, but her strong feelings about India remained.

We were both now citizens of the most beautiful country in the world, and so was our eldest daughter, Ratika Priya. We were officially Indian-Americans. In reality we were caught between two worlds. When I reflected on India I thought about the extended families, spirituality, scintillating colors, and enchanting sounds. But when I thought about my new, adopted country, I reflected on freedom, the land of unparalleled opportunity, the country where I wanted to see my children have roots.

I have now traveled the world. Not too long ago I came across a billboard that read THE ONLY TRUE NATION IS HUMANITY. That truly resonates for me.

15

An Obscure Light

Deepak

Deepak enjoying time with his grandchildren
Tara, Leela, and Krishan, 2011.

W E HAVE WORDS IN ENGLISH for illumination and parables about the road to Damascus. The sudden stroke of awakening is very dramatic. But it would be helpful to have a separate word for a slow-motion epiphany. The reason it doesn't exist, I suppose, is that slow epiphanies often aren't recognized until years later, with a backward glance.

After storming out of my residency and severing all ties with the Tufts-affiliated hospital, the way forward seemed hopelessly blocked. Endocrinology didn't seem to be in my future anymore. I felt stymied. On the positive side, my replacement job at the ER in Everett paid a living wage, much more than my fellowship had. When I showed up there, expecting to moonlight for hourly wages, I was met by the only full-time ER doctor, who was overwhelmed, and he offered me a full-time position on the spot. I protested that I wasn't really qualified in emergency medicine, but he waved away my objections, saying that he would train me. Rita was pregnant with our second child at the time, but my work was so demanding that we barely saw each other in passing.

One night while I was on duty, Rita called me in the emergency room. "Congratulations, you have a son." At first I didn't understand what had happened.

When she had started having contractions, Rita gathered her maternity things and drove herself to the hospital (her mother, who had come from India to stay with us, was the nervous passenger), and hours after giving birth she phoned me. It's an accomplishment to make it safely downtown through the tangle of Boston traffic in the first place. It was strange to hear all of this in between trauma cases at work and I was sad that I couldn't break away when I got the news. But that was our life.

We decided to name the baby Kabir, in tribute to one of India's most revered poets. My mother used to have friends come in for *kirtan*, ceremonial singing and chanting. Someone would play the harmonium while the ladies sang songs that were often by Kabir.

The poet Kabir has a lovely story attached to him as well. He was an orphan in Benares, and no one knows what religion his parents followed. As a baby he was adopted by a poor Muslim couple who taught their child the weaving trade that he pursued his whole life. Kabir looked beyond Islam, however, and tricked a guru named Ramananda into giving him a Sanskrit mantra to meditate on. But this didn't signify that he thought of himself as Hindu, either. When Kabir died in 1518, the Muslims wanted his body in order to bury it, while the Hindus wanted the body to cremate it. A heated argument arose. Someone drew aside the cloth that was draped over the corpse. Miraculously the body had turned into a bouquet of flowers. This was divided, and the Muslims buried their half while the Hindus burned the other.

My mother loved Kabir, but she had a social qualm about giving the baby his name. She didn't want him to grow up with strangers assuming that someone named Kabir, which is Arabic for great, was Muslim. Rita and I went back and forth. In the end we chose Gautam instead, a common name in north India; we were pleased by the association with the Buddha, who went by Gautama when he left home and took up life as a wandering monk.

The ER job paid $45,000 a year, a dreamlike sum to us. We had graduated from a savings account to credit cards, feeling more and more American along the way. We bought our first house for $30,000 in the comfortable bedroom town of Winchester. But nothing brightened my anxiety that I was at a dead end professionally. It took almost a year for anything to move. Then I got an unexpected call from an academic researcher, a colleague I'd known for some time but had almost forgotten about. He was chief of medicine at the Boston VA Hospital in Jamaica Plain.

"I hear you're looking for another fellowship," he said. "How would you like to come work for me and finish your endocrine boards?"

"You know my history," I said cautiously.

"Yeah." I could hear the smile in his voice.

Later it occurred to me that he meant "That's why I'm calling you." My former adviser was personally disliked among other research doctors. He had treated all of us junior fellows with disdain, in the apparent belief that insulting other people's intelligence was a way to prove his authority. None of this dislike was out in the open when I was hired. The only condition that came with the fellowship was that I would serve as chief resident at the VA. In itself this was a coup for them, since it was unusual to get a board-certified internist for the role.

After my residency in endocrinology was completed I passed the boards in 1977, which meant that I was now both a board-certified internist and an endocrinologist. Since I had lost two years along the way, Sanjiv took his boards in gastroenterology at the same time as me. But I was satisfied. All my educational aims were fulfilled. On the research side I spent my time at the VA studying the thyroid gland, as I had before. I wound up publishing a couple of papers and was rewarded with a small but growing reputation. The black marks from my previous altercation were erased.

If I vaguely questioned how the system worked, I still had every intention of working within it. Rebelling wasn't the only way to get things to change. I would be complimenting myself without cause to claim that rebellion ever crossed my mind. As brilliant as scientific medicine can be, I was walking through the wards completely blind to another reality. This was the reality of a patient entering the hospital. Almost always he is frightened and sometimes concealing deep dread. His health and perhaps his life are at risk. The admissions process is impersonal. If there is the looming prospect of a huge hospital bill at the end, as there often is, more anxiety is piled on. The probing and prodding from doctors carries a measure of indignity as the patient sits naked under a flimsy green gown on a cold metal table.

These are not superficial changes from normal life. Doctors talk in a jargon that is mostly unintelligible to the average person. A mechanical routine is imposed once you arrive at your hospital room, an antiseptic and alien place. Orderlies and nurses come and go with only a passing interest in your human side. The interview with the surgeon, if surgery is what you have been admitted for, lasts barely fifteen or twenty minutes, and you are too nervous to remember all the questions you wanted to ask — they run obsessively through your mind as you lie sleepless in bed staring at the ceiling.

The two realities of patient and doctor are almost like victim and persecutor, even though there are good intentions on both sides. No one addresses how terrible it feels for a patient to be depersonalized, even as it is happening. We've all seen enough TV to know that doctors talk about "the pancreatic cancer in room 453," not "anxious Mr. Jones in room 453." If a surgeon successfully removes a malignant tumor, he thinks to himself — at least at that moment — that he has "saved" the patient, without much concern for what is often a dire prognosis and, ultimately, death. It's not a tribute to human nature that the one who holds all the power, the physician, is inured to the plight of the one who has no power at all, the patient.

I was ensconced in America, but India was about to reclaim me. It didn't feel as if she needed to. Our friends included many Indian doctors, just as in Jamaica Plain. Sanjiv had brought his family to Boston, so there was no rupture in our relationship. We felt as close as ever. The way we talked was no longer like two boys growing up. Career and family took precedence. We weren't twin stars circling each other anymore. But the constellation felt secure with wives and children filling it out. Once I moved into private practice, Boston medicine provided what it had promised all along, a community of the best hospitals staffed by physicians who also thought of themselves as the best.

This doesn't turn into a story about disillusion. Cynicism didn't corrode my heart and spoil my contented life. Once I gave up working the inhuman hours of a resident and the all-nighters at an emergency room (two things that had been a constant for six years), I did what established doctors do everywhere.

My day began around five in the morning. I would get up, grab breakfast on the run, begin stoking my energy with strong coffee, and drive to the hospital. I was affiliated with two hospitals, located in Melrose and Stoneham, which meant that I was an attending physician. These were the places where my private patients were admitted if they needed surgery or hospital care.

I would make morning rounds, checking in on my admissions, and then drive to my office around eight. The next nine hours would be filled with appointments. My rapport with patients was still good, and I built up a sizable load — at its peak I think my practice had more than seven thousand patients on file. As the day wound down it was back to the hospital for evening rounds, and then home again. The whole cycle, which was repeated for the next decade, mirrored the routine of every other doctor I knew. Out before dawn, home after dark. Rita and her friends, who were also doctors' wives, raised their families around the demands of their husbands' work. It was simply accepted.

Medical training postpones the process of maturing as a person. I had been a full-time student until I turned thirty. One aspect of surviving in such an immature station was to remain immature, listening to authority, staying at the bottom of the ladder, reassuring yourself that you had more to learn. American doctoring is incredibly selfish if viewed as a climb into the elite echelon of moneymaking. The American dream at its crassest is the American paycheck. Once my annual income crossed $100,000, Rita and I were staring at money that felt surreal. The house we finally settled in, which was in Lincoln, another comfortable bedroom town outside Boston, cost six times what the first one had. The Seventies were our coming-of-age decade. Hidden from view was something I barely considered: If you don't mature on time, you may never get a second chance.

What I began to notice instead was that my world was narrow and filled with rituals. In Jamaica Plain our Little India had been glamorous in a reverse way, with the nervous excitement of high crime and the daring of living from hand to mouth. One day I came home exhausted and collapsed in bed. Rita had gone out on errands. Suddenly there was a crashing sound from the living room. Jerked awake by adrenaline, I rushed into the living room. A threatening black man had invaded my home. He stopped in his tracks, sizing me up. My mind raced immediately to the baby, who was asleep in her crib. I grabbed a baseball bat and charged at him. (The bat was a present from an American friend who wanted to coax me to stop fixating on cricket.) Before he had a chance to react, I swung hard at the intruder's lower back and knocked him down.

The scene instantly became chaotic. Neighbors rushed in. Rita came home with groceries in her arms to see the baby screaming with fright on the living room floor next to a stranger swearing and writhing in pain. The police arrived, and I was trying not to seem jacked up on adrenaline — it wasn't lost on me that I was under the influence of an endocrine hormone. It turned out that the intruder was an escaped convict who was quickly returned to prison.

Being in the suburbs among well-heeled Indian doctors was a duller existence. We kept our roots by doing the daily puja ceremony at home with an oil lamp and incense. As the children grew up, the girls went off to learn traditional Indian dances, called *Bharatiya Ratnam,* while the boys devoured Indian comic books filled with the exploits of Rama and Krishna. We drew into a tighter circle from knowing that, to many white doctors in Boston, Indian doctors were less skilled and suspect. Their silent rejection didn't keep us from copying their lifestyle, however.

The American customs we were most proud of showed how insecure we actually were. Weekend barbecues and cocktail parties were indistinguishable from the ones seen in television commercials for charcoal lighter fluid and Kentucky bourbon. Among the men conversation consisted of a running contest over the cars we bought and the size of the color televisions in our living rooms. I heard about one doctor who was worried that being Indian meant his offspring would grow up too short to play varsity football. He undertook the drastic measure of putting his preteen kids on human growth hormone, which was illegal. As an endocrinologist I wished that I could warn him about possible side effects, including cancer, but we had no personal contact.

Being in private practice was satisfying, but it had its faults. At the most mundane level my day was filled with overweight women who looked at me with hope in their eyes. They had been told that getting fat could be traceable to a "gland problem." Ninety percent of the time or more I dashed their hopes. The problem wasn't low thyroid but high calories. Their disappointment bothered me. I no longer played the hero in an emergency room, and the intellectual challenge of laboratory research was gone. I had learned what a good doctor understands: There is a limit to what he can really accomplish.

Is that why a new aspect of the self began to emerge? Perhaps I had kicked out some invisible bricks without knowing it, leaving an aching hole. All that I noticed was a sense of disappointment in myself. I was smoking and drinking too much. The stress of eighteen-hour days couldn't be shrugged off anymore. I wondered whether the answer might lie in meditation. No one in my Indian circle gave meditation a second thought. You weren't going to win the race by sitting in lotus position.

The Americans had given it a new twist, though. Ever since he sprang to worldwide fame as a guru to the Beatles, Maharishi Mahesh Yogi had accomplished a cultural shift. "Mantra" had entered the English language as a hip word. (In the background of a Woody Allen comedy a Hollywood agent is anxiously saying into a telephone, "I forgot my mantra.") With everything too foreign stripped away, meditation was now about stress release and increased energy. You didn't have to sit in lotus position. It was promised that you could still win the race even if you had inner peace at the same time.

When I decided to try Transcendental Meditation, the Sixties were long past. In the early Eighties TM was already so established that it had become passé. American popular culture thrives by making sure that there is always room on the shelf for something new. Inevitably that means shoving something old out of the way. In my case, however, three streams of influence were merging. I respected my mother's religious nature, as a physician I kept wondering about the mind-body connection (although at that point it was purely a chemical fascination), and I knew that my stress level wasn't going to decrease on its own. No one had yet coined the phrase "a perfect storm," but I was at the eye of one.

"How can you follow a guru?" one friend said. "I'd never surrender my life to somebody else."

Others turned away discreetly with obvious embarrassment. The synonym for guru that readily came to American minds was charlatan. At home, sitting on the bank of the Ganges with matted hair, rags for clothes, and a begging bowl, gurus had their place. But something bad happened when they came West. Here, gurus led cults. They pretended to be God. They practiced tricks of mind control, and their followers were hopelessly brainwashed, which they came to realize too late, long after their wallets had been cleaned out. Silent or spoken, a deep suspicion of spiritual teachers from India had fouled the nest.

The tainted image is a tragedy. Now Maharishi is dead — the obituaries in February 2008 called him "the Maharishi," but he used the title "great sage" like a first name, without "the" — and my association with him ran the gamut of gurudom. He was such a domineering figure in my life for a decade that it's only fair to see him outside the context of my reactions. Something important had come into the modern world.

Maharishi Mahesh Yogi started out as one kind of cultural curiosity — a lone Hindu monk who aimed to teach meditation to everyone on earth — and ended up as a different kind, the one-time guru of the Beatles. He came remarkably close to fulfilling his original intent, though. In the Seventies millions of Westerners learned Transcendental Meditation. He thrived long after the departure of the Fab Four, who decamped almost as soon as they sniffed the thin air of Maharishi's Himalayan retreat. Only George Harrison turned into a genuine seeker and remained a quiet ally.

Maharishi owed his survival to two things. He was sincerely a guru, a dispeller of darkness as the word means in Sanskrit, who had the good of humanity at heart, despite the wags who turned TM into "the McDonald's of meditation" and the cartoonists who morphed his white-bearded image into a pop cliché. Sincerity would have served him little if Maharishi hadn't also been a gifted teacher of India's ancient traditions. Many visitors who came to gawk went away moved by what he had told them about the self and the soul.

Millions of baby boomers owed as much to his meditation teachings as they did to LSD, both gateways to another state of consciousness. The parallel was fatal, however. If dropping acid equated with dropping out, becoming a drug freak, and flouting respectable society, then what a guru teaches must somehow be nearly as corrupting.

I wasn't American enough to consider "guru" a suspicious term in this way. Superficially I was a stressed-out doctor who needed an alternative to Scotch and a cigarette. I read about TM in a book, so in October 1980 it wasn't momentous to seek out a TM teacher in Boston to initiate me into the practice. Culturally, however, I was carrying around some deep impressions dating back to the times when my uncle Sohan Lal, the traveling field hockey salesman, took me as a boy to sit with the saints. My uncle took a very simple attitude to these excursions. He wanted the darshan of a holy man, and he was satisfied with setting eyes on one—the blessing of darshan required nothing more. A restless boy sees the situation differently. I didn't find the half-naked bodies and long, matted beards exotic. They were everyday sights. What impressed me was the charged atmosphere that existed around these saints.

Walking into the presence of a holy man, if he is the real thing, causes an instantaneous change in you. The air seems calm but infused with vibrancy. Your thoughts quiet down and approach silence. At the same time your body feels twice as alive. My uncle had become addicted to soaking up this kind of influence. I had only a passing acquaintance with it, but after I learned TM, that would change. Beginning in the mid-Eighties, I had the opportunity to know Maharishi as an intimate. Whenever my medical practice permitted, I joined his inner circle, which at that time often stayed for periods of time in Washington, D.C., where the TM organization had bought a hotel on H Street to use as a live-in meditation center.

If I had qualms about a guru pretending to be God, they were needless. It wasn't necessary to be reverent in Maharishi's presence. He made a point of not being seen as a religious figure but as a teacher of higher consciousness. He gave a memorable answer when someone asked him if a guru should be worshipped.

"No, the proper attitude is openness. Accept that he may be telling you the truth, no matter how strange it seems to your ordinary way of thinking."

Of the many recollections I could offer, here is the most intense: Maharishi had fallen mysteriously and gravely ill on a visit to India in 1991. My father was consulted on my advice because I immediately suspected heart trouble. He ordered Maharishi to be rushed to England for emergency care. Soon I was standing outside London's Heart Hospital, watching an ambulance navigate the snarled traffic, sirens wailing. Just before it arrived on the hospital's doorstep, one of the accompanying doctors leaped out, running up with the news that Maharishi had suddenly died. I rushed to the ambulance, picking Maharishi's body up — he was frail and light by this time — and began carrying him in my arms through the traffic jam.

I laid him on the floor inside the hospital's entry and called for a cardio assist. Within minutes he was revived with CPR and rushed to intensive care on a respirator. The doctors fitted him with a pacemaker that took over his heartbeat. I became Maharishi's primary caretaker during this crisis, tending to him at a country house outside London. It quickly became apparent that he was totally indifferent to his illness, and he made an astonishingly rapid recovery. The hospital expected lasting health problems, but there were none apparent. Within a few months Maharishi was back to his round-the-clock schedule — he rarely slept more than three or four hours a night. When I approached him one day to remind him to take his medications, he gave me a penetrating look. In it I read a message: "Do you really think I am this body?" For me that was a startling moment, a clue about what higher consciousness might actually be like.

As he saw himself, Maharishi had come tantalizingly close to changing the world, as close as any nonpolitician who doesn't wage war can. He held that humanity could be saved from destruction only by raising collective consciousness. In that sense he was the first person to talk about tipping points and critical mass. If enough people meditated, Maharishi believed that walls of ignorance and hatred would fall as decisively as the Berlin Wall. This was his core teaching in the post-Beatles phase of his long career before he died peacefully in seclusion in Holland, age ninety-one, his following much shrunken, his optimism still intact.

Before we ever met, I had a sense of respect for him: Maharishi had single-handedly brought India to the West. The price he paid was that fame makes people assume they know you, for good and ill. Maharishi imprinted in everyone's imagination an image that could be adored or reviled. The West projected the wildest notions of divinity on him, and once the Beatles disappeared, Maharishi faded from sight.

Starting in 1980 Rita and I became regulars at the TM center on Garden Street in Cambridge. (With a note of pride, people at the center said that because Garden ran into Chauncy Street, the savant-like character that Peter Sellers played in the movie *Being There* got the name Chauncey Gardiner. But the film was more than ambiguous about whether he was a holy fool or just a fool, so the character's other name was Chance.) Two weeks after we learned TM, so did Sanjiv's wife, Amita.

Meditation was something I instantly loved. I became exuberant about it and probably an annoying proselyte that people avoided if they saw me coming at cocktail parties. I felt no insecurity that India was reclaiming me. If I was going into the light, it was hardly a brilliant flash. What lay ahead was unbelievable, however. Maharishi's ambition to change the world hadn't died as his reputation faded. He needed a younger surrogate to make his dreams come true and, unwittingly, I was about to step into that role.

16

Being and Bliss

Sanjiv

Sanjiv and Amita on vacation in St. Martin, 1975.

TWO WEEKS AFTER DEEPAK and Rita learned Transcendental Meditation they were at our home in Newton, telling us that it was undeniably the best thing they had done in their lives. I listened with a high level of skepticism. My brother has always been a person with great curiosity, and when something interested him he pursued it with vigor. Rita had encouraged him to try meditation, she explained, but insisted on joining him because otherwise she knew he just wouldn't stop talking about it. She had to learn it or she would never hear the end of it. We all laughed, knowing this to be absolutely true.

TM appealed to Amita immediately. Growing up she had been a very spiritual child. Her father, a very practical man, an engineer, would sit cross-legged in the lotus position on a deerskin rug every morning at the break of dawn to meditate. On Sunday evenings her parents would take her to the Ramakrishna mission, a worldwide spiritual movement dedicated to helping people, and while they were inside listening to monks giving a discourse on the Vedas, the sacred and ancient scriptures of Hinduism, she would sit in the meditation hall, in front of the marble statue of Ramakrishna, trying to imitate his posture and find the peace that was so evident in his splendid demeanor. As she later understood, she was yearning for some kind of spiritual experience.

When she was eleven years old Amita went to her father and declared that she wanted to join the ashram of the followers of Paramahansa Yogananda, one of the learned spiritual teachers who had first brought Hinduism to America. She even cut off much of her long flowing hair, a remarkable thing for a child to do, to show that she was very serious about this calling. Her father understood her feelings and took her to a meeting at the ashram. There they told her that she was far too young but that after she completed her schooling, if she still wanted to join the ashram she would be most welcome.

A year later, when she was only twelve years of age, her father died suddenly of a massive heart attack. After that Amita tried to teach herself meditation, practicing how to control her breathing as she had seen the monks doing. And at times, completely on her own, she had been able to reach a certain distinctly different state of consciousness. But then her studies and social life had become more important and she had put this quest aside. So when Deepak and Rita came to us bursting with excitement she was immediately receptive.

But not me. By this time I was as American as an Indian immigrant could be. My career was progressing very well, I had a nice home for my family in the suburbs and I had become a pretty good tennis player. I didn't want anything at all to do with that meditation stuff. I associated meditation with people who wore saffron robes and walked around banging drums, chanting hymns, and often carrying begging bowls. No, sir, thank you, I'd seen too much of these folks in India, and to me it had always looked like some sort of scam in which they were selling spiritualism for a few dollars the way con artists sold miracle cures for every malady. It was the kind of stuff Deepak had always been more interested in than I was. I liked my life just the way it was and I didn't see any need to change it. So when Amita said she wanted to learn how to do it, I told her please go ahead, good for you. You'll probably like it. But it's not my cup of tea.

I actually had three very specific reasons for not wanting to begin meditating: Years earlier, as a gastroenterology fellow, when I'd walk into the radiology department to look at X-rays two of the radiologists would be sitting there smoking their pipes. I would take out my pipe and we would begin seeing all the X-rays of the patients of the gastroenterology service. But before we started we would have a discussion of the different kinds of tobacco. I also liked to drink Scotch to relax, and so I wasn't about to give up my pipe and my alcohol.

Second, as assistant chief of medicine at the West Roxbury VA, on a few occasions I had to discipline interns and residents. I saw that meditation made people very mellow and I couldn't afford that to happen to me. Lives were at stake every day.

Third, my exercise and relaxation came from tennis. I wasn't interested in having my competitive edge dulled by spirituality. I had no desire to applaud my opponent for making a great passing shot. I was a fierce competitor and wanted to win every match.

Amita went without me and learned the technique. After a month there were noticeable changes in her; she would walk around with a smile, which was not that unusual for her, but it seemed distinctly more peaceful and beautiful. And, to be honest, I felt a little resentful because in the evening dinner was delayed for twenty minutes because she had to go meditate. She did not try to talk me into learning meditation, but my resolve was weakening.

One Saturday morning about a month after she'd started meditating Amita wanted to go to the TM center for a check-up and I volunteered to drive her.

"I'll come with you," I said, "but I'm not going into the center. I'm going to wait for you in the car and read a book about tennis." As I sat there a man tapped on my window and introduced himself as Ted Weisman. I had heard his name.

"You're the instructor who taught my brother, right?"

I invited him to sit in the car with me. It was a little uncomfortable as I didn't know what to really talk about. So I suggested he tell me a little bit about TM. After he'd given me an overview, I decided to share the three things that really concerned me about the practice.

"First," Ted said, "in terms of drinking and smoking the only thing we ask is that people not be on drugs or intoxicated when they first come to be initiated into the practice of TM. Second, you'll probably be more assertive at work, but from a stronger and more quiet place. Without losing your temper. And third . . ." he paused and told me he would be right back. He returned with a pamphlet entitled *The TM Programs in Athletics: Excellence in Action,* which included testimonials from many athletes, including baseball star Willie Stargell, football Hall of Famer Joe Namath, and an Olympic diving champion. In different words they all claimed that TM had actually helped them become more focused and far more competitive. "I can't guarantee that you'll win your tennis tournament," Weisman told me. "But I will promise you that if you lose you won't feel that bad." He had literally given me the introductory TM lecture in my BMW.

"Sounds good," I said to him. "Please sign me up." I learned Transcendental Meditation the following weekend. It turned out to be nothing at all like what I had expected. I didn't suddenly want to start wearing a robe and chanting. Instead, within a few days I noticed that I was no longer smoking my pipe. And I realized that smoking that pipe gave me heartburn, so I was able to stop taking antacids.

One day I was stopped at a traffic light when I glanced at the driver in the car next to me, who smiled at me. That's odd, I thought. Why is that person smiling at me? During a group discussion, one of the other new meditators pointed out that I had a big smile plastered on my own face, and suggested the person in the other car was simply responding to that.

I began meditating regularly, twice a day for fifteen to twenty minutes. I enjoyed the practice, but also the benefits that accrued as a result. Rather than becoming the center of my life, as I had feared, meditation made me more energetic and enthusiastic about the things I was already doing. It was a very profound experience. I found that I was more creative at work, and that I had become a far better thinker. My career blossomed.

While Deepak had opened a private practice, I enjoyed working in a teaching hospital. For the most part the fact that we were Indian immigrants made no difference at all. The only problem I remember was that the *Boston Globe* once printed a story criticizing foreign-trained doctors who had been licensed to practice in America. The tone of the article suggested that doctors trained outside America were inferior to doctors who had graduated from American medical schools. As I saw the evidence to the contrary around me every day, I considered it a ridiculous thing to have declared. Deepak was furious and sent a long, angry letter objecting to that article, arguing that it was not based on any factual information. In response, the *Globe* interviewed him and put his picture on its front page. Deepak received a lot of calls of support from immigrant physicians who were pleased he had spoken up; within almost every immigrant community there is an unspoken fear about attracting too much attention, as if people might object to their presence. But Deepak also received many more calls from American doctors who were angry at him for airing some of the friction that existed between American and foreign-trained physicians. They did not want people outside the medical field to know about this tension.

My experience was very different from my brother's. Generally I was welcomed and treated respectfully. Compared to India, where position and rank meant everything and we were never allowed to be casual with people ahead of us, I found there was great camaraderie among all the colleagues I worked with. In 1975, for instance, I was doing the first year of my gastroenterology fellowship at St. Elizabeth's Hospital. I was the only fellow and by virtue of that I was on call every single night and every single weekend other than my three weeks of vacation. It seemed like I never got a day off. I didn't complain — I loved what I was doing. The learning trajectory was steep and I soaked it all in.

One Friday after we finished our rounds everyone was furiously writing notes about their patients for me; this person needs this, that person needs that. Make sure you check these results. This is an exercise called a sign-out. And as they got ready to leave for the weekend, everybody told me to have a good weekend and that they would see me the following Tuesday.

Tuesday? I asked them what happened to Monday. It was the Jewish holiday of Yom Kippur, I was told, and at that moment I realized every single person there, the four attendings, the two residents, the two medical interns, the two fourth-year medical students, the GI secretary, the GI nurse, and the GI technician were all Jewish. I thought about that for a minute.

"Well, you know what? I'm not coming to work Monday, either! Who's covering?"

The room got very quiet. No one knew if I was serious or joking.

Finally one of them asked me, "Sanjiv, what do you mean you're not working on Monday? Why not?"

"I've decided to change my name," I announced. "From now on, please call me Choprastein!"

In fact, I think there was only one time I ever felt even a slight bit uncomfortable. I had taken up the game of golf and joined a country club. My first day on the golf course I was introduced to one of the long-standing members, an optometrist. When I told him my name was Sanjiv Chopra, he said, "Well, I can't pronounce that. I'm going to call you Sonny."

I thought that was rather impolite and culturally insensitive.

"No," I said, "you will not. You have three choices. You can call me Sanjiv. It's not that difficult to pronounce, it's just like 'sun' and then 'jeeve.' Or you can call me Dr. Chopra, or you can call me sir." That spread very quickly throughout the country club, that this new member had politely reprimanded a senior member. But if I hadn't put my foot down, three hundred members of this historic club would have been forever calling me Sonny.

I knew about Deepak's growing doubts concerning modern medicine, but I didn't share them. For me, it was simple: Science had provided us with a body of knowledge. Often we could use that knowledge to improve our patients' health and sometimes even save their lives. I felt that the single most fulfilling words in the English language, words I've always used very carefully, are "You're cured."

The best doctors, I learned, are detectives. They have a knack for looking for the right clues and asking the right questions. After I started teaching, I emphasized that to my students: Don't hesitate to ask more probing questions, as many as might be needed to get to the root problem. As a sculptor chips away at a block of stone, keep going until you get the information you need. I found that patients sometimes try to hide the truth from their doctors, from the very people they have trusted to protect their lives. I once had a patient with jaundice tell me he did not drink alcohol. I was skeptical, given that his laboratory tests pointed to alcoholic liver disease.

"Really?" I asked. "When did you quit?"

"Last week," he admitted with a sheepish grin.

If there is one lesson that I've drilled into the ten thousand students I've taught during my forty-year career, it is to ask that extra question. I tell them about an incident that took place during hepatology rounds at the Beth Israel Deaconess Medical Center, the major teaching affiliate of Harvard Medical School.

I would tell all of the medical student interns and residents and fellows on the hepatology service, "Every time you see a patient in consultation or after they've been admitted to the hepatology service, in addition to asking all the usual questions about alcohol and drugs and alternative medicines, make sure you also ask them how much coffee they drink. And whether they drink regular or decaf." I did this because numerous studies done over the last several years have shown that coffee appears to confer substantial protection against liver disease. In medicine we call this hepaprotective.

I'd emphasized the benefits of coffee to the liver so much that it became a little joke, Dr. Chopra and his coffee.

One Friday as I began rounds, I noticed all of my students were smiling. As soon as I sat down they told me that, at long last, they had encountered a patient with advanced liver disease who drinks coffee.

"Did you ask him whether it was regular or decaf?" I'd taught them that decaf can be beneficial for people with a variety of diseases, including type 2 diabetes, but only caffeinated coffee appeared to provide protection against liver disease.

"He drinks four cups of regular coffee every day," the intern who had admitted the patient replied, and then added, "I even asked him about the size and it's a normal cup." The team was convinced that they finally had proven me wrong.

"You know, he may be the exception," I said. "These studies are not ironclad. They're observational, they're epidemiological studies. But let me take my own history."

We went through our rounds. When we got to this patient's room, I shook his hand warmly and introduced myself, then pulled up a chair and sat down. I always sit down when talking to a patient. Some thirty years earlier a colleague pointed out to me that if you stand by the patient's bed for twenty minutes they believe you were only there briefly because you looked like you were ready to turn on your heels and walk out, but if you sit for five minutes it seems like you have given them all the time in the world. So I've made it a practice to always sit down.

I began taking a detailed history. The patient told me he did not drink alcohol. He did not use drugs, not even herbal medication. Finally we got to tea and coffee.

"Doc," he said, "I don't like tea. I love coffee."

"Good," I said. "What type of coffee do you drink?"

"If I'm going to have coffee, I'm going to have regular coffee. Otherwise, why bother?"

"Good. How many cups a day do you drink?"

"Four," he answered, "regular size." All around the bed I noticed the young doctors trying hard to repress their smiles while maintaining a professional decorum. Then I asked this patient one more question, a question the young doctors hadn't thought to ask.

"How long have you been drinking four cups of coffee a day?"

"Oh, ever since my liver transplant. Doc, it was the strangest thing. I never liked coffee, but right after I had my transplant I had this great craving to drink some. Now I drink at least four cups of regular a day. Why, you think I should stop?"

The house staff nearly fell over when they heard his response. As I told them afterward, the information you're going to need is there, you just need to keep digging until you find it.

For me teaching brings the greatest satisfaction. I feel that by sharing my knowledge I am fulfilling my dharma. At the time, I was very ambitious, much like my brother, and I couldn't slow down. I was doing everything possible to move my career forward, seeing patients, writing articles and books, learning new techniques. But there came a point when I had to make a career choice: Did I want to stay in academic medicine or open up a private practice? Should I continue working at a hospital? Elements of each of these options appealed to me. I had watched my father at work; I'd seen him on the wards in the hospital and also in his private practice. What I noticed, though, was that his greatest joy seemed to come from teaching young doctors. He enjoyed sharing his information. Deepak had decided to open his own practice and had been quite successful. I never really had to make that decision; from the first day, I enjoyed teaching and I made the decision that I would work in a teaching hospital affiliated with a prestigious medical school.

Amita followed a different path, going into private practice, which she enjoyed thoroughly. She was completely devoted to her patients. However, in the early Eighties she took two years off to spend with our children. They were growing up and she didn't want to miss those magical moments of their childhood. During that time, so we could afford for me to accept a gastroenterology fellowship, she would moonlight several nights a month at St. Elizabeth's Hospital. But she also enjoyed teaching, and even when she was in private practice she would have medical students shadowing her. In fact, for most of her career, spent in a private practice, she was affiliated with a number of major teaching hospitals. So she had her responsibilities to her private patients and responsibilities at the hospital for teaching students and junior doctors; she called it "the best of all possible worlds."

Not for me, though. Early in my career I had been asked by Dr. Eugene Braunwald, the chairman of the Department of Medicine at Brigham and Women's Hospital, which is affiliated with Harvard Medical School, to take morning report there. Morning report is an exercise where the interns and residents get together first thing and jot down on a blackboard all the admissions to their service from the previous day. A couple of cases are selected to be discussed as a teaching exercise. Even though I was still based at the West Roxbury VA, I told Dr. Braunwald that I would truly be honored to do so. I started to go to the Brigham and Women's Hospital on a regular basis and take morning report. I decided to bring with me ultrasounds and CAT scan images of the most interesting patients that I had seen at the West Roxbury VA. I'd present the cases and I would use mnemonics and alliterations to embellish the teaching.

"What do you notice here? Here is calcification of the gallbladder wall. What is this condition called? What is the significance? What are the other conditions in which there is an inordinately high risk of gallbladder cancer?"

If you loved the mysteries of medicine, these were exciting meetings. The young doctors spoke out, ideas were thrown around — naturally lots of coffee was consumed — and medicine was learned. I would often use repetition; it's a great tool for adults to remember new facts. I'd repeat what I'd said, then say it again. I took morning report at the Brigham for ten years. During this time I taught but I also learned a lot from my young colleagues. It was a wonderful experience.

There is an annual honor that is given by the house staff at the Brigham called the George W. Thorn Award for Outstanding Contribution to Clinical Education, to honor Brigham's legendary former chief of medicine, who had an unusually distinguished career and was the personal physician to President John F. Kennedy. It is bestowed on one of the faculty in the Department of Medicine. The medical house staff votes on the award with no input from the chairman or vice chairman of the Department of Medicine. When I started taking morning report there in 1985 I set my goal to win this award someday, although I knew well it had never been given to anyone based outside the Brigham. But I received the award that very first year.

That was also the year that Deepak called one day to tell us that he had decided to close his private practice and begin working at the behest of Maharishi Mahesh Yogi at an Ayurvedic clinic in Lancaster, Massachusetts. I'd thought I knew my brother well, but this decision really surprised me. Deepak had always enjoyed using his intellect to push back the walls, but he had always stayed within the room. This was very different. This was giving up the core of his career: his training as an endocrinologist. It meant giving up science-based medicine to become a practitioner of what many of us believed was folk medicine. It wasn't my place to discuss this decision with my brother; it was up to him and Rita, and he was firm about it.

By every measure, especially in the quality of patient care, Deepak's practice was a tremendous success. Medical students from Boston

University and Tufts University School of Medicine rotated through his office, so there certainly was an academic element to his private practice. His life was well established and his family was quite comfortable. This decision would change all of that.

It was a very courageous thing for him to do. By that time Amita and I had been meditating regularly for a couple of years and understood all its benefits. Everyone in TM had emphasized that it should become an integral part of your life, but not your whole life. It seemed like Deepak was making it the centerpiece of his life. But when we discussed it I could see his excitement and his passion. Deepak had always enjoyed finding a new path. I remember thinking of what Emerson once said, "Do not go where the path may lead; go instead where there is no path and leave a trail." Deepak was truly a trailblazer.

When I responded with some concern in my voice that I was a little nervous about his decision, he said, "I'll keep my medical license current. That means I can always go back."

One of my favorite sayings is from the Danish philosopher and theologian Søren Kierkegaard, who wrote, "To dare is to lose one's footing momentarily. Not to dare is to lose oneself." I've always felt that anyone who takes a bold step to transform their life or undertakes a major challenge or takes a bold step in leadership is incredibly courageous.

And that was the step my brother had decided to take. Of course we all loved him dearly and supported his decision, but I did so with some trepidation.

17

The Pathless Land

Deepak

The Way We Were—Deepak and Michael Jackson after a dance
practice session in Michael's studio. Deepak showed him a few steps,
and Michael couldn't stop laughing, in the late 1980s.

I NDIA HAS HAD A ROCKY road producing messiahs for the West. There's been a fine line to walk between wisdom and wonders. Some gurus crossed the line willingly. Wonder-working is in the air in India. There is always a saint at the next holy site who can perform miracles, to the point of raising the dead. Some never eat food but live solely on *Prana,* the life force. A great many have the healing touch.

Sadly, when I was growing up, I never met anyone who had actually witnessed a miracle firsthand. My father's gaze had turned West before I was born. It wasn't respectable to take wonder-working seriously. Maharishi reached me with a new idea—meditation was a simple, practical technique that changed your consciousness. By this time, however, the West was asking for instant gratification from gurus. A cynical observer dubbed it karma cola.

Rita and I were invited to meet Maharishi in the winter of 1985, so we drove down to Washington, D.C., for a conference that had attracted meditators from all over the country. Maharishi's visits to the U.S. had become more and more infrequent. By that time we had been meditating for four years. In the most fundamental way I could attest that TM worked. Our more indulgent Indian friends would say, "I'm happy that it works for you." The implication in "for you" was obvious. They wanted to be left alone. But I was very enthusiastic about this new discovery. The mind did have a level of peace and calm that could easily be reached using the mantra I had been given. I gave up smoking and drinking. My everyday existence was easier and less stressful. Unfortunately one of the reasons that TM had become passé, as far as the marketplace of popular culture was concerned, was that these benefits were no longer flashy enough.

Western disciples wanted miracles from a guru and a facade of Godlike perfection, unblemished by human frailty. The standards were impossible to reach, and so a backlash had also set in. Partly it was the temptation of excess. The West offered a luxurious lifestyle to a successful guru, along with devotees who would do anything for their master. Some gurus were being accused of sexual impropriety. Their miracles were hyped and then quickly debunked.

I was on a plane seated next to an American couple who were on their way to spend time at their guru's ashram in south India. At the height of my desire to tell everyone about TM, I held aloof from playing the game of "my guru is better than yours." But this couple had some amazing tales.

"We have his picture on the mantelpiece," the husband explained. "We do puja to it every day, and in return things appear."

"Things?" I asked.

"Mostly holy ash," he said. Applying a dab of ashes to the forehead of a devotee is a common blessing in India.

"But sometimes we get other things," the wife added quickly.

"Such as?"

"A gold necklace one time. Another time a gold watch."

These objects appeared out of the blue, the couple insisted. The messiahs from India were keeping up with their Christian counterpart in the wonders and miracles department, and doing even better, since their miracles might happen in your living room by long distance. A devotee didn't need to regret that he wasn't alive two thousand years ago to see Christ walk on the Sea of Galilee.

Nothing uncanny surrounded Maharishi, but our first meeting carried a hint of that. Apparently he felt a spark of recognition. Rita and I were standing in the lobby of the H Street hotel that had been taken over by the TM organization and converted into a residence for people who had joined the movement full-time. We were near the elevators, waiting for a glimpse of Maharishi as he left the exit hall. As he came through the crowd, a number of people handed him a flower and murmured a greeting. Somehow he spotted us and immediately broke free, walking in our direction. From his armload of flowers he picked a long-stemmed red rose and handed it to Rita, then found another one for me.

"Can you come up?" he asked. "We can talk."

Why he singled us out we never asked. Perhaps it was because we were Indian, or because someone told him I was a doctor. Whatever the reason, we were thrilled. Only later did I hear a more esoteric reason: gurus, it is said, spend a good deal of time rounding up lost disciples from a previous lifetime. I can't say that I felt a spark of recognition on my side.

Maharishi was treated with awed devotion by his Western followers, and it made Rita and me uncomfortable. We were grateful to be allowed to be ourselves. From the beginning there was a relaxed, congenial atmosphere, with Maharishi making clear that we were accepted as two people from India who understood the spirituality we had all been born into. But this led to its own strains, especially at first, because in reality I knew very little about my spiritual heritage. What eased my way was that Maharishi had long ago decided that the West needed to be addressed on its own terms. This meant using science. I was embraced as a physician, someone who could translate meditation into brain responses, alterations of stress hormones, reduced blood pressure, and other benefits to the body.

If this had been my only role, I might have drifted away fairly soon. TM had been publicly circulating in America since the early Sixties. There was already a cadre of scientists, including at least one Nobel Prize–winning physicist, who had been attracted to TM. Research into the benefits of meditation, although still arcane, had become respectable. Dr. Herbert Benson, a cardiologist at Harvard Medical School, had taken the scientific side of meditation to its logical conclusion. In a bestselling book, *The Relaxation Response,* Benson set out to prove that the brain can reach a meditative state, complete with all the benefits to the body claimed by TM, without the rigmarole of a personal mantra and the trappings of Indian spirituality. Using the same style of meditation as TM, a person could silently repeat any common word (Benson recommended "one") and an autonomic response would be triggered in the brain. Benson had considerable research to back up his claims.

The response was mixed in the TM camp, where the medical benefits of meditation had been a way to get Westerners through the door. Maharishi deserved credit for insisting that meditation delivered such benefits in the first place. Without them, Indian spirituality would have languished, so far as the West was concerned, in a warm bath of religious sentiments and mysticism. Turning the exotic into the practical was a brilliant stroke. Because Benson and others with an antispiritual bent felt they could get all of meditation's benefits without its tradition however, the spiritual core of TM was ignored. I felt quite differently: It was wrong not to see meditation as an avenue to higher consciousness. I knew that was controversial as viewed from the West. I couldn't produce any medical validation for the existence of higher consciousness. And so it was somewhat odd to be treated like the prodigal son returning to the fold, a medical expert with Indian spiritual underpinnings.

Two years earlier, while we were in India, Rita and I had traveled with a good friend to Maharishi's academy in Rishikesh where TM teachers were being trained. (Because of its religious connotations, I suppose, the word "ashram" was never applied to any TM facility in India or in the West.) We knocked on the gate, assuming Maharishi would be there. He wasn't, but among the people we spoke to was Satyanand, a monk who had joined Maharishi's movement and was put in charge of the Rishikesh facility. He was much more like a traditional disciple in an ashram than a Western meditator. Like Maharishi, he had a long, white, untrimmed beard and was wearing a dhoti, the traditional monk's garment wound from a single piece of white silk. When Satyanand asked us if we meditated, using the Indian word for it, *Dhyan,* I explained that we had learned in the United States, in the city of Boston. He laughed in delight.

"Indians go to Boston to learn dhyan. It's wonderful!"

Why did I accept the attentions of a famous guru in the first place? Some experiences as yet untold had happened to me. Years back in medical school I had a professor who took an interest in how the brain controls basic responses like hunger. Everyone experiences a daily rhythm of autonomic responses that arise without being willed:

We eat, breathe, sleep, have sex, and become aroused to fight or flight by sudden stress. This man had done pioneering work in locating the hunger center in the brain, but he was also interested in how automatic responses can be controlled at will. In India yogis and swamis put on demonstrations of extreme bodily control as proof that they have attained mastery over their bodies.

One can read accounts going back to 1850 of a local yogi who has been buried in a box underground without oxygen and emerged unharmed. To endure such a trial, a person would need the ability to slow down respiration and heartbeat quite drastically — in effect, the yogi goes into a state of hibernation. (As reported in a 1998 article in the journal *Physiology,* a seventy-year-old yogi survived for eight days in a sealed box underground. He was connected to monitoring devices, which revealed, quite astonishingly, that "his heart rate was below the measurable sensitivity of the recording instruments.") On medical grounds I became fascinated by the prospect that the mind-body connection had profound implications. Claims about meditation leading to a reduced metabolic rate seemed natural to me, and probably only the tip of the iceberg.

I also had begun to wonder about the mind-body connection in a way that some might call metaphysical. Before I met Maharishi, a small announcement had appeared in the *New York Times* saying that J. Krishnamurti was giving a talk at the Felt Forum in Madison Square Garden. Immediately my interest was piqued, because a remarkable figure was just then emerging from obscurity.

Krishnamurti was nearing the end of a long life — he died in 1986 at the age of ninety — but the most astonishing events had swirled around him in his youth. One day in 1909 he was playing on the beach of the Adyar River near Madras (now Chennai) on the east coast of India. He was the eighth of eleven children, five of whom died in childhood; his mother also died when he was ten. Among high-caste Brahmins who strictly observed their obligations, the eighth child was customarily named after Lord Krishna.

The family lived a nearly impoverished existence in a small crowded cottage without sanitation. Krishnamurti was sickly as the result of untreated malaria; he was considered dreamy and vague, perhaps mentally impaired. He looked unkempt without a mother's care, and like his brothers, he was infested with lice.

The conditions were totally unlikely considering what happened next. A former English clergyman in his fifties, who was also at the beach, suddenly focused on the boy. He started making excited claims about the boy's "perfect aura." Using his power of clairvoyance, the man declared that the next world teacher had been discovered. Krishnamurti had no idea what any of this meant, but he was soon swept up in one of the twentieth century's most vertiginous spiritual journeys. The ex-clergyman, named Charles W. Leadbeater, took major control over the bewildered boy's existence. As "the vehicle for Lord Maitreya," young Krishnamurti was told that he had a destiny to fulfill, one that might change life on earth.

A good deal of exotic background needs to be filled in. Not all Westerners disdained and ignored Indian spirituality. Some became immersed in its mysteries. Books were written about living masters in the Himalayas who rivaled Christ in their wisdom, holiness, and miraculous powers. The most prominent group who announced such wonders was the Theosophical Society, founded in New York City in 1875. They were at the forefront of the late-Victorian craze for the occult. An intricate belief system arose around theosophy, a quasi religion that reached out along many avenues of mysticism, from ancient Egypt and the Jewish cabala to table-rapping séances and communication with the dead. Its peak of popularity may have passed, but the Theosophical Society still exists and has matured into a sophisticated center for many spiritual pursuits. Mysticism is very much welcomed.

Krishnamurti's father, Jiddu Narianiah (the family name was Jiddu) worked as a clerk for the Theosophical Society in India, which was how his children came to play on the beach at Adyar. He was astonished that one of his sons, who had always seemed the least likely to make his way, suddenly became the focus of wild excitement. It resembled nothing that an orthodox Hindu like him believed in. Theosophy was awash in esoteric knowledge. It taught about the ex-

istence of higher beings known as Ascended Masters, spiritual luminaries who had passed from a human lifetime to an exalted station in
the other world.

Leadbeater, who was coleader of the Society's international head-
quarters in Adyar, claimed to be in touch with the other world. He
expected the imminent arrival of someone who would be the vehicle
(physical embodiment) of the next world teacher, known as Lord
Maitreya, successor to the last Ascended Master, the Buddha. I knew
little of this lore at the time, and I've barely hinted at its occult complexity. (Looking back seventy-five years later, Krishnamurti only
remembers a willingness to do whatever he was told, to the point of
subservience.) But I knew that for a time the young Krishnamurti had
been groomed as the world teacher and unabashedly worshipped. A
sect was formed around him known as the Order of the Star in the
East.

Who could resist such a tale? The general public had long forgotten Krishnamurti, but with a sudden resurgence of interest he now
gathered large crowds. Rita and I decided to drive down to New York
to hear him talk. Krishnamurti grew up to be strikingly handsome
— it was said that he was one of the most photographed celebrities of
the century — and as he climbed the steps to the stage of Felt Forum,
he remained a striking figure with white hair, an aquiline profile, and
the trappings of an English gentleman in a three-piece flannel suit
with a pocket watch.

Loud applause broke out. Krishnamurti, who had a sharp glance,
turned it on the audience.

"Who are you clapping for? Perhaps for yourselves?" he said.

Quiet descended, and he made his way to a simple wooden chair
in the center of the stage. For the next two hours he talked, and it was
such talk as I had never heard before. Nothing occult or mystical was
touched upon. You became aware of a mind that had gone beyond
anything in your own experience. Krishnamurti asked deep questions — Where does thought come from? What does it mean to be
free? Why do we talk about finding God but never reach God? — and
then he spun out a line of reasoning that led to strange answers.

Where does thought come from? No fixed answer is valid. Each person must go inside and follow the trail that begins with a thought. The trail leads into unexplored territory, back to your very source. Only when you arrive there will you know, with total certainty, where thought comes from.

What does it mean to be free? Freedom isn't a goal you can pursue. Freedom comes first, not last. It comes when you realize that the only way to be free is to become timeless. As long as you are imprisoned by time, freedom is an illusion.

Why do we talk about finding God but never reach God? Because we are trapped inside our limited minds. The God we seek is merely a projection of thought. There is no reality in such projections; when talking about God, we are just talking about trifling ideas, a kind of religious gossip that keeps being repeated generation after generation.

Krishnamurti's tone was challenging to the point of being abrasive. He radiated total seriousness. He made spirituality seem like the most sober calling a person could follow. When the two hours were up, after glancing at his pocket watch and apologizing for going a few minutes over time, Krishnamurti left an elusive presence in his wake. He wasn't a conventional guru. Every other minute he would pause and say, "Look into this for yourselves. Don't listen to me. Don't listen to any teacher." He was that rare thing, a leader with thousands of followers who told them all to go away.

Poring over his life, one discovers that Krishnamurti renounced his destiny as the world teacher in 1929, dashing the hopes of the theosophists. His motivation wasn't simple disillusionment. Seven years earlier he had had a profound spiritual awakening, and it entailed considerable physical agony. He called it the process, and although worried spectators witnessed a young man in delirious spasms racked with pain, Krishnamurti reported a profound experience of unity. After days of undergoing "the process," he would return to consciousness with a sense of extraordinary sensitivity to the tiniest things around him: "The blade of grass was astonishingly green;

that one blade of grass contained the whole spectrum of color; it was intense, dazzling and such a small thing, so easy to destroy."

It was a moving story. I was touched by Krishnamurti's suffering and isolation. A part of me longed for a different ending. What if a world teacher had come before the rise of Nazism and the horrors of the Bomb? Would humanity have stopped on its self-destructive course? (In his early days in America Maharishi knew that the odds were against him. He used to say that if a modern person met Jesus on the street, he would politely say, "I'm sorry, but I can't stop right now. I'm on my way to the movies. I'll be happy to listen to you later.")

On and off during his entire life Krishnamurti never escaped "the process," and it transformed him into something no one quite understood, including himself. He would end a talk in a lovely natural setting and wander in the woods, he recounts, wanting nothing more than never to return again. "Ninety-nine percent of the people have no idea what I'm saying, and the one percent who do are already ninety-nine percent there." In the end Krishnamurti wondered aloud if he was some kind of biological anomaly.

I was betting that he wasn't. After being struck by his presence, I needed a way to start "the process" for myself, although I didn't know what it actually entailed. I only knew that in India the way is always open for inner transformation. The first time I sat in a room with Maharishi, more than the blessing of darshan emanated from him. He had arrived. His journey was almost the reverse of Krishnamurti's. He rose to public attention when he was around forty, already a monk, or *Brahmachari,* who had served his spiritual master until the master's death in 1953. He had followed a classic discipleship, renouncing the world and taking a vow of celibacy. Maharishi also took literally the classic notion that complete dedication to spirituality is a second birth; therefore, even the most basic facts about his actual birth are vague.

He was born around 1917, as a best guess, and his given name was Mahesh. The family name was either Varma or Srivastava—he had relatives with both names. His father's occupation is given as civil servant, either in the Indian tax department or its forestry service. At times Maharishi welcomed his family into the inner circle; over time I met two nephews, a niece, and a cousin, as I remember. What struck me about his past was that Maharishi was born in Jabalpur (most likely), the same place my father had been stationed, and he graduated from University of Allahabad in 1942 after studying physics. The scientific bent of TM had deep personal roots.

Having any past seemed irrelevant when you met Maharishi, because he embodied what a second birth means. No one could have been more like an enlightened sage. He presented a jolly face to the world (the media dubbed him the giggling guru), but in private he could converse on any subject with experts in the field. When he brought in a spiritual perspective, one felt his total authority, as if a rishi from the ancient Upanishads had stepped out of history. When he first decided to leave his Himalayan retreat in 1955, the younger Maharishi made a profound impression speaking around India, a land that is used to its fair share of saints, real or assumed. He left no doubt that he was a master, although he could be quite humble. His motto was that you should let others make you great, not proclaim your own greatness. Maharishi also declared that once a person becomes enlightened, everything he says and does is dictated for the good of humanity; there is no longer a personal self — God has burnt it away — and therefore no personal desires.

Before he arrived in San Francisco in 1959, Maharishi found himself standing on a platform at a spiritual conference in south India declaring, without forethought, that he was going to lead a movement to regenerate the world. This hypothetical organization became known as the Spiritual Regeneration Movement. Only later did Transcendental Meditation and TM become brand names. The early American followers considered themselves to be part of the world's spiritual transformation. That ambition never left Maharishi; it was evident from the first time he came out of India.

This brings us to a fork in the road. Viewed as an enlightened master, Maharishi pursued his huge project without ulterior motives.

He was a selfless teacher who embodied higher consciousness; he had only the good of humanity at heart. But viewed as the head of a profitable multinational organization that focused everything on a charismatic celebrity from India, he was a kind of spiritual entrepreneur. He was taking advantage of the exotic impression he made on Westerners, giving them diluted knowledge that couldn't compare with the real thing.

To me the first view was right and the second one jaded and cynical. Whatever the goal of enlightenment is, I sensed that this small man with a rose in his hand and a wise smile on his face had walked the pathless path, as it is known in India. The year I met him was the same year that Krishnamurti died. I couldn't help thinking that the pathless path, which was thousands of years old, resembled something Krishnamurti had imparted to his theosophical followers in 1929 when he told them to go away: "I maintain that truth is a pathless land, and you cannot approach it by any path whatsoever, by any religion, by any sect. That is my point of view, and I adhere to it absolutely and unconditionally."

The only difference was that Maharishi didn't want me to go away. He wanted me to stay close and learn everything he had to teach.

Inner circles are like families. The one around Maharishi had existed for many years. It was bound by various feelings — devotion, ambition, the need for approval, shared ideals, and more. The family members came from everywhere. Hundreds of thousands of Westerners had casually picked up TM in its heyday, mostly college students attracted by the media glare surrounding the Beatles. The vast majority stopped meditating after a time, usually brief — as I was reminded, meditation is meant for a lifetime, but it only takes a day to quit. For a core of TM meditators, however, the practice was profound enough that they devoted themselves to it completely. After leaving India and appearing in California in the late Fifties, Maharishi picked up a retinue. Since I arrived late on the scene, the original followers were now mostly old and no longer active publicly. They seemed to be composed of spiritual seekers who were ready to accept an unknown Indian monk as a guru. They were not as congenial to the later guise of TM as a brand name marketed to a wide, largely naïve public.

The family I met around Maharishi was a small coterie of people for whom he was at least the equivalent of a world teacher. They revered him and jealously guarded their intimate relationship with him. The fact that he had laid an approving eye on me was as good as giving written orders. Gurus have whims of iron. If I was just a whim, the inner circle would still treat me as one of their own. I tried not to be self-conscious about how green I was.

People padded silently up and down the corridors of the converted hotel on H Street. The upper floor was reserved for Maharishi when he was in residence — as it turned out, he soon left the United States and spent the remainder of his life in a specially designed house in Vlodrop, an obscure village in the Netherlands. The colors surrounding him were soothing pale pastels. His flower-bedecked suite was old-fashioned and ornate in decor, like a room at the Ritz done up in pink. He saw visitors sitting in lotus position on a silk-covered divan. Directly under him would be a deerskin, the traditional seat for meditation as dictated in the Bhagavad Gita.

The reverential behavior on display in the inner circle exists around any guru, and it's a reason many Westerners suspect gurus in the first place. But I was struck by the genuine benevolence that greeted me. Maharishi had laid down a code of conduct through his own example. Because he was friendly, approachable, highly adaptable to new events, and never less than optimistic about the future of the world, the whole TM movement reflected those qualities. In an early book, I wrote that TM meditators were the only genuinely happy people I had ever met, an exuberant outburst that earned me some scorn with reviewers. But at the time I meant it, not out of naïvety but because meditation is supposed to deliver bliss, or *Ananda* in Sanskrit. "Bliss" has become an iffy word, as if it is mindless or an enemy to reason, but I felt blissful once I began to meditate, and I saw blissfulness in the people around Maharishi, most of whom were high-performance types in the Western mode, the same as I was. They included psychiatrists, physicians, businessmen, and Ivy League or Oxbridge graduates. There was nothing McDonald's about them.

The only truly unsettling thing was the scope of TM's ambitions. Maharishi was fond of making announcements that I couldn't readily accept. He had announced in 1979 that world peace had been achieved. He knew as well as anyone that there were hot spots of war, as there always have been. But his whole perspective focused on raising collective consciousness. He was always looking for signs of a tipping point (the phrase only came into use decades later, but Maharishi was publicizing the concept in the Seventies). If a seed core of humanity actively practiced meditation, a peaceful influence would affect everyone else's consciousness. Without knowing the cause, human beings would find themselves resorting to violence less and less, and in time—a very short time, as Maharishi saw it—war and crime would fade away. He found the tipping point in 1979, and typically for Maharishi, he wanted to let the whole world know.

I loved the idealism this expressed, and I was intrigued about collective consciousness. No one could doubt that spiritual luminaries like the Buddha and Jesus had, in fact, altered the global mind and moved history in a new direction. But Maharishi was using mass media to declare the same thing, and to focus the change on himself and his efforts to spread TM everywhere. As he did when TM produced the first evidence for the health benefits of meditation, Maharishi urged social scientists to provide data for decreasing hostility in the world. They did, but by this time the wider audience for his pronouncements had shrunk. Thirty years later, a body of findings from outside TM verified that deaths from armed conflicts started to decline around 1980 and have sharply declined ever since. More than eighty despots have been overthrown; democracy movements brought down the Soviet empire and continue to this day in the Arab spring. Can a guru be credited with foreseeing all this? To say yes or no requires a closer look at the ancient Indian world view that Maharishi stood for. I was just standing on the threshold.

Once I crossed it I would be stepping into the middle of a spiritual enterprise that was boundless. I would have no choice but to adapt quickly, which meant that my own boundaries would have to expand enormously. Maharishi had issued other media releases to the effect that the earth was about to experience a new Age of Enlightenment. This was a variant on the ancient Indian concept of historical cycles, or *Yugas*, that rose and fell over spans of thousands of years. Maharishi telescoped the time drastically, declaring that humanity was about to leap from *Kali Yuga*, when people struggled in the darkest depths of ignorance, to *Sat Yuga*, when every person's life would be illuminated and happy.

To prepare the way, he formed TM teachers into the World Government for the Age of Enlightenment, whose task was to prepare the way for a global rise in consciousness. I quickly discovered that such pronouncements, seemingly absurd to the outside world, had to be taken with total seriousness inside the TM organization. The immediate transformation of the world into a place of peace and harmony was discussed and planned for the way Ford and General Motors plan next year's car models.

Which presented me with a dilemma. It was obvious that Maharishi wanted to sweep me up into the swirl of activity surrounding him. I could temporize, keeping my distance for practical reasons. It was a long way from Boston to Washington, and I had a medical practice to run. These obstacles were nothing to Maharishi when I brought them up. If I came on board, it was understood that I would be provided for. On the plane ride back home, I struggled with my conscience. I couldn't espouse the Age of Enlightenment. The claim that TM had already brought world peace made me uncomfortable. It wasn't possible for me to adopt the official jargon of the TM movement, either — among meditators it was simply called the movement.

As it turned out, Maharishi didn't put any limitations on me. I could speak the way I wanted to. I could carve out my own area of activity. Any demands to conform, which were often quite strict for teachers in the movement, wouldn't apply to me. I was being offered carte blanche because Maharishi placed his complete trust in me. To

my mind there was very little of "the process" that had transformed Krishnamurti. In India surrendering to a guru meant giving yourself over body and soul. All Maharishi wanted was for me to give talks wherever he sent me and to sit in meetings with his inner circle. I had arrived at the pathless land. As much as anyone, I hope that it led to the truth.

18

Soothsayer or Charlatan

Sanjiv

Sanjiv's family, Thanksgiving, 2012.

ONE DAY IN MID-NOVEMBER, when my daughter Kanika was six years old, she came home from school looking very unhappy.

"I want to ask you a question," she said to Amita. "Are we Christian or Jewish?" As we discovered, all the kids in her class were talking about Christmas and Hanukkah. They were going to get gifts, and they were going to celebrate with family and friends. But when they asked Kanika what she was going to celebrate, she was bewildered.

"We are Hindu," Amita explained. One of the most difficult challenges faced by immigrants is whether to integrate the traditions and lifestyle of the culture you left behind into your life in America, and if so, to what degree? "Assimilation" is a very important word in immigrant communities. Sometimes, in the desire to be thought of as completely American, to fit in, almost all of one's own homeland culture is forgotten or buried. People want to leave their old life behind. I have a colleague in Boston, for example, whose name is Roger Komer. In India it was Raj Kumar. But more often, as in our family, we tried to find a way of combining our Indian heritage with our American life. We wanted our children to understand and respect where they had come from. And as Deepak had proved when he became an advocate for Ayurveda, sometimes the traditional ways have great benefits. Even in America.

There is nothing more important than discovering your own identity. When we arrived in America the relatively small Indian community kept a low public profile. Very few Indians were known to the American public. In fact, one of the people who first brought visibility to Indian immigrants here was my brother. The irony is that he did so by bringing the benefits of traditional Indian medicine — which we had been skeptical and dismissive of while growing up — to the West.

Kanika asked that question because she was feeling left out. We explained to her that Hindus, rather than celebrating Christmas or Hanukkah, celebrate Diwali, the festival of lights which symbolizes the triumph of the god Rama over evil. In India it is a very special holiday. Even poor people exchange presents, and everyone dresses in their best clothes. In fact, Deepak was born on Diwali, which is the origin of his name. It occurred to me that for Kanika, Diwali couldn't possibly be as important as Christmas or Hanukkah because nobody got off from school. We usually celebrated this festival on the weekend. But from that time on, Amita and I decided our family would celebrate the holiday on the day it actually fell. I went to the Indian grocery store and purchased a calendar that colorfully depicted Hindu religious festivals. For the next several years, we would take off from work and the kids would stay home from school, and we would take them out for a special lunch and buy them presents. We would even (carefully) set off fireworks in our backyard. The next day our children would go to school and their friends would inquire about their absence.

"We were celebrating Diwali," they would reply with glee, and then explain the holiday to them. We also celebrated *Holi,* a festival that welcomes spring's glorious colors after the bleak winter, the traditional way — by flinging colored powder on each other.

We also encouraged our children to celebrate the holidays of their friends. Ammu married a wonderful Catholic man, Joseph Sequeira, and our family would celebrate Christmas with them every year. For us it was a celebration of faith, good deeds, and sacrifices; it didn't have a religious connotation. One year we even had the kids' Irish nanny help us put up and decorate a small tree in our house. On Easter we would color eggs and invite everyone's kids to our house for an Easter egg hunt. We attended many bar mitzvahs, and our kids dressed in costumes for Halloween. The best part of assimilation is having more excuses to celebrate, more joy in our lives.

Probably the most important aspect of life in India that we missed by being in America was the constant presence of our extended family. We were surprised to discover that the family unit is not nearly as strong in America as it is in India. What our kids missed in America was being smothered in affection from their aunts and their uncles, that huge, wonderful extended family and all the stories they would hear time and time again. It helped create a strong sense of identity; this is who you are, this is where you come from. They didn't get that here.

Our cousin Dipika lived in America for several years but finally decided to return to India.

"When we were looking to buy a house in San Francisco," Dipika told me, "we would go to a nice place with the Realtor and she would tell us that the best thing about this house and this neighborhood was that we wouldn't hear a pin drop. That actually scared me terribly because I wanted to hear a pin drop. We were brought up with noise and chaos and people just walking in our house at any time."

Her sister Ashima, who lived with her family in Mumbai, came to visit Dipika.

"I thought San Francisco was such a lovely place," she recalls. "Everything was so beautiful there, but I couldn't get used to the silence in the house. When I was there I felt it was too easy to be alone."

When their father, my uncle Rattan Chacha, died, they agreed that one of them would have to move back to Delhi to care for their mother. Eventually, though, both families moved to Delhi and now the entire family, fifteen people, live together in one large house. As Dipika says, "It's one hundred and eighty degrees opposite from what my life was in California, where my husband, our child, and I lived in a nice suburban home. Now they should put cameras in the house and do a reality show, because there are fifteen people constantly running up and down the steps and bumping into one another. But we are one happy family."

To make up for that we did what many immigrants do: We formed a community with other Indians living close to us. When we first moved to Boston we lived in an apartment complex in Jamaica Plain with several other Indian families. About half of the thirty apartments in that complex were occupied by Indians, most of them doctors. Because many Indian doctors had immigrated to America and worked at the hospitals in Boston, we were part of a rather large group of friends who often got together and whose children played together and celebrated Indian events together. They included Chander and Kanta Nagpaul, Madan and Piki Zutshi, Raj and Shashi Chawla, and Bimal and Sharda Jain. We have remained best friends for almost four decades and have shared our common experience.

And because we could afford it, as often as possible we returned to India with our children. It was there, really, that our children learned about their Indian heritage. They spent time with their family, ate traditional foods, dressed as Indians, played Indian games, heard the languages spoken, and listened to the music. In addition they could see the snake charmers and the cows in the streets, ride elephants, and learn how to deal with poverty unlike anything they had ever seen in America.

It was my parents, their grandparents, who showed them total and unconditional love — and best exemplified the heart of India.

My son, Bharat, remembers sitting in a small room, just off the kitchen on the entrance floor of my parents' home. "This was where my grandmother would play the harmonium and my grandfather had his library," he recalls. "It was a great place to sit and read the comic books, the *Amar Chitra Kathas,* which told the story of the entire Indian mythology: the saints and the holy men, the gods and the goddesses, the noble warriors.

"One day I was sitting there with my grandfather, who described heaven and hell to me. It was just the two of us, and I've never forgotten it. In the Hindu philosophy, he said, there is no physical heaven and hell. They are states of mind. Then he told me a fable: A robber was running through the forest and met a monk. He asked the monk to tell him the story of heaven and hell. The monk looked him up and down and said, 'I'm a noble monk. Why should I waste a moment of my life teaching a filthy scoundrel like you what heaven and hell are?' The robber was filled with rage and anger. He took out his sword and raised it above his head. And just as he was about to bring it down to cut off the monk's head, the monk said, 'That is hell.' The robber was stunned. He dropped his sword to the ground and was overcome with gratitude, love, and compassion for this monk, who had risked his life to teach him the meaning of heaven and hell. He smiled benevolently at him. As he did that the monk looked up at him and said softly, 'And that is heaven.'"

It was important for our children, we believed, to maintain as many Indian traditions as possible. We wanted them to be culturally literate. At times it was a struggle for them to figure out exactly where they belonged. Whenever it became a problem for them we would remind them how lucky they were to have been brought up in two cultures, although sometimes that was hard for them to accept. For a time they attended a school in which they were the only Indian children. That was hard for them; kids don't want to be different. When we had the opportunity we tried to teach the popular aspects of Indian culture to American kids. When Kanika was in third grade, for example, Amita went to her school and spent the day teaching children how to wrap themselves in a sari, which they dearly loved. Our daughter Priya attended dance school to learn the classical dances called *Bharat Natyam*. Every Saturday for years we would drive her to those lessons. She celebrated her sixteenth birthday with an *Arangetram,* to which we invited scores of our friends. An arangetram is a coming-of-age celebration like a bar mitzvah or a sweet sixteen, the difference being that the young woman is required to demonstrate her mastery of classical Indian dance for several hours. Our American friends were fascinated and impressed.

"When she applies to college send a tape of her performance," one of them said. "This will be her ticket to any Ivy League school."

All of our children played American sports. Our son, Bharat, played baseball, basketball, and tennis, our daughters played tennis and softball — and a little field hockey.

Once, when we took our children to India, Priya wanted to play cricket with her cousins, and when she smacked the ball she immediately dropped the bat, as is done in softball, and started running. And all her cousins laughed at her.

I think our attempt to assimilate our children succeeded so well that Bharat, an absolutely fanatical Boston Red Sox fan, once told me,

"Instead of thinking of the Pakistani cricket team as the enemy, to me my biggest enemy is the Yankees."

And when he attended NYU he lived on a floor with about nine other Indian students. His first day there an Indian girl knocked on his door and asked him where he was from.

"I'm from Boston," he told her.

"No, no," she explained, "I mean really, where are you from?" Then he thought he understood.

"I'm from Weston, it's just outside Boston."

What she actually wanted to know, she said, was where in India his family came from.

"My parents are from New Delhi," he finally said. At NYU, Bharat realized, other young Indians defined being Indian as being able to speak the language and knowing the popular Bollywood movies and Hindi music. He didn't know any of that. For him, being Indian meant understanding the mythology and having strong connections to his family there.

For Priya assimilation meant becoming a vegetarian. Although many millions of Indians do not eat meat, that has always been a personal choice. Indian restaurants, for example, will usually offer nonvegetarian options. Our children ate meat as they grew up. But when Priya was a teenager she started eating only chicken and fish and after a visit to India in 1997 she became a vegetarian. She used to wonder about the animals' karma and for her the decision to not eat meat is a form of individual prayer. In some ways that's a peculiarly Indian way of thinking.

In our house it was natural to speak English, as that was the language Amita and I had grown up speaking in India. We didn't insist that our kids learn Hindi. But whenever there was something we didn't want the kids to know we would speak to each other in Hindi. That was our secret language, although the habit had its drawbacks.

During a visit to India, Amita and I were in a shop debating how much we would spend on a wall rug depicting a beautiful hunting scene. The dealer named the price. Amita turned to me.

"*Yeh hamara bewakuf bana raha hai,*" she said in Hindi, which means "This guy is treating us like fools."

I smiled at her. "This is India," I said. "This guy speaks Hindi better than we do."

The shopkeeper was standing there grinning at us. I told him that we would come back in a few minutes after making up our minds.

"No," he said, "please stay, and I'll be back in a minute." A few moments later he returned with tea and pastries. The rug now adorns our living room.

I think every immigrant parent worries about how well his or her children will adjust to America, especially if they look like they come from another culture, as ours did. So both Amita and I were pleased that in only one generation our kids were mostly American.

The fact that our children didn't speak Hindi made it difficult for them to communicate with their cousins when we visited India, but they made do — as kids will — with a composite called Hinglish. It was basically Hindi with an English word stuck somewhere in every sentence. When we did go to India our kids were smothered with affection from our extended family. They had a difficult time getting used to the fact that everyone wanted to hug them and kiss them. Their cousins referred to them as ABCDs, which stands for American-born confused desi; desi being another word for an Indian.

Watching our children adjust to the culture in which we had been raised — and wanted them to appreciate, if not embrace — was fascinating. Everything there was new and different for them, especially the food. We encouraged them to at least try everything, even street food, and almost inevitably the result would be someone suffering from traveler's diarrhea, a common affliction when people from a developed country visit a developing one. In Delhi it's called Delhi belly, and in other parts of the world it's called Montezuma's Revenge, Aztec two-step, Hong Kong dog, Poona Poos, Casablanca Crud, and, if you get it in Leningrad, the Trotsky's. I guess I knew I had truly become an American when I, too, suffered this ailment.

While they loved all the exotic stuff they saw in India, the most difficult thing for them to deal with was the poverty. In the United States poverty can easily be hidden; Americans are lucky in that most of the time we don't have to deal directly with in-your-face desperate poverty. That's not true in India, and it was confusing to our kids. They came from an affluent society and suddenly had to deal with children their own age living on the streets, dressed in filthy clothing, begging for morsels of food. When we stopped our car at a traffic light, young children covered in dust and holding a baby in their arms would approach our car, stick their noses to the window, and beg for a few rupees, the equivalent of a few pennies. How do you explain that to children who have grown up in America in a way that makes sense to them?

And it was difficult to explain it to them because we weren't sure that there is a right answer. When you grow up in India the poverty becomes part of the scenery, part of your life, and after a while you don't even notice it. But when you return after living in America it has a tremendous impact. It's impossible to be adequately prepared for it. A colleague and friend of mine, Gina Vild, and her husband, Nigel, were on holiday in India and were visiting Agra to see the Taj Mahal. A very young boy tried to sell her wooden camels with sequins. He was following Gina and tugging at her sleeve. Finally she told him to stop.

"He did stop and just looked at me," she recalls. "This young boy, about ten years old with huge brown eyes, said, 'To you it's a very small amount of money. It would mean so little. But for me it would make a world of a difference.'"

She bought two camels.

We had a lot of discussions with them about the accident of birth. There are things that are not under our control, we would explain. If that beggar had been born into a different family, his life would have been completely different. We encouraged them as much as possible to have a sense of responsibility toward those people.

"It's terrifying," Kanika said once when we were talking about it. "When I saw children my own age I kept thinking, how is this possible? When I was looking at a beggar it was really hard not to think that it could have just as easily been me. Rolling down the window and giving them a few coins doesn't seem like very much."

My daughter Priya said once, "It's such a helpless feeling. You want to help all of these people, but you don't know how." That really is the difficulty, we told the kids, the problem is so huge that it's beyond the ability of one person to make a difference. You simply do what you can to help as many people as you can. When Priya was nineteen, for example, she spent a summer in India teaching English at a school for children with artificial limbs.

On these trips to India the children were also exposed to a different kind of spirituality than they experienced in America. While many Americans tend to be skeptical about those things that they can't experience with their physical senses, the Indian culture widely accepts mysticism as part of life. Maybe because our children had learned to meditate while they were young they were always very open and curious about these things. Priya once went on a pilgrimage to a hill station high in the mountains with her cousins and her aunt. To get there they had to walk on a somewhat narrow path on the side of a mountain. Walking ahead of them was a blind man feeling his way with a cane. He was by himself and he was walking close to the edge. If he had taken just one wrong step he would have fallen three hundred feet into a ravine and died. But as Priya remembers, he walked with complete confidence.

"He was praying to God, and every step he took was a prayer," she told me. "We watched him for a long, long time. We probably were a little afraid for him, but his devotion to God was so beautiful that we cried."

I think that there is some part of all of us that wants to believe there is far more to this world than we know. That there are some things for which there is no scientific explanation. The path that Deepak followed heads in that direction. And growing up in India we did see and hear of real examples of that, for example, the monk who was buried for several days. But we also knew that many of these spiritual people were complete frauds. Maybe living in America made me forget that, or made me want to believe in the existence of the magical powers of the human mind. Once, on a trip to India, Amita and I took my parents, our children, and Deepak and Rita's children, Gautam and Mallika, on holiday to Kashmir. While they were all busy shopping I was standing by myself outside a store. Mallika had gone inside a shop to get a soft drink. As I stood there by myself a holy man dressed in a saffron robe approached me. Opening a copy of the Gita, he looked directly into my eyes with an intense stare and said in Hindi, "You live abroad, don't you?"

Here we go, I thought. I was wearing Western clothes, including Adidas sneakers, so it wasn't very difficult to figure out I lived in the West. But before I could shoo him away, he continued, "And you're a doctor." That was an interesting observation. There was nothing about my appearance that would have suggested that. I began to get intrigued. "And you have three children, and your son's name resonates with India's name." My son's name is Bharat; another name for India is Bharat. I didn't know how he was doing this, but it was impressive. He continued, "You live in Boston in Massachusetts and you work at the Harvard Medical School." Now this was getting seriously interesting. How could he know this?

My father, always the voice of reason, came up and saw what was going on.

"Don't get caught up," he warned me, speaking English. "If he asks for money, don't give him money."

It was too late for that. I was hooked. If this was a trick, it was an impressive one.

"Give me a hundred rupees," he said, asking for the equivalent of about two dollars. I gave it to him and he continued. "You're passionate about tennis." I nodded. "And you've been to Manchester, England."

"Yes and no," I said. This was the first wrong statement. I had won many tennis tournaments, but I had never been to Manchester.

He smiled with confidence and corrected himself, "You will soon go to Manchester." And then he told me to give him a thousand rupees — about twenty-five dollars. When I refused he repeated his demand, staring at me — practically through me — with that unblinking, hypnotic gaze.

"No," I said firmly. I was vividly remembering the charlatans of my childhood. "Leave now. Be on your way. And go in peace."

He left just as my niece came out of the store with her soda.

"Chhota papa," she said, meaning small or younger father. (My kids call Deepak Barra Papa, the older father.) "Chhota papa, what was that man telling you?"

"It was quite uncanny," I admitted. "He knew that I was a doctor who lived in Boston and had three children and that I worked at Harvard."

"That's very strange," she said. "Because when I was buying my soda a man came up to me and asked me who you were. I told him you were my uncle. Then he asked me all these questions about you and whatever I told him he repeated it into the air in Hindi."

I laughed, both at my desire to believe him against all scientific evidence and the fact that I had been tricked so easily. That was the India I knew and loved so much, where many things are not what they appeared to be.

In addition to returning to India, members of our family would occasionally come to America to visit us. That gave us the opportunity to see America again through Indian eyes. The young people loved going to the various American amusement parks. They were fascinated by how much American people ate and the fact that they would see so many overweight people at those parks. As they got a little older the shopping mall culture became exciting to them and they loved to go to the large malls with their cousins. And while we wanted our kids to at least appreciate Indian music, before MTV arrived in India our kids were making tapes of the Top 40 hits in America and sending them to their cousins.

Their parents were impressed by how easy everything seemed to be in America. Until the mid-Nineties, when cell phones became available, it could still take many months, sometimes as long as a year, simply to get a telephone line installed. And Deepak enjoyed showing visitors things like the electric garage door opener that enabled people to perform the amazing feat of opening their door without having to get out of the car! But for most visitors, the biggest adult amusement parks were big-box stores like Costco. Walking through the aisles with them reminded me of Amita's and my first trip to an American supermarket, which of course was considerably smaller than the big stores. After they got microwaves in India they would always buy the big cartons of popcorn to take back with them.

As a result of the way our kids were raised they identified themselves as Indian-Americans. While many marriages are still arranged in India, we never even approached that subject with our children. But as it turned out Kanika married Sarat Sethi, a distant relative whom she met through the family. In fact, when her future husband's grandmother was sick, the doctor she generally would go to was my father, Kanika's grandfather. Her mother-in-law's cousin is Deepak's wife, Rita. This is the way it often works in Indian families, even Indian families in America. When Kanika and Sarat began dating they decided to keep it a secret in case it didn't become serious. When Amita found out who Kanika was dating, at first she was somewhat reluctant, pointing out that we didn't know him at all. But I felt very differently when I heard about him. I knew I would like him as soon as I found out he was an avid golfer!

Our son, Bharat, had a somewhat different experience. Several years ago he was living and working in Singapore, and he learned that in that culture there was a very distinct pecking order in which respect is given. Because of his name and his appearance it was immediately obvious to everyone that he's Indian, and that got him to a certain level — but when he started talking and people heard his very American accent they realized he was actually an American, and in Singapore being an American expat got him much higher on that corporate and social ladder.

19

....

Science of Life

Deepak

Maharishi Mahesh Yogi with Deepak in a forest grove outside
Vlodrop, the Netherlands, late 1980s.

I N NO TIME AFTER MEETING Maharishi I made a life-changing decision. Standing in the Boston airport, while still waiting for our baggage to be unloaded, I told Rita that I would be flying back to Washington. I was going to do as Maharishi had asked.

She was quite taken aback. "You're not even coming home?"

"I can't. I have to go back."

My wife knew that I could make impulsive decisions. I had over-turned our lives once before, when my fellowship in endocrinology ended badly. But this decision still came as a shock. She had been present for the meetings with Maharishi when he had painted a pic-ture of changing American medicine, with me as his chief spokes-man. She loved and respected him as much as I did. But that wasn't the same as throwing away a thriving medical practice, along with the practical considerations of paying a mortgage and raising two children with college looming in the future.

Maharishi had spent hours assuaging my doubts, and now I tried to reassure Rita. The transition out of private practice wouldn't be abrupt, I explained, and eventually I could find a buyer for the prac-tice at a good price. I'd make sure that I remained board-certified in endocrinology and internal medicine, so that no one could chal-lenge my professional respectability. And I was chief of staff at New England Memorial Hospital in Stoneham, a position I wouldn't leave for a while.

Still, I was proposing a huge leap that brought unknown risks with it.

"I know this is right," I insisted, buoyed by an irresistible wave of enthusiasm. I had no right to announce what our future would be without taking Rita's opinion into account, but all I could think about was that I had found a calling. Maharishi insisted that I was the right man to tell the world about his new initiative. He had made a snap decision singling me out of a crowd. Who resists an enlightened master?

I was about to make a snap decision of my own. I would be pioneering a kind of medicine completely different from what is practiced in the West. Because he had made TM a household name, Maharishi wanted to do the same with another aspect of India's cultural tradition: Ayurveda. As a system of indigenous medicine, Ayurveda went back thousands of years, but its age gave it little credibility in my father's eyes. Ayurveda was village medicine to him, practiced by vaidyas, the local doctors whose training had scant scientific basis. As part of transforming India into a modern society, the old ways were being ignored, if not discredited. Who needed remedies made from herbs and fruits plucked in the fields? I was being asked to promote something that my father considered superstitious, importing folk ways to America, the most advanced center of medical science in the world.

The irony was lost on me. I was too eager to jump into the abyss. At the airport I walked Rita to the car, and she drove home upset and bewildered. I took the next flight back to Washington, prepared to learn everything about the science of life, which is the literal meaning of Ayurveda (or as the press releases called it, Maharishi Ayurveda —turning everything into a trademark was a lesson in the American way that Maharishi took seriously). Everyone in the movement was delighted by my decision. In short order I was established as the medical director of a facility that the TM movement had bought outside Boston, a sprawling mansion in Lancaster, Massachusetts, built by a wealthy railroad tycoon at the turn of the last century. An imposing brick pile, it had once been surrounded by extensive formal gardens and staffed by household servants. The gardens were dilapidated now, the servants gone, and the interiors in need of extensive repairs. The former owners had used the mansion as a Catholic girls' school, and they had not lavished care or money on the place.

I wasn't entirely walking into a vacuum. Meditation had attracted any number of highly educated people, among them some physicians with much the same credentials as mine. The American and European doctors in TM were enthusiastic about Maharishi's new campaign, and the Indian ones tried to be, although I suspected they were as baffled as my father. The real connection to this ancient tradition came from the Ayurvedic vaidyas who were brought over in a steady stream from India. Needless to say, they were thrilled that the West was finally paying attention to them. The Washington press stared at this cadre of exotic visitors with undisguised skepticism; Maharishi had as much work to do as when he first won the media over in the Sixties.

The vaidyas presented a contradictory face, as Indians do. They acted like authorities while sometimes breaking out into heated arguments among themselves. (During one public presentation an eminent vaidya got so angry that he ripped a page out of an Ayurvedic text and shoved it in another vaidya's face to prove his point.) They could be charming and wise, but they also liked to keep their professional secrets to themselves. None were village doctors; these were important figures in their field. The clash with Western culture led to some comical interchanges.

At one press conference a senior vaidya got carried away extolling how Ayurveda could cure any disease. A newsman stood up and asked about AIDS. Was the vaidya saying that Ayurveda had the cure?

Without missing a beat, the vaidya, who was old and a little deaf, said, "Age? Everyone should live to be a hundred. That is normal in Ayurveda." The reporter raised his voice.

"Not age. AIDS."

Shocked, the vaidya exclaimed: "Horrible! One man, one woman. That is what the scriptures say."

It soon became clear that while Western medicine prided itself on establishing scientific facts that every doctor could agree upon, each Ayurveda practitioner prided himself on knowing more than any of his rivals. Certain ancient texts dating back a thousand years before Christ, especially the encyclopedic *Charaka Samhita*, were taken to be authoritative. This didn't prevent the current practice of Ayurveda from being a confusing, often contentious field where few assertions were backed up with research that would pass credibility tests in the West. (On their own terms, I hasten to add, the Ayurvedic medical schools did conduct research to prove the efficacy of what they taught, but nothing about that appeared in Western journals. Thirty years later, the situation remains much the same.)

The grandiose claims made by the vaidyas, eager to impress Western audiences, were distressing. My anchor was an eminent Ayurvedic authority named Brihaspati Dev Triguna, the most powerful ally in the field that Maharishi could have hoped for. Dr. Triguna, who was born in 1920, came from my father's generation. He was a large, imposing figure who exuded authority. When you met him it was almost as if he was holding court, but in fact Triguna saw hundreds of poor patients from his clinic behind the railway station in New Delhi, in a historic section populated by villagers who had migrated from South India.

It added a glow of prestige that Triguna was president of the All India Ayurvedic Congress, but my first attraction was to his diagnostic skills, which were remarkable. My father had built his career on the same skills, which are as much instinct as science. Triguna's method was entirely based on taking a patient's pulse. It was startling to watch him touch three fingers to a person's wrist and immediately diagnose all kinds of maladies, congenital disorders, predispositions to weakness, and so on. When I asked him how he accomplished such a feat, he replied, "Take four thousand pulses first. It becomes clear."

Triguna also dispensed Ayurvedic remedies of the highest quality, prepared according to meticulous ancient formulas. In essence his practice came down to taking pulses and writing prescriptions all day. I couldn't adopt such a practice without years of practical training, but I did immediately begin to learn pulse diagnosis. The clinic in Lancaster began to offer *Panchakarma,* the "five actions" used in Ayurveda to balance the body and avert illness. Unexpectedly this became a major attraction. Going through panchakarma was more like a spa visit for the people who came to us. Daily massages with warm sesame oil and a treatment where sesame oil is gently dripped over the forehead were part of the regimen, along with constant personal care. Dietary advice was tailored to each person's individual needs. Without knowing anything about Ayurveda's heritage, celebrities got the word and began to come. When Elizabeth Taylor came for panchakarma, she was so delighted that a regal scene ensued. In departing she slowly descended the huge main staircase of the mansion, with staff members lining her way as she gave each one a silky pashmina shawl embroidered with her monogram.

We had arrived.

With her usual graciousness Rita forgave my sudden leap, and our lives remained intertwined with the rest of the family. Sanjiv and Amita continued to practice meditation. Amita is a pediatrician, but she remembers the spiritual leanings of her father, who died when she was young. On meeting Maharishi, she seemed fascinated by the revival of Ayurveda, and I think she would have explored it more if her busy medical practice hadn't made so many demands.

The most positive response came from my father, who was dismayed at first that I would throw over my medical career. But as I became more deeply interested in *Vedanta*, the purest and oldest spiritual tradition in India, he took it up too. He and my mother met with Maharishi when he came to his center in Noida, an hour or so outside Delhi. Maharishi would spend hours discussing Vedanta with my father while I sat on the sidelines, rather awed. Once my mother realized that a meeting with the guru was likely to go on for eight or ten hours — Maharishi had indefatigable energy and little need for sleep — she declined to go back.

Awkwardly and by fits and starts, Sanjiv and I did what brothers must do as we passed thirty and then forty. We faced the fact that our childhood bond wasn't enough. A new relationship had to be forged. At times this was like being teammates in a relay race, trying to pass the baton with the risk of dropping it in the attempt. Two factors were always a given: We were brothers, and our families loved each other. I still keep a photograph taken of us for an article in *Harvard Magazine,* where we are sitting side by side, half embracing. Our beaming smiles could be taken as pure affection, self-satisfaction at having arrived, or rekindled nostalgia.

We made the most of not seeing the fork in the road that was separating us. There were still islands of joy and companionship even as we drifted apart. Sanjiv's close ties with Harvard Medical School, first forged soon after he arrived in this country, were a testimony to his abilities and drive to succeed. It felt strange to see him climb a ladder that I was kicking away. Whether Maharishi Ayurveda became the second TM or fell on its face, I wasn't welcome back in the medical establishment to the same extent as before. If anyone found it inexcusable that a real doctor, a chief of staff at that, would shift allegiance to such quackery, I intended to head them off.

My timing was fortunate. The prestige of scientific medicine wasn't waning, but for millions of people something crucial had shifted. They were seeking alternatives to the drugs and surgery that are the mainstay of mainstream medicine. In part this shift gained official approval. It was being widely recognized that all kinds of lifestyle disorders were preventable. Thirty years later it's common knowledge that exercise, diet, and stress management can make major inroads in preventing heart disease, stroke, and type 2 diabetes; in the latest advance for prevention, it is estimated that up to 90 percent of cancers may be preventable with the right lifestyle changes.

At the time, however, there was a trickle of approval compared to a flood of disapproval. "Alternative" was a dirty word to every doctor I knew, and their complaints ranged from irrational outrage to disdainful ignorance. Prevention didn't figure into a physician's everyday practice. He hadn't studied it in medical school; the very thought of teaching a med student about diet and exercise was considered laughable. Equating herbal remedies and natural cures with pharmaceuticals was considered everything from absurd to flagrantly illegal. Traditional medicine from around the world was bizarre and alien.

The only crack in the facade, so far as the medical establishment was concerned, was acupuncture. The West had seen propaganda footage from China where smiling patients waved at the camera while undergoing surgery without anesthesia. They were totally conscious and free of pain. Debunkers quickly came forward with explanations about brainwashed people putting on a show as good Communists, but these arguments were singularly unconvincing. Nothing quite erases the sight of a patient smiling and awake while a scalpel is cutting into his thorax. The clincher came from James Reston, one of the most respected reporters and columnists at the *New York Times*. In the summer of 1971 Reston's appendix became inflamed; he was rushed to the hospital in Beijing where it was removed using conventional surgical methods. But in his recovery period he agreed to let his postoperative pain be treated with acupuncture. The endorsement Reston gave in a dispatch sent home made a big impression.

So it was naïve of me to think that I could stave off censure. At first there was no such threat. Then I wrote a book, *Creating Health,* which predated my decision to jump ship. In 1985 Ayurveda was far from my mind, but a host of anomalies grabbed my attention. Outside the mainstream journals were all kinds of strange medical events that were impossible to explain, such as the spontaneous remission of cancer. The placebo effect hadn't been explained satisfactorily, yet on average 30 percent of patients felt relief from it. This totally contradicted the accepted notion that the body cannot duplicate what pharmaceutical drugs can do. The more I delved into it, the more I saw problems with medicine as I had learned it. I was taught that each disease has a standard history, a course of progression that goes through roughly the same stages and timing for each patient. So why did some patients die so much faster than others, or survive so much longer? Just shrugging it off as "dying from their diagnosis" wasn't good enough.

Creating Health gathered evidence from many areas that seemed unrelated at the time. Within a few years, however, alternative medicine was talking about a mind-body connection, which if examined closely explained almost every strange anomaly. The proposition that the mind could influence the body was greeted harshly by mainstream medicine (at a conference another doctor told me how ridiculous the concept was, and I said, "If there's no mind-body connection, how do you wiggle your toes?").

For me the real breakthrough wasn't Ayurveda but a pioneering book, *Space, Time & Medicine,* that I pored over like a seeker hungry for a revelation. The author was Larry Dossey, a Texas physician (and later a good friend) who was intent on going far beyond the mind-body connection into such foreign realms as quantum physics and the healing power of prayer. His open-mindedness was remarkable, with no sense that medicine should obey strictures and boundaries just because some authority said so. Writing in 1982, Dossey poured the thrill of discovery into his book. His references to quantum physics made most doctors look hopelessly parochial, and the challenges he laid down couldn't be ignored.

The main challenge was a demand that the human body move out of the Newtonian universe that Einstein and the other quantum pioneers had exploded once and for all. If atoms were no longer tiny bits of matter but ghosts of swirling energy, if the universe operated as a whole rather than as a machine with countless separate parts, if time can bend and two particles separated by billions of light years can communicate instantly, disregarding the speed of light, our understanding of the human body needs to be totally reframed. For what is the human body but a construct of matter and energy that must obey the new quantum rules? Dossey's passion and insight floored me. I wanted to answer his challenge, and what I saw as a farseeing vision fueled everything that was to come. If Larry Dossey was right, the next age of medicine wouldn't resemble the age of Pasteur and Salk at all.

I set out on the quixotic quest of reinventing the human body.

At first, practicing Ayurveda was like going through the looking glass, to a place where ancient is better than modern and intuition more reliable than science. I had no desire to go there, and fortunately Maharishi gave me great leeway. When the time came to write a handbook for the general public, eventually published as *Perfect Health,* he cautioned me, "Don't turn this into a kitchen pharmacy."

This came as a great relief, because as eye-opening as Triguna and the other vaidyas were, it would be a sham for me just to perform a pulse diagnosis and prescribe traditional herbal remedies. The challenge was to turn Ayurveda into something useful and reliable for the West. In the Eighties alternative medicine implied a rejection of mainstream medicine, largely as a reaction to the American Medical Association's overt hostility to anything not taught in medical school. It would take time for an uneasy truce to be declared, and even more time for "complementary medicine" to evolve, which eased the standoff between two opposing camps.

I was at the center of a clash of world views. In India, if you seriously followed an Ayurvedic regimen, you began as a young child and kept it up for a lifetime. A vaidya would examine you to determine your basic *Prakriti*, the general nature of your constitution. It's highly significant that this same word is used for nature as a whole, because in Ayurveda, the elements of life are universal. A person's constitution was said to be composed of *Vata* (air), *Pitta* (fire), and *Kapha* (water). One or more of these dominated, and once you knew if you were Vata-Kapha, for example, certain predispositions for disease could be taken into account. Ayurveda essentially comes down to imbalances of Vata, Pitta, and Kapha, and yet as simple as that may sound, the Ayurvedic system gets incredibly intricate.

Not that a Western doctor would care. The whole system sounds like a retreat into the medieval system of the four humors, when patients were diagnosed by imbalances in phlegm, black bile, yellow bile, and blood. The prescribed medicines of Ayurveda presented their own problems, since they were untested in laboratories, poorly controlled at the manufacturing end, and at times contained toxic substances, the most notorious being mercury, that supposedly had been purified of poison through intricate procedures of burning and refining that amounted to alchemy.

Despite these obstacles, Maharishi Ayurveda caught on. Its core audience consisted of the thousands of meditators who trusted Maharishi implicitly. They flocked to the center in Lancaster for panchakarma, and my mind was easy on that score. The purification treatments involved no medicines, and when these were needed, ours were made under the best conditions in India and passed inspection at U.S. Customs.

People were astonished by how accurate the prakriti system is, even on casual acquaintance. I remember a movie star who came to me for an evaluation — TM had made considerable inroads in the Hollywood community. When I took her pulse and considered other telltale signs about her body type, it was clear that she had a strongly Pitta nature.

"You are organized and like to be in control," I told her. "You have lots of energy but wind up exhausting yourself because you don't know your limits. You used to be able to eat anything without gaining weight, but as you've gotten older, that's changing, much to your surprise. You are attracted to hot, spicy food. You don't do well in warm, humid climates." She sat back, incredulous and impressed.

"Do you read minds?" she asked.

I could have told her much more about herself, and did. The prakriti system, which goes beyond body types, can reveal many things about a person. Pitta types, for instance, are good with money but tend to spend on extravagances. Their discomfort with heat can be eased by drinking something that is bitter and sweet, like tonic water. When *Perfect Health* was published, the associated doctors and I did our best to compile the most reliable list of body type characteristics and the diets and health suggestions that went along with them. But it wasn't credible for this to pass itself off as "real" medicine by Western standards — or my own. Patients tended to make a fetish of eating the foods that were suitable for a Vata or Kapha, if that happened to be their Prakriti, and at its most superficial, cocktail party chat went from "I'm an Aquarius" to "I'm a Vata-Pitta."

The challenge for me, as set by Maharishi, was to reframe Ayurveda for the West. No one in America outside a few Indian immigrants lived an Ayurvedic lifestyle beginning in childhood, but the vaidyas who had signed on with Maharishi could dispense traditional Ayurveda to anyone who was interested. I became the public face of Ayurveda (arousing more than a little annoyance among the small

cadre of traditional vaidyas who had immigrated to America and established small local practices, since they felt that they owned the
knowledge), but I wasn't an Ayurvedic doctor. My assignment was to
merge "modern science with ancient wisdom," a catchphrase that the
media latched on to. It also happened to be the real challenge.

Ayurveda makes no sense as viewed from a scientific model if you
already assume that you know what the human body is. Medical science certainly does. The body is a biological machine with thousands
of intricate moving parts. At the finest level cells operate through
chemical signals and processes dictated by DNA, whose active twin,
messenger RNA, controls the switches for making enzymes and pro-
teins. All of these facts lead directly to medical treatments. A doctor
tinkers with the machine when it's broken, either by offering chemical help (drugs) or by repairing the larger moving parts (surgery).
I'm describing this simply here but I'm not being simplistic. Modern
medicine is a sophisticated outgrowth of the common-sense premise
that our bodies are free-standing objects in space, far more complex
than a rock or a tree but no different in their physicality.

Dossey's book introduced a quantum-based objection to this basic
assumption, and I enthusiastically pursued that line with my own
book, *Quantum Healing*. It specifically addressed a prevailing medical mystery, the rare occasions when cancer spontaneously goes away.
Spontaneous remissions fascinated me; I felt that I had witnessed one
in a patient I called Chitra. She was Indian, a flight attendant who
lived in Washington, D.C., and like many young Indian wives, she
was dominated by her mother-in-law. There's a certain "What can
you do?" resignation among daughters-in-law who live in a matri-
archal society, but Chitra was unusually intimidated. When she detected a lump in her breast that was diagnosed as breast cancer, she
couldn't bear to let her mother-in-law, who lived with Chitra and her
husband, know that she was sick. So she took the irrational step of
keeping her condition a secret and pursuing no treatments.

Some months passed, and when her doctor saw her next, he examined her and sent her for tests. The astonishing finding came back
that there was no sign of malignancy. Chitra was overjoyed at first,

but then she succumbed to anxiety. What if she wasn't really cured? What if the cancer returned? She fell into a state of desperation, which is how I met her. She wanted me to use Ayurveda or something else — anything — to keep her disease away and give her peace of mind. *Quantum Healing* was written on her behalf, taking me on a journey into the healing response.

I discovered immediately that healing is a thicket of confused findings and beliefs. The body's ability to heal can be observed under a microscope by a pathologist discerning cellular changes, and of course we've all experienced what it's like to get well. But these visible signs are like watching iron filings dance on a piece of paper without seeing the magnet that is moving them from below. Healing is a process so complex that it is the essence of what "bodily intelligence" means.

We tend to assume that intelligence is a human property, the product of an advanced brain, that arrived on the evolutionary scene billions of years after life began. Only in the Eighties did researchers begin to talk about a silent kind of intelligence built into the immune system. (The turning point came when it was discovered that the neurotransmitters and neuropeptides that brain cells communicate with are present throughout the body.) Witnessing the uncanny precision and accuracy that the immune system employs to fend off disease and heal wounds, some medical writers began to refer to the immune system as a floating brain — its primary home being in the fluid lymphatic system and blood vessels.

What was utterly mysterious was the placebo effect — and its reverse, the nocebo effect — which showed that merely the expectation of getting better can trigger the healing system. This led naturally to the possibility that unseen influences such as emotions and personality traits can drastically affect healing. I found remarkable things to discuss. In one trial patients suffering from nausea were given a pill they were told would cure nausea, and in a certain percentage it did — despite the fact that the pill was actually an emetic, which induces nausea. In one published case, a man with advanced lymphatic cancer, so advanced that his lymph glands were swelling bulges, went into complete remission over a single weekend. The doctors thought he was on death's door and therefore untreatable. So they had injected him with nothing more than saline solution, while telling him that he was receiving a particularly new and powerful form of chemotherapy. Later the patient read in the newspaper that this cancer drug had failed in clinical trials. He lost hope, his lymphoma returned, and he died within a matter of weeks.

The mind-body connection wasn't a curiosity, and no reasonable person could doubt it. Leaving aside the doctors who rejected the placebo effect as "not real medicine," which was blind prejudice, the doctors who were sympathetic couldn't figure out how to harness the mind for healing purposes. Various dead ends arose. There was a flurry of interest in so-called type A personalities, people who were impatient, demanding, tense, and susceptible to the triggering of stress. Type As had been correlated with higher risk for a premature heart attack. Yet predictably this neat classification blurred around the edges, and mainstream medicine was too caught up in warning of the dangers of cholesterol to bother with a psychological condition for which there was no drug.

The closer I looked at the mind-body connection, the more I realized that the entire healing system had to be redefined. No one could deny that the mind can do both great harm and great good. Every new finding pointed to an understanding of the body as a holistic system. Billions of cells throughout the body were intimately connected; they eavesdropped on a person's every thought and mood. This led me to an inescapable conclusion: Medicine would never understand mind and body without seeing them as a single entity. Mind creates matter. That can be observed in brain scans, because those areas that "light up" on an MRI are actually manufacturing brain chemicals, not emitting visible light. Brain scans provide a picture of invisible activity in the mind. The link between injecting someone with saline solution and having his cancer go away had to be mental. For the first time healing came down to consciousness.

Reviewing the literature on thousands of cases of spontaneous remission, I found that the people who had cured themselves of cancer hadn't pursued the same program — far from it. Everything from faith healing to grape juice, laetrile from apricot pits to coffee enemas had been tried. These modalities were scorned by mainstream medicine without exception. They had produced a handful of cures but also many thousands of failures. There seemed to be only one strong correlation. People who spontaneously recovered from cancer knew unshakably that they would. One found anecdotes of farm wives who, on discovering a lump in their breast, would visit the doctor once to be diagnosed and then return home, too busy to bother with treatment. Had some of them recovered as their relatives later swore?

I pondered this riddle and decided that something far more powerful than positive thinking must be at work. A turbulent mind can force itself to be positive while remaining disturbed below the surface. Instead of a certainty about their recovery, the people who successfully recovered from cancer may have reached a state of peace, and after that it wasn't a matter of dread and helplessness whether they got well or not. They had surrendered to the outcome without interference from fear, agitation, mood swings, and the fragile hope that is so common in cancer patients. This state of surrender wasn't resignation, which is a mask for defeat. Instead, the body was given a chance to draw upon its own healing powers, to regulate itself back into balance. Was this the hidden key?

For Chitra my explorations had no good outcome. Her dread was prophetic. The cancer returned after a brief remission and she died. But this didn't disprove the notion that the mind holds the power to create change in the body. If anything, the mind-body connection had worked in reverse, turning her fear into illness. Because I hadn't entirely turned my back on my Western medical training, I asked oncologists how they explained spontaneous remissions. It seemed to me that if even one person recovered from a deadly cancer like melanoma, a massive research effort should be launched. (Melanoma was a good example, since it is highly malignant but also exhibits a higher than usual number of reported spontaneous remissions. We are still talking about a minute number of patients, though.)

The oncologists I spoke to all shrugged. Cancer is a numbers game, they said. Spontaneous remissions were rare, idiosyncratic cases. Studying them wouldn't help treat the hundreds of thousands of normal cancers that appear every year. Normal, it seems, meant the total exclusion of the mind.

I can look back on my years with Maharishi Ayurveda as a tight-rope walk where I wobbled but never fell off. In clinical practice I developed a complementary approach. Patients with serious illnesses were treated with Ayurveda but strongly advised to seek conventional medical care. It would have been unethical to do anything else. I squirmed when Maharishi or one of his devoted followers with an MD spoke of Western medicine solely in terms of harming patients and leading in time to a society rife with incurable illnesses. The claim was undeniable. I knew the litany of charges against modern medicine. A shocking number of patients undergo treatments that grossly compromise their immune systems. Others die of illnesses brought on in the hospital, what is known as iatrogenic disease. A fixation on hygiene has resulted in "super germs" that have grown immune to antibiotics. All drugs have side effects, and over time drugs lose their effectiveness. When you paint this grim picture, you can't leave out the unspoken deaths that occur because people are so dependent on the magic-bullet approach that they neglect prevention — the neglect of self-care is a massive killer.

None of these things can be discounted. They drove me deeper and deeper into alternative treatments. That's different from jumping into Ayurveda as the one and only solution, which unfortunately is what Maharishi wanted. The flaws of Western medicine made Ayurveda look promising. There was a long way to go, I told him, before the evidence was strong enough to claim that Ayurveda actually cured diseases that Western medicine couldn't.

Taking this position created the first signs of friction between us. Meetings would drag on, with Maharishi planning a worldwide campaign to "put Ayurveda in every home," and using inflated rhetoric as a substitute for research. This tactic had worked brilliantly with meditation. TM made claims that took decades to verify with solid findings. Medicine demands the findings up-front. Maharishi was impatient with that reality. The minute that a new Ayurvedic product was ready to market, he insisted on putting an exorbitant price tag on it (Ayurvedic medicines are generally cheap in India, except for those with exotic ingredients like gold or pearls), and he had only to lift a finger for devoted meditators to rush forward with endorsements about the health benefits they were receiving.

I began to grow restless during the meetings, and then increasingly frustrated. It seemed absurd to be torn in two by opposing forces when they could work together. The tide had turned for alternative medicine. By the beginning of the Nineties the editorial page of *The New England Journal of Medicine* had to confront a fact that deeply distressed the medical establishment: More Americans were going to alternative practitioners than to MDs. It was no longer viable to tell all these people that they were deluded, superstitious, or the victims of scams. Yet that was still the official position of mainstream medicine, which went to extremes of alarmist reactions if need be. When a few cases of poisoning from herbal remedies were reported, a huge cry arose that herbs should be regulated by the Food and Drug Administration, overlooking the fact that fatal reactions to surgical anesthesia and antibiotics were vastly more common.

The rise of alternative medicine was unstoppable, and Maharishi had been early to catch the tide. There was no need to turn Ayurveda into an absolute, an either/or choice between medicine that healed and medicine that killed. What bothered me more, since I wasn't coerced in any way to talk in either/or terms, was the tendency to turn Ayurveda into a mirror of the drug-pushing that a doctor does all day in private practice. It was herbs instead of pills from Big Pharma, which was promising. Still, the profound basis of Ayurveda was being shifted aside. The real revolution in medicine would come about only through consciousness. People needed to see that matter was a mask for mind. A human being isn't a machine that learns to think; we are thoughts that learned to build a machine.

I was touring the world using these aphorisms. They were simplistic, but I put all my idealism behind them. People seemed mesmerized, which to me indicated a yearning for a new way to heal and stay healthy. They knew that they were hopelessly dependent on the medical profession, and yet health is a natural state, one that each person should be able to maintain.

Much of America was too jaded to listen to idealism, perhaps. In other countries, from South America and Ireland to Australia and Great Britain, the reception was more open-minded. I would go on a nationally televised program to talk about the unlimited potential of the mind, with sentences that made the interviewer lean forward with genuine fascination.

"You go to the same place to see the image of a rose as the universe goes to create a star."

"The macrocosm is the same as the microcosm. Quite literally, your body is the universe."

"Every cell in your body is part of the cosmic dance."

Because these things fascinated people, I could distract myself from the troubles that were brewing with Maharishi. Or to be more specific, with his inner circle. Ashram politics are notoriously vicious. The TM inner circle wasn't an ashram, but people had been jockeying for favor with the guru for years before I arrived on the scene. The international tours grew longer and longer. I sold my practice and within two years resigned my position as chief of staff at the hospital. So far as the media was concerned, my name was synonymous with Ayurveda. Unless they were coaxed into it, reporters almost never added the "Maharishi" part. In that minor slip lay the source of a rift that would never be repaired.

I didn't see it coming. It wasn't an impossible strain to feel restless and frustrated. When an enlightened master tells you to compromise some of your beliefs and repress some of your doubts, he knows better than you what is good for your soul. Crusades are fueled by a sense of total righteousness, as long as it lasts.

The path that I was to follow had become clear to me.

20

Finger on the Pulse

Sanjiv

Sanjiv relaxes with his daughters Priya, eight, and Kanika, two, in their Newton, Massachusetts, home, 1978.

W E GREETED DEEPAK'S SUCCESS with happiness. He had taken an enormous risk, giving up his successful practice, to follow his heart. That is a definition of courage. I remember thinking of Sir Winston Churchill's remarks: "Courage is rightly esteemed the first of human qualities . . . because it is the quality which guarantees all others." Initially, when Deepak threw himself into his new life with such passion, I was somewhat skeptical about it. Deepak was an intellectual explorer: He'd find something that intrigued him and immediately want to learn everything about it. But in a few months that might well pass and he would be onto a new and glorious pursuit.

For example, after I became a passionate golfer Deepak and I played a round one day in California. He'd been playing the game barely six months but clearly it intrigued him. During the round he asked me why I enjoyed golf so much.

"Deepak," I said, "it's outdoors, it's all about collegiality, focus, integrity, honesty, and commitment." And as I said this I could see the wheels spinning.

About six months later I was in my office and his new book, *Golf for Enlightenment: The Seven Lessons for the Game of Life*, with an introduction by professional golfer Jesper Parnevik, arrived on my desk. Deepak had thrown himself into the game of golf, trying to understand it on an intellectual as well as a physical level. The book was more about the mental approach to the game of golf rather than nuts-and-bolts golf instruction. It was indeed a very good book. However, I could be biased; in the book's dedication he wrote, "To my father, Krishan, who inspired me to play the game of life, and to my brother, Sanjiv, who taught me that the game of golf mirrors the game of life."

A writer for a golf magazine wanted to do a story about Deepak taking up the game and writing a book about it, and suggested that they play a round together. Deepak was quite nervous when he discovered this writer was an excellent golfer. In preparation for their match, Deepak played every single day and took lessons from a gifted instructor. His shot-making improved. The two of them played a round and Deepak acquitted himself well. That was the height of his passion with golf, as after that he pursued many other passions.

TM and Ayurveda proved to be very different, of course. TM very quickly had become an important aspect of all of our lives. Amita and I went to Fairfield, Iowa, to learn advanced meditation techniques, including what is known as yogic-flying, and sometime later we also got to spend time with Maharishi. The first time I met him I was introduced as a doctor who had written a book entitled *Disorders of the Liver.*

"Dr. Chopra," he asked me, "in that book, did you include a chapter on how Western medicine can cause liver disease?"

"Maharishi, I have written a chapter on drug-induced liver toxicity and there are many drugs that can even cause fatal liver disease. So, yes, of course there is a chapter on it."

He was pleased, I think.

Then he said, "You should abandon Western medicine. It is a sinking ship, and you should embrace Ayurveda."

As much as I respected him, I knew that was not the path I intended to follow. But to be polite, I told him, "I will think about it." My path in life is to be a teacher; that was my passion. At the same time he also invited Amita to give up the practice of modern medicine and join his movement. Amita was probably more intrigued by the possibility than I was, but as she explained, "My home and my heart and my path lies with Sanjiv and my children," so she chose to continue with her career in Boston.

But having grown up in India it was impossible not to know about Ayurveda; it just wasn't an important part of our lives. My father practiced Western medicine and both Deepak and I followed him. While occasionally we would use natural remedies to heal minor cuts and bruises, for any serious medical problems we relied on science. But after Deepak became so deeply involved in mind-body medicine, both my father and I investigated it further. It certainly was impossible to dismiss it, as some modern physicians insisted on doing. And, in fact, I did see things that couldn't be explained by the medicine I practiced. For example, one morning when we were vacationing in Delhi, a TM teacher named Farroukh, who was a friend of my father's, told me, "Sanjiv, I'm going to see this amazing Ayurvedic physician to get some herbs for a friend of mine. Come along, you will find it an amazing experience."

Off we went in his car. Farroukh told me several amazing stories about the man we were going to see. His name was Dr. Brihaspati Dev Triguna and he was quite well-known for being able to diagnose people by feeling their wrist pulse. He said he had accurately diagnosed a colleague, saying to him, "Years ago you had a hyperactive thyroid, and when you were young you had surgery for kyphoscoliosis." All of this by taking his pulse for a few seconds. This colleague's wife also went to see Dr. Triguna. He took her pulse and then he asked her, "Do you have problems having an issue?"

She had no idea what he meant. "Issue?"

Dr. Triguna's assistant then explained: "He's asking if you have any problems conceiving and having children."

They were flabbergasted. They had been trying to have children for years without success. Then Dr. Triguna told her, "You have a very large but benign tumor of your uterus. That's why you're having difficulty getting pregnant." Sure enough, back in Boston they did a uterine ultrasound and the doctors discovered a large uterine fibroid. I listened with rapt attention, though, truthfully, stories like this were not all that uncommon for Deepak and me when we were growing up in India. But I had never encountered somebody who had firsthand experience with such an amazing skill. So I was indeed quite curious to meet this learned Ayurvedic doctor.

About three hundred people were waiting quietly in the courtyard to see him. From the way they were dressed it was obvious they came from all social classes, very rich and very poor. There were even several Westerners there. I was even more curious, but equally skeptical.

Farroukh took me right away to the front of the line and I sat down. Dr. Triguna was sitting cross-legged on a divan. We were propped down directly in front of him. He quickly dispensed the herbs to Farroukh, then said to me in Hindi, "So what is the matter?"

I replied in a polite, but admittedly somewhat confrontational voice, "I'm fine. You're supposed to be this amazing and gifted Ayurvedic physician. So please tell me what's wrong with me."

"Okay," he agreed, "put your wrist out."

Using three fingers he felt my pulse on both my left and right wrists, holding his hand there only for a few seconds. Then he said, "There are three things wrong with you. The first one is you get serious heartburn."

I was astounded because I did take medicine on a regular basis to counteract my heartburn. But heartburn is quite common, so it could have applied to almost any Westerner whose pulse he was reading.

"Okay," I said, "what else?"

"You have difficulty breathing through your nose."

That, too, was true. I have a markedly deviated nasal septum. I thought, maybe when I sat down and looked up at him, being an astute clinician, he had noticed it.

Finally he said, "Okay, done. Next."

"Wait," I said. "There were three things, you said. What is the third thing?"

He shrugged. "The third thing is *Mamuli*," meaning totally trivial, really inconsequential.

"No, no, please." I was incredibly fascinated. "Tell me what it is."

"Every time you take a shower your eyes turn fire-engine red."

I was absolutely blown away. That's exactly what happens. In fact, when Amita and I were first married she thought I was drinking in the shower. It's some type of reflex. But it was astonishing that he was able to diagnose that simply by holding my pulse for a few seconds.

"Could you teach me how to do this?" I asked him. "Specifically can you teach me to take a patient's pulse and accurately diagnose their liver condition?"

"I can," he said. "It will be a two-year apprenticeship. When would you like to start?" There was no way for me to take a two-year sabbatical and make a foray into unchartered territory.

In some ways he reminded me of the diagnostic skills displayed by Dr. Elihu Schimmel, who was able to determine a patient's medical history by looking at his X-ray. What I did learn from Dr. Triguna was that there is so much more to the practice of medicine than we already know. He and Deepak eventually became friends and Deepak brought him to America, where he demonstrated his remarkable ability to diagnose patients with a variety of medical disorders simply by taking their pulse for a few seconds. I think from that point forward I began to pay at least a little bit more attention, and perhaps even gained a modicum of respect, for the ancient and current practice of Ayurveda.

What also pleasantly surprised me, at least mildly, was that our father at a later stage of his life was able to embrace aspects of the mind-body connection. My father was always open to new experiences. He and my mother had started meditating. He met Maharishi Mahesh Yogi many times and they would have long conversations late into the night. As our father began probing the power of the mind to control the body he recalled experiences from his own life that couldn't be explained by Western medicine. His mother — my grandmother — had sustained a serious head injury in an accident and had fallen into a coma. He and my mother had rushed to the hospital. When they arrived his mother was in critical condition, both of her arms were paralyzed and physicians could not feel a pulse or detect any blood pressure.

"It appeared," he wrote years later, "that she was waiting for me. I went to her bed and leaned over her face. Immediately her breathing became noticeable and quicker. She opened her eyes, whispered my name, and lifting her paralyzed arm around my neck, pulled my face toward hers and kissed me on the cheek. Then she fell back and stopped breathing . . . Her will, so dynamic and strong, must have been operating from outside her individual consciousness, from what I could think of as only a cosmic level, directing the paralyzed limb of the pulseless body to lift and embrace me. I kissed her face over and over again."

Although he never embraced Ayurveda completely, our father did integrate important aspects of it into his own cardiology practice. When treating Maharishi, for example, he relied on Western medicine when he felt it was necessary. When Maharishi suffered his heart attack, it was the techniques of modern medicine that kept him alive and allowed his body the time to recover. But at the same time he also stressed the importance of stress reduction, diet, and the other elements of Ayurveda in his work.

Toward the end of my father's life he published two books, including *Your Life Is in Your Hands*. In that book he summed up what he had learned, writing, "I believe that you can heal yourself more effectively by changing your lifestyle, and by engaging in activities and relationships that raise waves of love, happiness, compassion, and other positive thoughts and emotions." Of course that's sensible advice from any doctor. But in that book he also headed a section, "Our Thoughts Can Even Influence Whether We Live or Die." There he told a story of one of Deepak's patients when Deepak was an intern. The patient was an elderly man who decided it was time to die, but Deepak, who was preparing to leave the hospital for a month, told him, "You can't die until I come back to see you again." That man waited an entire month until Deepak returned—and then he died peacefully.

But what was more telling was my father's own life, and his death. Dr. Krishan Lal Chopra was a man of science; he had an insatiable appetite for knowledge. For twenty-five years he was the head of the Department of Medicine and Cardiology at the prestigious Moolchand Khairati Ram Hospital, where fact-based medicine was practiced. He was eighty-three when my daughter Kanika got married. The wedding was held in India because her husband, Sarat, wanted the blessing of both sets of grandparents. So about one hundred and fifty people traveled from the United States to India. Indian weddings are large celebrations and as many as six hundred people attended the five functions we had there. At the wedding my father sang and danced and blessed every guest. It was a time of great celebration and joy for him. In addition to this wedding, his second book, *The Mystery and Magic of Love*, was completed and about to be published.

About two weeks later, at midnight, he said to my mother: "Pushpa, I am departing. I love you." And after he had this premonition, he passed away. He had lived his life as a saint, and he died that way.

We all returned to India, this time for a parting. After the cremation we asked my mother to come back with us to live in America.

"You can stay with us," Amita said, "or you can stay with Deepak and Rita. Your children are in America. Your grandchildren are in America. Come and be with us."

She refused.

"I'm going to die in India," she said. "I don't want to die in America." It was frustrating to all of us who loved her.

"What is India? America? It's all one world," I said. But she was adamant. India was her home and she would not leave. And then Deepak and Rita, Amita and I decided that one of us, including our kids, would go to India every month and spend at least a week there with her. Maybe we had become Americans in so many ways, but when it came to family we were still Indians. There were some members of our family in India who were totally skeptical that Deepak and I would follow through with this plan, but every month for almost six years Deepak, Rita, Amita, our children, or I was there so she would know that next month, every month, somebody was coming to be with her.

Each of us knew that every time we left, for the entire six years, it was possible this would be the last time we were seeing our mother, or our grandmother alive. There is no way to describe that feeling, except that it heightened every greeting and every departure, and made us appreciate the importance of family.

Like my father I have certainly looked into the potential benefits of all forms of alternative medicine. I have always had an open mind and I understand that not all forms of medicine can be judged solely by science. For example, surprisingly there is very little scientific evidence that acupuncture has any real benefit at all. There is no single accepted form of acupuncture; different practitioners probe different points on a patient's body with their needles to achieve results, which makes it impossible to test by the traditional scientific method. But several years ago I had an operation on my right knee for two torn menisci and afterward on occasion it would swell up quite painfully. When that happened it became difficult for me to walk. In the past I had seen an acupuncturist for back problems and found substantial relief, but at the same time I was also losing weight, doing abdominal core exercises, and incorporating other treatments, so it wasn't possible to be certain that the marked improvement was directly a result of the acupuncture treatment. I decided to see this practitioner about my knee.

One Friday afternoon I hobbled into her office. An hour later the session was over. I got off her examining table and looked at my knee. The swelling was gone. As I wrote in my book, *Live Better, Live Longer:* "My first reaction was, *My goodness, how did this happen?* My second reaction was, *There's still daylight, maybe I can play nine holes!*" Which I did, with alacrity and without pain.

I don't have to see scientific evidence to know that in certain situations acupuncture can be beneficial. Using that same criteria I can't dismiss the possibility that Ayurveda is beneficial just because there isn't a lot of science to support it. My general feeling is that Ayurveda or, in fact, any type of holistic medicine, may have a role in prevention. But I've yet to see a single non-Western drug that eradicates the hepatitis C virus; or if a patient needs a liver transplant or bypass surgery or a replacement for a broken hip, I haven't seen any alternative to traditional Western medicine that would be effective. When you get a rusty nail in your leg you need a tetanus shot to prevent infection; as far as I know there isn't any Ayurvedic medicine or Chinese herb that will replace that shot. If a patient has reoccurring pneumonia due to a bacterium, that patient better get the right antibiotic. So don't tell me that this is six thousand years old and it has been practiced through the centuries and therefore that in itself makes it meritorious. Certainly there may be benefits to it, but what I find appalling is when people believe they can abandon all of the miracles of Western medicine and safely replace them with alternative treatments.

They are not alternatives. The term that is fortunately now commonly used is "complementary medicine," or "integrated medicine," which means a practitioner can integrate all or some of it into his or her practice. But to me it's not a replacement for Western medicine.

When Deepak initially became involved in this we would discuss it, debate it, the way we had discussed so many other topics through our life. Deepak, being a forceful debater, always brings insight to the discussion. We had our arguments about it.

"It has a role in prevention," I would agree. "But show me a patient with long-standing diabetes who no longer needs frequent daily doses of insulin because of an herb or Ayurvedic medicine that you give him. Show me a single patient." And of course he couldn't.

My brother has never been afraid to take on difficult or controversial issues, but I was especially concerned that his work might prevent people from getting the care that they need. Unfortunately I have seen that happen in other instances. There is the story of one patient who had a neuroendocrine tumor in his pancreas and spent more than a year trying to treat it with non-Western medicine. More than twelve months. A neuroendocrine tumor generally is slow growing. If it hasn't spread, the prognosis is extremely good if it's removed surgically at an early stage. But in this instance by the time a year had elapsed it had spread to the liver and the patient eventually died. If you have a malignant tumor in your pancreas, you should see an excellent surgeon, have an operation and get that damn thing taken out. You shouldn't procrastinate or waste a year seeking alternative treatments.

"Deepak," I told him, "you have to be very careful when you're dealing with the lives of patients."

But at least some of what Deepak has said about Ayurveda has been misunderstood. He has always been very clear about the fact that there are medical issues that require treatment by accepted Western methods. The patient with the neuroendocrine tumor was not one he consulted on, for example. If he had, he probably would have given him the same advice he has offered to many other patients. "Here's what I recommend," he explains. "Talk to your oncologist or liver specialist and follow my recommendations only with their approval." Wise advice indeed.

It also turns out that there are lots of herbal and Ayurvedic medicines that have significant and detrimental interactions when they are taken together with medicines that are prescribed by physicians practicing Western medicine. Years ago I reminded him of a patient of mine, who had undergone a liver transplant. He was on a drug called tacrolimus. A friend told him that grapefruit juice had miraculous health benefits, so he started taking it. Guess what? That was dangerous advice. There is a well-recognized interaction between grapefruit juice and the way tacrolimus is metabolized. This advice could have caused an extremely serious reaction.

Deepak assured me that when one of his patients has lung or colon cancer, for example, he always tells them to follow the recommendations of their oncologist. The advice he gives to them, he points out, is not in lieu of the therapy, but rather something that will help them with the surgery or its side effects. He has been very careful about making sure they discuss everything with their primary care physician and their specialist.

But I also listened to my brother. And indeed, over the years I have taken a number of Ayurvedic medicines and supplements and found some to afford singular relief.

21

Birth Pangs

Deepak

Chopra family celebrating Gotham and Candice's wedding, New York, 2002.

WITHOUT MEANING TO, I BECAME a walking culture clash. Limousines met me at the airport to take me to a luxurious home in the Hollywood Hills or a president's palace in South America. I would absentmindedly run my hand over the butter-smooth leather seats and wonder how to explain Vedic knowledge to the person who had invited me — an actress who had become the highest paid in the world, the head of the Czech Republic, a Hollywood mogul, the prime minister of wherever I had landed. I was a version of them all, a spiritual seeker who presented the image of success to the world.

These two impulses came to a head in a book that brought me more attention than any other I've written, *The Seven Spiritual Laws of Success*. It argued that success must be measured in fulfillment, not in terms of external rewards. The world's wisdom traditions map the road to inner fulfillment, and if you distill them to their essence, they speak about the value of achieving what you wanted by relying on spirit. This became the Law of Least Effort in my book, and I was consciously separating it from Christianity, even though Jesus said, "Ask, and you shall receive," while also not referring to Maharishi, who said, "Do less and accomplish more." The Law of Karma derives from a worldwide belief going back many centuries that good actions lead to good results, bad actions to bad results. I didn't have to quote the New Testament when it said, "As you sow, so shall you reap."

This effort to treat every wisdom tradition as equal was ingrained in me. I have no tolerance for dogmatism (I love the bumper sticker that reads MY KARMA RAN OVER YOUR DOGMA), and in our house when I was growing up, the kids running in and out were Hindu, Muslim, Christian, and Parsi. But more than an ecumenical impulse was at work. I refused to write about anything I had not personally experienced. Everyday life didn't deliver the sort of inner experiences I wanted. Being with Maharishi did. The key is that gurus break down boundaries. They aren't your best friend; they may look like wise grandfathers, but in Maharishi's presence the situation could be maddening, exhausting, boring, and sleep-inducing as well as inspiring, joyous, and full of light. He and I had a special relationship, and when I told that to a man who had been in the movement for decades, he laughed.

"That's the big secret," he said. "Everyone thinks they have a special relationship with Maharishi — because they do, in here." He pointed to his heart.

For all the tales spread about spiritual charlatans, no one knows what it's like to enter into intimacy with a guru until they actually do. Externals are misleading. Imagine trying to explain love to someone who has never felt it. Ah, but he's seen people who are in love. They are distracted, moody, fixated on their beloved, and torn between laughing and crying. You can't talk to them any more than you can talk to a madman. None of this behavior comes close to the actual experience of falling in love. From personal experience I can testify that the cauldron of emotions that is love comes close to the inner turmoil aroused by a guru. Arrows that aren't romantic can still pierce the heart.

After one ridiculously exhausting and ultimately pointless campaign to establish a thousand Ayurveda centers in America — Maharishi wanted it accomplished over a weekend! — an old TM hand shrugged his shoulders.

"It's always been like this," he told me. "Wherever Maharishi is, you find pure creation and pure destruction. It keeps you churning."

This accords with Indian texts that speak of the spiritual disciple's lack of equilibrium: "always stumbling but never falling."

When my relationship with Maharishi came to a crisis, the cause was petty, and to me it seemed unreasonable. I had returned home from a speaking tour to find Maharishi fuming. A TM group in Australia had promoted my lecture with a poster that sized my picture larger than his. Even though I had no control over publicity in a country thousands of miles away, he was cantankerous and put out. Clearly the messenger was about to be punished for the message.

"You need a rest," Maharishi said. "You've been working too hard. Stay with me for a while." Any disciple in a Buddhist parable or the New Testament would have rejoiced over the opportunity to spend a year with the master. But I had seen Maharishi put more than one important member of the inner circle out to pasture this way. "Rest" was code for being shunted aside.

I sidled away from his offer. My workload was heavy, I explained, but it had been like that ever since I became a doctor. Taking a year off posed risks for my livelihood if I stopped seeing patients and giving talks. Maharishi listened impatiently, shuffling his silk shawl from shoulder to shoulder as he did when he was agitated. He insisted. I resisted. Then he laid down an ultimatum. Either I would stop touring for a year and stay by his side, or I could leave. It was a stunning moment, and many threads began to unravel.

Without another word I got up and walked out of the room. The next day, as I heard later, Maharishi looked around and asked in bewilderment, "Where's Deepak?" He didn't understand that I had taken his ultimatum seriously. In his mind, shifting from one mood to the next was perfectly normal. I had to live with the guilty knowledge that I had been wanting to run away for a long time.

I felt hemmed in. I wanted a creative outlet while the movement wanted an official spokesman. Which showed just how much I had become a walking culture clash. It wasn't America that rejected India; it was the American in me. At one point I met the aging Laurance Rockefeller, one of the legendary five Rockefeller brothers. Their mother was an intense Buddhist (her private collection of Buddhist art was unmatched in the West), and Laurance, I believe, was the one son who carried on her spiritual interests. He was soft-spoken and gracious when we met, and he let me do almost all the talking.

At the time, I was seeing at least six people a day, so I don't recall exactly what we spoke about. But as I was leaving, he said, "You're going places. You'll go even farther if you aren't hanging on to the Maharishi's coattails. Cut yourself loose."

The remark startled and tempted me at the same time. In my mind my relationship to Maharishi was pure. It mirrored the classic guru-disciple role that I had read about in ancient texts. A guru has the right to put the disciple through any number of tests. In one classic story a disciple is told to build a stone hut by hand. He labors at the task, and when he is finished, the guru looks at his work and says, "Now move it three feet to the left."

I had spent seven years moving the hut.

When I couldn't get Rockefeller's advice out of my head, it wasn't because I was ready for another impulsive leap. I began to see a pattern inside me, and it wasn't about cutting and running. Instead, I somehow was tuned into a silent voice, and when I made sudden changes, it was as if I observed myself going through them. My behavior spoke of someone who had reached a breaking point and needed to be free. But inside I felt calm, and the freedom I needed was inexplicable. It was the soul's absolute freedom, which is why Krishnamurti was right to call it "the first and last freedom."

The paradox was that by walking away from Maharishi in 1992 I became more certain than ever of my spiritual mission.

Every self is built like a mosaic, piece by piece, with the baffling difference that no matter how many pieces fit in, you still don't know what the picture is supposed to be. I spent years constructing a version of Ayurveda that fit Western needs, but somehow the picture wasn't about Ayurveda. It was about reinventing the human body. I briefly touched upon this theme, and now it needs to be fully expanded, because in or out of the TM movement, stark realities have to be faced about what healing and medicine actually mean.

In my forties I could see, from an experienced doctor's perspective, the rifts and tears that were happening in old conceptions that once seemed completely true. Treating the body as a machine, which is fundamental in science-based medicine, is a flawed approach to begin with. Machines wear out with use; our muscles and bones grow stronger with use. Machines are assembled from separate working parts. The human body is a holistic system that is organically knit together. Every cell is a microcosm of intelligence inside a macrocosm of intelligence. What excited me about Ayurveda was that it could be the opening wedge for changing the whole system, but reinventing the body had no chance as long as mainstream medicine stood in the way.

Doctors, being highly trained technicians, scorn the kinds of objections I am raising as metaphysics. To them, healing the body requires no philosophy. What counts are results. But I knew that the results were fraying around the edges. One glaring area was heart disease. Every year around half a million heart patients undergo CABGs (coronary artery bypass grafts), pronounced *cabbages,* to correct their clogged arteries. Sometimes the patient is a middle-aged man who feels chest pain, the classic symptom of angina pectoris. More likely he has no pain but becomes winded with mild exertion or does poorly on a treadmill stress test.

He has friends his age who have undergone bypass surgery. They tell him that it hurts like hell for a while, but modern surgical techniques have you up and walking within a day of the procedure. The surgeon pulls a clean artery from elsewhere in the body, usually the leg, and once it is sewn into place, the heart receives an unimpeded flow of blood. The procedure entails few risks; it's almost become a midlife rite of passage. So with some anxiety but lots of reassurance, the man has the surgery, paying on average $100,000. A whopping amount, he thinks, but his life is at stake.

It would upset the apple cart — and should — if he knew that only 3 percent of patients are actually given a longer lifespan by having bypass surgery. From the start it was conceded that CABGs should be used in limited cases, chiefly when the heart's left descending main artery is so blocked that the risk of a fatal heart attack is high. Otherwise, the procedure largely improves only the patient's symptoms, and within two months the newly implanted artery has become clogged again, unless the patient has undertaken drastic lifestyle changes — and few do, since after all they expect the surgery to cure them.

Having your chest cracked open is frightening, and there is another procedure that doesn't involve open-heart surgery: coronary angioplasty, where a tiny balloon is inserted in a coronary artery and inflated. The point is to expand the constricted blood vessel and allow better flow of oxygen to the heart. Usually a stent is inserted to keep the vessel open. As of 2006, 1.3 million angioplasties were done annually, at an average cost of around $48,000. In actuality, however, balloon angioplasty and stents benefit only 5 percent of patients in terms of added longevity. The procedure carries the very real risk of dislodging some of the hardened plaque inside the clogged artery. When even a speck of plaque floats free, it can lead to stroke or a pulmonary embolism (a clog in the lungs' blood supply).

On all fronts the number of unnecessary surgeries and office procedures performed every year is in the hundreds of thousands — the precise number is a matter of controversy. Drugs are far less efficacious than they are advertised to be. In recent years the distressing news came out that the most popular antidepressants, all of them billion-dollar drugs, are little more effective than placebos in mild to moderate depression. That's only the latest instance of a continuing story as miracle drugs lose their gleaming reputation.

Add to this the number of people who die from mistakes that doctors make. Between 1999 and 2012, as I am writing, the number of deaths related to medical error rose from nearly 98,000 to an estimated 200,000, making it a leading cause of death in this country. Such errors are caused by various factors, including overwork and the increasing complexity of modern medical procedures. Yet ironically, doctors are trying to avoid mistakes by running endless tests. In the period from 1996 to 2012, the number of visits to the doctor that resulted in five or more medical tests tripled, and the number of MRI brain scans, often for no valid medical reason, quadrupled.

Raising such objections irks the medical establishment, and I knew that if I continued, my credibility would suffer. There is only so much criticism that a system can bear before the whistleblowers are punished. When I was the public face of Maharishi Ayurveda, my role was so far outside the mainstream that such worries were irrelevant. Fortunately I could carry my shield with me. If I was satisfied with being a New Age doctor, perhaps *the* New Age doctor, everyone would know the niche I belonged in. America is tolerant of eccentric lifestyles and oddball beliefs. At a science-fiction movie the audience laughed when one character turns to another and says, "I think Jerry's channeling Deepak Chopra?" I laughed, too. But the silent pressure inside me wouldn't stop.

Rita was anxious about my abrupt move away from TM, but she has wonderful powers of adaptation. Our friends in Boston were still mostly Indian doctors, and if they raised their eyebrows over Ayurveda, fame was another matter. It brings a golden silence when the phone rings and your wife says, "Deepak, it's Madonna," or anything in that vicinity. Thanks to their mother, Mallika and Gautam grew up in a stable, loving home with complete insulation from the media machine that chewed around the fringes of my life. Maharishi himself took an enigmatic attitude toward me. I was invited to celebrate his birthday every January, and if he had any medical problems, his relatives called me up as if I were his private physician. The consternation that was felt in the TM movement after I left was what you'd expect when a true believer turns into an apostate. The biggest favor that anyone had ever done for me was Maharishi's offer to let me move beyond the conventional drugs-and-surgery lockstep. This only increased the great letdown over my change of heart. As the old guard closed ranks in the aftermath, some privately understood my situation. Most didn't.

They were captivated by everything implied in the phrase "enlightened master." No matter what Maharishi told them, he could never be wrong. But I kept alive in my heart a belief that was the ultimate in culture clashes: Maharishi knows what I'm doing. This is my dharma, and he wants me to follow it.

There is no separation between dharma and Dharma, the big and the little. If an individual heeds a calling, the same voice speaks to everyone. We each play a different role, but on the wider front we evolve together. I sincerely believed that, and my driving ambition to change mainstream medicine hardly made me isolated. By 1992 the facade of drugs-and-surgery medicine was crumbling. Pioneering researchers like Dean Ornish at Harvard were proving that lifestyle disorders were treatable without drugs and surgery. Heart disease, diabetes, prostate cancer, breast cancer, and obesity account for three-quarters of American health care costs, and yet these are largely preventable and even reversible by changing diet and lifestyle.

No one with a conscience could stand by idly and watch American medicine become a crushing financial burden to millions of people when the alternative was inexpensive and available to virtually everyone. A study published in 2004 in the leading British medical journal, *The Lancet*, followed thirty thousand men and women on six continents and found that changing your lifestyle could prevent at least 90 percent of all heart disease. Yet for every dollar spent on health care in America, ninety-five cents goes to treat a disease *after* it has occurred.

We exist, the Vedic scriptures say, to undergo a second birth in the name of spirit. In a strange way, that would happen for me only if I attended the birth pangs of a new medicine.

If reinventing the body was still a faraway hope, reinventing myself was an urgent need that had to be met right away. My private practice had been sold off. It wasn't feasible for me to return to endocrinology as if nothing had happened over the past seven years. Is it possible to have an interrupted destiny?

Strangely I don't remember discussing alternative medicine with Sanjiv at any length. It just became my department, as he had his. He was worried, as I recall, about people being drawn away from the proven treatments of mainstream medicine. He was echoing a familiar establishment warning that has never held water with me. It implies that a doctor like me, working outside the box, is encouraging his patients to forgo "real" medicine. Sanjiv wasn't saying that. But he was definitely a rising figure in establishment medicine. To an outsider we were a strange pair: one brother becoming an authority on a single organ, the liver, while the other brother devoted all his attention to treating the whole person.

It wasn't clear that my viewpoint would ever be accepted. Meanwhile Sanjiv had thrived by being a specialist. If you want a real mouthful, how about "holistic gastroenterologist"? If I could have shown Sanjiv that such a thing was possible, he might have had his doubts eased. (We had no way of knowing that twenty years later there would be doctors using that title.) Why shouldn't the gut, which is what gastroenterologists treat, be intimate to every cell of the body? Our gut feelings are chemically transported from the abdomen to the brain. It can't be a one-way telephone line.

On the one hand, the stark contrast between us was undeniable. I fervently believed in the holistic approach and valued farseeing visions of the future. Sanjiv believed in the scientific method and trusted that it would be just as strong in the future as it is today. These were matters of deep conviction. On the other hand, there was no real rift between us because we trusted each other. I trusted Sanjiv's scientific knowledge; he trusted that I would never say a word to harm a patient, no matter how far-fetched my thinking got to be, as viewed by the very skeptical mainstream. I'm sure he was as amused as I was whenever an irate doctor would challenge me and be floored that I actually knew conventional Western medicine. (Did I keep a strain of my father's determination when the British ignored him on grand rounds, such that he had to be twice the doctor they were?) At a certain point I told my book publishers to leave off the MD after my name. It wasn't worth it to keep proving to other physicians that I had respectable credentials. (Later on I also gave up charging patients for consultations, just to avoid any hint of profiting from their distress through false hope.)

Somehow, a niche was made so that I could put all the pieces together. At an Ayurveda conference I met Dr. David Simon, a neurologist who was also a trained TM teacher. We hit it off immediately, beginning when he came out unexpectedly with his favorite Jewish doctor joke:

Two Jewish friends are arguing over when a fetus becomes a human being.

"I know," one says to the other, "let's ask a rabbi."

They find a group of wise old rabbis and pose their question. The rabbis put their heads together and find an answer.

"A fetus becomes a human being," they said, "when it graduates from medical school."

David was a human being by rabbinical standards. He was whippet thin, with glasses, an enthusiastic demeanor, and a sharp mind. He had devoted more years than I had to a deep study of alternative treatments, and they had become his passion. He also knew what it was like to be an outsider in his field.

"If you're interested in consciousness," he said, "the last person to ask is a neurologist. They're all brain mechanics."

David had begun meditating long before we met, when he was a seventeen-year-old anthropology student at the University of Chicago, focusing on the role of shamans in non-Western cultures. In a short time he invited me to do grand rounds at his hospital in San Diego, one of several run by Sharp HealthCare. I spoke about the mind-body connection to some assembled doctors and staff. Some were interested, and I was already accustomed to the hints of professional disdain from the rest.

Then invisible wheels began to turn. The CEO at Sharp, Peter Ellsworth, had a sense of where medicine should be moving. He foresaw the merging of mind, body, and spirit into an integrated whole. David recommended that he visit Lancaster. Ellsworth brought two colleagues, and their experience was positive. He felt that I might be the point man he was looking for. When they got back home, Ellsworth proposed to Sharp that they open a center for "integrative medicine," a term barely used at the time. So far as we knew, this was the first center of its kind in America. I was to be the director. David, who was chief of staff for Sharp Memorial Hospital, would be codirector.

On the face of it the proposal was too radical to get past the complex politics of a major hospital. But CEOs are persuasive, and I told Rita that we had been pulled out of limbo. My new job was as a salaried doctor for a health care provider twenty-six hundred miles away.

Since the children were still in school, we would have to be a bicoastal family for a while, and I recall that the new house in La Jolla gained its furnishings gradually, a sign of caution on Rita's part. There was the human factor, too, since Rita had endured with good grace the role of grass widow to a husband who traveled three hundred days a year. The Little India in Jamaica Plain had become a Chopra colony in the nice suburbs. Rita had friends and family around her in Boston —her sister Gita and her husband had also come over by now after ten years living in England.

For two years, during the time that Sharp funded our center, David and I had complete freedom to teach patients how to go beyond being healthy. The mind-body connection, we were convinced, made well-being possible, and well-being meant a fulfilled life. At first the patients were mostly drawn from readers of my books. But David was the engine behind changing their lives in practical terms. They were taught meditation and yoga. They learned about breathing exercises and diet. They were given personal programs based on Ayurvedic body types; even the mantras were personalized, using ancient formulations from the *Shiva Sutras*.

David had followed the same arc that I had. His enthusiasm for Ayurveda, stoked by the revival Maharishi envisioned, turned to frustration with the movement's constraints. At the Sharp center he could soar, with only one small difficulty: We didn't make money. Outside the people who had read my books, nobody seemed very interested. The other doctors at Sharp were mostly dismissive as well.

I deeply admired David's way with sick people, which was both precise and caring. Once, at an alternative medical conference, a patient in her forties was presented with intractable inflammatory bowel disease. She had almost constant pain and had been recently hospitalized. I was in the audience while David was on the panel. Each practitioner was asked how he would treat this woman.

The Western doctor said that he would attack her inflammation with steroids and proceed with higher doses and various medications depending on how her symptoms responded. The acupuncturist on the panel said that her condition depended on several meridian points that he could treat. The naturopath said that he would begin by examining her mouth, since he suspected that she might have mercury fillings in her teeth.

When it came to David's turn, he offered no treatment. He came down from the dais and sat next to the woman, taking her hand.

"Tell me, when did you first feel this pain?" he asked. He had detected something elusive about her complaint. At that moment she burst into tears and unfolded a dreadful story. Her young son had died in an automobile crash, and soon after she began to feel abdominal pain. This increased when his estate fell into the hands of lawyers, whose unending battles led to enormous expenses. It had gotten to the point that she could no longer afford her mortgage payments, and meanwhile, her sense of shock and grief was overwhelming.

David listened to the woman, and as her rage and sorrow poured out, something cathartic seemed to be happening. David looked up at the audience.

"You all see what we should be treating? Her body is inflamed, her emotions are inflamed. These pent-up energies have made her sick."

With some irony I can point out that all the things we prescribed in the early Nineties — diet, exercise, yoga, meditation, etc. — are now covered by Medicare in various parts of the system. More importantly, it has become accepted that the mind-body connection is vital. Hundreds of genes are affected by lifestyle changes. But when we reached out to other Sharp doctors — referrals from them would have been very helpful — one attending patiently explained, "Around here, we call what you do hucksterism."

After two years David and I left Sharp, no doubt to their general relief, and we opened our own center in La Jolla. It was a point of pride that the place would be called a center for well-being. We intended to practice higher medicine. Like me, David fervently wanted this dream to come true. He also pointed out that it wouldn't hurt if we prayed for more customers.

The first time that most Americans learned of my existence was when I appeared on Oprah Winfrey's television show in 1993, invited to talk about "the new old age." The concept itself wasn't new. Longevity has been a sliding bar since civilization began, with people living longer for all kinds of reasons. These were external for the most part: between them, better sanitation and the rise of modern medicine played the biggest part. But the new old age is different. It came about through rising expectations. Instead of expecting to become useless and feeble around age sixty-five and then going downhill from there, the baby boomer generation reframed old age as an extension of middle age, and possibly better. It would be an active time, when physical and mental vigor is maintained, and free of the stresses of work, retirement would be fulfilling in a new way. People could be free to live the way they had always wanted to.

Oprah didn't need me to tell her audience things that were already being widely publicized. To a statistician the new old age was just a matter of creeping numbers. Baby boomers had already experienced unprecedented good health; their parents and grandparents had lived longer than previous generations. There was no reason for the trend not to continue. But I leaped in to promote a more radical idea. Aging is a mirror of a person's consciousness. There is no biological imperative that cuts off human longevity. Our bodies respond to every kind of input, and the more consciously you respond, the better you will age.

Because aging hits home with everyone eventually, my idea caught on. Oprah was at the height of her influence — she also has a deep streak of spiritual seeking, as I discovered when we became close allies almost twenty years later. By having me on her show, she turned my book *Ageless Body, Timeless Mind* into a bestseller. Many more people began to shout "Deepak!" when I was walking down the street. But for me the whole issue of aging was the opening wedge in my campaign to reinvent the body.

It was the perfect issue. Although everyone ages, no one dies of old age per se. It's not a disease. At the moment of death, more than 99 percent of a person's genes are intact, and if a key system of the body hadn't broken down (typically the respiratory or cardiovascular system), more than 90 percent of cells could keep on living. It isn't even clear why aging should exist. The theory that we are genetically programmed to age is countered by the theory that genes become distorted through accidental mutations or outside damage.

Finding an answer to the mystery wasn't necessary, however, if I could outline a way to keep aging at bay. A famous saying of the Buddha is that when you find yourself in a burning house, you should find a way to run out as fast as you can; you shouldn't wait to find out how the fire started. Aging is like a house burning down very, very slowly, at about 1 percent a year, the average rate that people age after they turn thirty. One thing is certain in the midst of much uncertainty. Every cell participates in how we live, eavesdropping on every thought, empathizing with every feeling, taking the brunt of every decision. No part of the body gets to opt out when you take a drink; alcohol permeates the system. Yet so does depression; so does stress.

Conscious aging makes the best sense because the new old age is already a change in consciousness. It's good for ninety-year-olds to go to the gym to keep their muscles from wasting away. This fact has always been true. What has kept ninety-year-olds from lifting weights or running on a treadmill was psychological: The whole thing was unthinkable, risky, or just not done. Aging as a whole can be reduced to one thing, the feedback loop that governs your body every minute you are alive. You receive inputs from every direction; your body responds. Into this automatic exchange you can either insert yourself as a conscious agent or not. Reinventing the body comes down to inserting yourself as the body's leader, the force that issues orders based on life-supporting beliefs.

As I write, the radical concept behind *Ageless Body, Timeless Mind* has become commonplace — almost. The envelope keeps moving. It has been well established that positive lifestyle choices, in terms of exercise, diet, meditation, and stress, cause profound biological changes, down to the level of our genes. One physical marker for aging is the fraying of telomeres, which are the tail end of each chromosome. In young people telomeres are long; they cap the chromosome like the period at the end of a sentence, keeping its structure firmly intact. In older people telomeres appear to be shortened, as if the genetic sentence is left dangling. The more a chromosome frays, the more a cell shows signs of aging. Yet it would seem that meditation increases the enzyme telomerase, which is critical for maintaining long telomeres.

By bits and pieces, the inevitability of aging has been pushed back. But that's not good enough. What's the point of reinventing the body? To regain something invisible, precious, and elusive: writing your own destiny. Each of us should be the author of our own lives. We are not meant to let biology write our destiny, or even karma. Karma is the accumulation of unconscious acts that return to bite us. Inject consciousness into the whole system — mind, body, and spirit — and the same thing always happens. Human beings become more human and acquire a sense of deeper being. Aging won't be solved until the most outrageous idea from ancient India turns into a cliché. The idea was expressed by perhaps the most eminent sage of Vedanta, Adi Shankara, when he wrote that "people grow old and die because they see others grow old and die."

To make this declaration less outrageous is within reach. But someone as persistent as me has to kick over the apple cart. All kinds of cherished beliefs need to roll into the gutter. The belief that aging is a curse, that the individual has no control over it, that dementia and memory loss are a roll of the dice, that cancer is looming in your future and cannot be stopped — all of these outworn beliefs are already shifting. They need to roll into the gutter once and for all.

God has been strikingly absent from this story so far. My life could be rewritten exclusively in terms of God, but that would require shifting gears. Everyone lives in more than one dimension. At the level of everyday life we pay attention to events around us. It matters deeply how we earn a living, raise a family, and handle the challenges that come our way before they become crises. Yet at a second level we intuit that something very different is going on. If you see your life only in terms of everyday events, spirituality can seem totally alien.

Put yourself in the place of a shepherd, stone mason, or farmer on the northern shore of the Sea of Galilee two thousand years ago. You climb a hill in the hot sun, joining a group of listeners whose eyes are fixed on a wandering rabbi sitting under a tree. He begins to tell you certain truths that he has heard from God: Providence takes care of a fallen sparrow, so how much more will Providence take care of you? You are beloved of your Father in Heaven. Store up your goods with him — that is far better than storing up wheat in a granary. The birds of the air do not toil. The flowers in the field do not spin thread, and yet Solomon in all his glory is not arrayed as they are.

You would be inspired, but wouldn't your reason rebel at the same time? Farmers who don't store wheat over the winter will starve. Weavers who stop making cloth will go naked. The mystery of doing as Jesus advised — being in the world but not of it — isn't peculiar to Christianity. Every spiritual tradition poses the same mystery, which comes down to surviving in this world while obeying the demands of a higher world.

The mystery can be solved only in consciousness. Is it possible to be aware of who you are in the world while also knowing your soul? I spent a long time too spooked about the whole issue to write about it. It was a point of pride that I didn't use the words "God" or "soul" in the first few books I wrote, simply to escape their associations with organized religion. When a wit said, "God handed down the truth, and the Devil said, 'Let me organize it,'" I laughed and nodded my head. But once you cross over from mind and body to spirit, there's no hiding behind terminology. God has to be faced.

One thing meditation shows, very directly and personally, is that the mind is more than a daily stream of thoughts and sensations. There is a deeper level of silence, and every spiritual tradition points to it. Silence in itself seems to have no value, but it has overwhelming importance if it is our source. "Be still and know that I am God" only makes sense if stillness is pregnant with the divine. Christ echoes the Old Testament with "the Kingdom of Heaven is within." This implies that you can pay attention to your life from a superficial level of the mind or from a deeper level. I became fond of a simple term, "second attention," to describe this deeper level of awareness.

You could ignore every event in my life if you went from first attention to second attention. Every question would change. Instead of "What's happening?" you'd ask "Why is it happening?" Second attention is about the meaning of life. First attention is about labels: name, address, college, occupation, bank account, spouse's name, and so on. It's not just in America that these labels, which are attached to externals, are considered the right way to make your life meaningful. India, especially the new BRIC-certified India (after it joined fast-growing Brazil, Russia, and China as an enviable economy), espouses the same values.

Materialism is a path. There is nothing immoral about this path, but as a substitute for God it reaches the wrong destination. I once saw a multipart documentary on public television about the search for God. The host, who was very British and civilized, went around the world asking people if they had experienced God. He sat in gospel church pews and swayed with the music. He interviewed an African tribesman who had not only experienced God but could also draw his picture (the deity has a spiky black beard and very bushy eyebrows). In the last episode, after his trek is over, the host asks himself if he believes that God exists. He does, because his definition of God has shifted. God is whatever you worship with deep devotion. Therefore, to a rabid soccer fan, soccer is God.

As I was blending into American culture, the animus against a foreigner who dared to challenge Christianity was disturbing—and misplaced. (I've written two sympathetic books about Jesus.) But the real issue came down to showing the difference between religion and spirituality. America is supposedly the most churchgoing of developed nations. Up to 40 percent of the population attends religious services as compared to around 10 percent in England and Scandinavia. But churchgoing, as I saw it, was primarily social. It showed that you conformed to the norm of religious worship, which means that you accept groupthink. You define God secondhand, through revelations given to prophets and teachers many centuries ago.

Spirituality is firsthand experience. It takes you on an inner journey from hope and faith to real knowledge that no one else has spoon-fed you. For someone who holds this view, my timing was right. Millions of Americans were quietly walking away from the faith they were brought up in. They no longer believed in the old verities, yet their yearning for God and the soul hadn't died — far from it. Being on the spiritual path, trying to wake up, seeking God in odd corners of the world, perhaps even aiming at enlightenment, all of these became far more common and acceptable.

It was very annoying to religionists, the churchmen and rabbis who didn't want the altars to topple. Yet I found pockets of openness, sometimes at places you'd expect, like the liberal divinity schools of the Ivy League, but also among some Jesuits. They wanted to sharpen their reasoning about Christ by understanding my logic. After several years speaking to every kind of audience, I set down my best argument in a book: *How to Know God.*

God, I began, has pulled off the neat trick of being worshipped and invisible at the same time. He is accepted without direct experience, feared without knowing if he even exists. So in practical terms one must ask if God makes a difference. If you followed a believer all his life with a video camera mounted on his shoulder and an atheist outfitted the same way, would their lives turn out any differently? In other words, God can only be known by the difference he makes. Drinking water ends thirst. Eating food ends hunger. What does worshipping God do for you?

To begin with, the question is too broad. God is defined as infinite, eternal, and all-knowing. Such a being cannot possibly be a white-bearded patriarch sitting on a throne above the clouds. We must begin by throwing out the popular image of God as a person. Every religion gives a place to an impersonal God who is pure essence or presence. The Holy Spirit in Christianity, Shekinah in Judaism, Shiva in Hinduism — every spiritual tradition names God in his spiritual essence as light or Being. But this brings us to a new problem. Pure essence has no form, and being infinite and all-pervasive, it can't be limited by images or thoughts in our minds.

To solve this dilemma, God has been shrunk to our size; the infinite became finite. We project human form onto God, but that is just a crude example. What we project at a subtler level is "God made in the image of man." This isn't blasphemous; it's just how the nervous system works. We experience love as human, and that gives us a way to view divine love. We want to feel safe, so we project God as a protective father. Our need for order instead of chaos makes us project God as a law giver. There are as many ways to project God as there are people. Still, God mirrors the needs of human beings in general. We need to feel safe, protected, and loved, and so God has those attributes.

For 90 percent of humanity, this is enough. If you add the intricate laws and rules that the ultraorthodox live by, whether Brahmins in India or Hasidic Jews in Brooklyn, God is already known. There is a kind of feedback loop, a circle that embraces God, creation, and the worshipper. The world you see, the deity you worship, and the person you see in yourself all fit together. Until history tore the circle apart — the Holocaust, a century of world wars, the Bomb, and totalitarian dictatorships made it impossible for believers to see how a loving, protective, very human deity could preside over a broken world and let evil run amok.

The only answer was to stop projecting, to rise above outworn conceptions and experience God's essence directly. Most of *How to Know God* was devoted to mapping out how a seeker might exchange religion for the spiritual path. The fact was that the West knew very little about Eastern paths. The Buddha had a halo of prestige about him, but the rest of India was sacred cows and religious riots. I felt a deep urge to modernize Eastern spirituality, putting it in everyday language that could fit modern lives. This time I went much deeper than I had in *The Seven Spiritual Laws of Success*, trusting that the reader wanted to reconnect with the divine out of a yearning for meaning.

Moving from a book to real life provided many jolts. I was sure that everyone harbored the same yearning, but to get at it one had to pass through a great deal of pain and pathos. I gave a course on how to know God in Agra, literally under the shadow of the Taj Mahal, and one evening I held a sobbing American woman in my arms for two hours as she released what seemed like a lifetime of sorrow. My role wasn't to be her therapist or her guru. We were on the same journey, and my only advantage was that I had the peculiar talent of looking out the window and describing the passing scenery. Dante's *Divine Comedy* begins with a man in the middle of his life lost in a dark wood. I had no authority to tell anyone what the absolute truth was, but I felt compelled to say, "We are all in the woods, and I can see up ahead. Believe it or not, we are safe."

To me this was evidence of God in motion, an invisible guide that shows the way from darkness to the light.

22

Miraculous Cures

Sanjiv

Sanjiv, with his immediate family, celebrating his daughter Kanika's
wedding to Sarat Sethi, New Delhi, 2001.

I REMEMBER A STORY MY FATHER had told Deepak and me about a patient of his, a man suffering from lung cancer. This patient, a wealthy businessman, heard about a Filipino faith healer who claimed he could perform bloodless surgery to remove the tumor.

"He insisted on going to see him for treatment," my father explained. "He was rich, he could afford it, and there was nothing I could say to change his mind."

When the man returned he said he felt much better, and he proudly showed my father an X-ray of his chest — and the lung mass was gone.

"Oh, come on," I interrupted. "The guy is a charlatan. He gave him an X-ray from somebody else, and fooled the patient."

My father continued his story. "A few weeks later he came to see me because he wasn't feeling well. We did a CAT scan and, unfortunately, we saw that his tumor had grown. There was nothing more we could do for him."

Any physician can understand this patient's desperation. I suspect we've all known patients like this man, who had tried the best and latest of Western medicine and it was not enough to cure him. His desperate need to believe that there was something more that could be done to save his life caused him to reach out to a charlatan. Unfortunately the world of medicine is riddled with people who are willing to sell a promise for a price. There is, for instance, a vast, multibillion-dollar supplement industry that exists without any scientific evidence that most of its products do any good at all. So at least for a time, when I heard terms like "alternative," "complementary," or "holistic medicine," I wondered about their value. And I worried that patients who might be helped by modern medicine would instead put their faith — and their money — into these unproven techniques.

But I have always been willing to listen and learn. In my current position as faculty dean for continuing medical education at Harvard Medical School, I lecture to as many as fifty thousand health professionals annually. I'm also the director for a dozen courses each year, which means at the beginning of a conference I'm the first person to step up on the podium to welcome the attendings and give them a sense of what they are going to learn over the ensuing days. I also deliver a number of talks at each conference and make sure that I incorporate the latest evidence-based medicine. What are the studies that show that this particular medication works in this situation?

In the introduction and welcome I always say the following: "I'm delighted to see you here. I'd like to begin by all of us taking a moment to reflect on our medical profession. Justice Louis Brandeis once said there are three attributes of a profession and for the medical profession the first attribute is that there is a specialized body of knowledge, known primarily to its practitioners. The second attribute is that we practice medicine more for the benefit of society than for personal gain. So, all of us make a decent living, some specialists make a pretty handsome living, but we're all here to serve society. And the third attribute is that society in return grants the profession great autonomy. Hence, we make the rules. How many years of medical school? How many years of internship or residency? How many years of fellowship to be a cardiologist? What about relicense, recertification, CME credits? So these are the three seminal attributes.

"Some years ago, Dr. Dan Federman, who was the first dean of CME at Harvard Medical School and one of my mentors, added a fourth: For the medical profession there has to be an encompassing moral imperative. And I would like to take the liberty of adding a fifth attribute: Learning. Learning is a lifelong privilege, not a process; pursue it with passion and zeal and see the wonder fill your world. We are in the most amazing profession where it is our moral obligation, our duty and dharma to engage in lifelong learning. We learn every single day, and we do so from textbooks and conferences, from medical journals. We learn from our colleagues, our students, the nurses and pharmacists we work with, and importantly we learn from our patients."

As I learned, for most people in the medical profession learning never stops. It's invigorating. It becomes a passion. Although it did take me some time to accept the value of complementary medicine. Admittedly Amita embraced it long before I did. Ayurveda had always intrigued her; she wanted to study it. But she never had the time she needed. As she explained, "I was so busy taking care of my patients that I really didn't have the time to go into any of the Eastern disciplines. But I finally got the opportunity when I was at a large group practice in Cambridge. We had as many as five hundred physicians at fourteen different health centers, and we decided to incorporate alternative medicine, which later came to be called complementary or integrative medicine.

"We started a pilot program at the Cambridge Center, which included chiropractic, massage therapy, and acupuncture, and we integrated those with modern medicine and it was so successful many other centers quickly adopted it. That was a beginning.

"I'm retired now, and when I think about it I would still love to integrate *Pranayama,* breathing techniques, into treating various physical disorders. For example, I'd like to teach breathing exercises to children with asthma."

The difficulty for a physician like me, who practices and teaches evidence-based medicine, is that there are many instances of dramatic benefits that can't be explained by modern science. These are the so-called miracle cures that can't be explained by the knowledge we have and often can't be replicated. We know there is something more than we can fathom taking place.

I once had a patient with metastatic osteosarcoma, a terminal bone cancer, who developed an infection in the lining of his lung. We suspected he had a condition called empyema. There was a spirited discussion among the students, interns, residents, and attendings whether we should even treat this patient or just make him as comfortable as possible and explain the dire situation to his family. And if we did treat him, should we use antibiotics, put him in the intensive care unit, insert a tube into his chest to drain the pus? We decided that since he likely had an infection, we would insert a chest tube to drain the pus and give him powerful antibiotics. We inserted a needle into his pleural space and sure enough out came pus. He did indeed have empyema. We treated him with broad-spectrum antibiotics.

The infection cleared up; he got remarkably better and he was released from the hospital. And then the miraculous happened: Six weeks later he said he felt great, his skin color looked healthy, and he was no longer in pain. A bone scan revealed that the multitude of metastatic cancerous bone lesions had disappeared. He was indeed cured, somehow. He was alive years later.

There is no good scientific explanation for this. The hypothesis is that it's somehow related to the empyema and that his body, in its infinite wisdom, mounted an impressive immune response to fight the infection, and while doing so eradicated his bone cancer. What is the actual mechanism? How did it happen? We really don't know. There is no clear answer.

I had another patient with chronic hepatitis C, which can evolve into cirrhosis or liver cancer. I happen to be considered one of the leading experts in America about this disease and have participated in clinical trials, written many chapters, and presented at prestigious national symposiums to educate physicians about this viral disorder. I've seen hepatitis C in all of its guises. It is a disease that at the time I saw him could be cured in about 20 percent of cases, but it took a year-long treatment with weekly injections and lots of side effects, some of them pretty debilitating. There are several options when it comes to treatment. In this case the patient had a mild disease, as ascertained by his liver biopsy. Given the 20 percent success rate and the difficulty of treatment, he and I decided the best course of action was to monitor him closely and simply wait for further advances in treatment. Over a ten-year period his disease remained stable; he was not drinking alcohol and he consumed at least two cups of regular coffee a day. So a conservative approach was very reasonable.

Then this patient went on a vacation to Martha's Vineyard and apparently was bitten by a tick. When he was admitted to the ICU he was deathly ill. He had a high fever; he had profound anemia, a high white cell count; and his red cells were being destroyed. He was seen by the infectious disease consultant, who correctly diagnosed Lyme disease; ehrlichiosis, a bacterial infection transmitted by a tick bite; and babesiosis, a malaria-like syndrome. It turned out he had all three conditions! This is most unusual and was testimony to the skills and acumen of the infectious disease consultant. He received transfusions and the treatment recommended by that doctor.

A week later, as his condition improved, I received an e-mail from the intern taking care of him informing me that this patient's liver enzymes, which had been abnormal for the past decade, were now completely normal. That was interesting, I answered, but suggested we repeat the liver enzyme test to make sure this was not a lab error. If they came back normal again we would send off a test called hepatitis C virus RNA by PCR (polymerase chain reaction).

Three weeks later the patient came to see me. When he walked into my office he looked quite healthy.

"Dr. Chopra," he asked. "What happened to my test? I hope my virus level didn't go up."

I looked at all his computerized results and, lo and behold, the PCR test, which can detect even minute traces of the virus, came back negative.

"This is a miracle," I said. "It's possible you're cured. I want to repeat this test in three months and again in a year, and if both those tests come back with no trace of the virus, then you're cured."

That is exactly what happened. A year later his liver enzymes remained completely normal and the most sophisticated possible test for the hepatitis C virus detected nothing. When I told him that he no longer needed to see me, he smiled.

"Dr. Chopra, is this a new treatment for chronic hepatitis C? Get a tick bite, get deathly ill, survive, and wipe out the virus?"

"No, that's not the treatment," I said. "But clearly there is an important clue here." What likely happened is that in fighting the three life-threatening infections at once, his immune system had waged a majestic interferon response and wiped out the virus. The basis of scientific evidence is that something is repeatable, and this certainly was not. In answer to my initial statement, there are no studies that showed this would work. It just did.

For me personally, I have also experienced things as a patient that I can't explain scientifically. I have a herniated disk in my back as well as mild spinal stenosis. At times it got extremely painful, and to deal with it I was receiving an epidural of Novocain and long-acting steroids, treatment that provided substantial relief—but only for about a month.

In 2008 I was giving a lecture to four thousand clinicians in Houston. After answering several questions I stepped down from the podium to speak with several physicians who had stayed behind to ask me some follow-up questions. Before the last person asked his question, he noticed that I was looking extremely uncomfortable. I explained to him that I was experiencing pain in my lower back and I really needed to sit down. I invited him to join me in the faculty lounge for lunch.

When I told him about my lower back problems he offered to show me a form of Chinese exercise that he had used successfully with many patients. I was polite—I had been to some of the most knowledgeable doctors in the world and they had not been able to afford much relief. I certainly didn't expect any better results from him. But right there and then, on the floor of the convention center, he demonstrated what he was talking about: Basically it consisted of bending at the knees and doing a hula hoop–type maneuver, left to right twenty-seven times, then right to left twenty-seven times. It had to be twenty-seven times, he explained. I tried it then and there and to my surprise felt significant relief. I made it part of my daily routine. I do it in the morning and on occasion in the evening—and since that time I have seldom needed an epidural. I have no idea how it works. There are no studies that show this mechanism, but it does work for me. I have a saying: I don't argue with success.

The late South African writer Lyall Watson defined nonsense as "that which from our present state of mind is unintelligible." Five hundred years ago, if someone had predicted man would one day walk on the surface of the moon, it would have been considered blasphemy, and the man might have been hung in the public square. I've learned that just because we don't have a mechanistic explanation doesn't mean something is hogwash. The relief I experience from back pain tells me that every day.

So I listened to my brother speaking and I read his books and I paid attention to what he was saying. I think Deepak has a lot of wisdom and is able to connect the dots. He has also met and collaborated with some amazingly brilliant scientists and has been more than willing to conduct a dialogue with his critics. He ardently seeks out folks who are supportive of what he is saying as well as his fiercest critics. I very much admire that. I understand what he is saying in somewhat simplistic terms, and I recognize that it has become important for health care professionals to have an understanding of his philosophy.

There is one place where we are in complete agreement, and we should be, because it was the strongest lesson taught to us by our father. All medicine should start with the healer — whether it is a physician, a nurse, a nurse practitioner, an Ayurvedic physician — listening to the patient. It starts with listening to their story, listening with heart as well as mind. As he often said, every patient has a story to tell. In 2012 a lecture I had given often was published as the book *Leadership by Example: The Ten Key Principles of All Great Leaders.* The basis of the lecture and the book is that each letter of the word "leadership" stands for a memorable quality common to great leaders. The first one, *L,* stands for listening.

A colleague of mine, Dr. Richard Mollica, who heads the Harvard Program in Refugee Trauma, was treating a Cambodian woman who was suffering from myriad common symptoms, but he couldn't seem to find the root cause. Finally he asked her to tell him about her family. She broke down and told him that most of her family had been massacred by the Khmer Rouge. She and one of her sons had somehow managed to survive and come to America — and then her son had died tragically. My colleague had asked; he had listened with compassion. He held her hand and they prayed silently. After many years and scores of doctor visits, none of which had helped her, her healing began that day.

In Western medicine we haven't learned how to listen to our patients. We ask the basic questions: How do you feel? What hurts? How long have you felt that way? We ask the same questions: What's the major complaint, history of past illnesses, current medications, social history, occupational history—and then we write it all down and recommend a procedure or prescribe a pill. We may never find out that the reason they have those severe headaches is because they are tense and deeply depressed. We stop the headaches, but we have not addressed the root cause.

This is changing. My colleagues are beginning to understand they have to bring the patient into the conversation. Give them an opportunity to tell their story, and it may help discover the root cause. Western medicine has some wonderful medicines, and we are able to affect some miraculous cures. But too often in the past we relieved the symptoms without addressing the cause. That's not a good fix.

This certainly is evidence of the impact Deepak and a number of the practitioners of complementary medicine, among them Dr. Dean Ornish and Andy Weil, have had on the medicine I practice. I sometimes think about the state of American medicine when we arrived in this country and how it has changed since then. We've moved a great distance from almost purely curative to recognizing the physician's role in prevention. The medical community has become much more open to at least examining alternative therapies. There is little doubt that Deepak has been a leading force behind the acceptance of these once ignored or even ridiculed techniques. In the late Nineties I was working with my colleagues, Martin Abrahamson and the chairman of the Department of Medicine at Beth Israel Deaconess Medical Center, Dr. Robert Glickman, planning our annual Update in Internal Medicine conference. Dr. Glickman suggested we invite Deepak to speak, and every year since then he's spoken as guest faculty and delivered the keynote address. It's often a two-and-a-half-hour session on spirituality and healing, or a new paradigm of understanding consciousness and how it can affect the way we deal with our patients. Many of the attendees consider it one of the highlights of the course.

As faculty dean for continuing education it is my honor and privilege to have 275 postgraduate courses come under my jurisdiction. In aggregate we reach out to seventy thousand clinicians each year. We are continually changing our presentation to reflect the evolution of medical thinking. A few years ago, for example, we added to our curriculum a new course directed by Dr. David Eisenberg that probably would not have been offered by Harvard Medical School in the past. This course is entitled Healthy Kitchens, Healthy Lives and recognizes the critical importance of diet in good health. The attendees learn medicine but are also taught to cook healthy meals. Indeed, half of the syllabus provided consists of recipes. They are encouraged to try them out and also share them with their patients.

For me that is simply additional evidence that modern medicine willingly embraces any techniques that can be proved to be beneficial to our patients. As Deepak has acknowledged, none of these mind-body systems are meant to be a replacement for sound medical practice, but rather they are meant to be integrated into our lives where they might help prevent or ameliorate disease.

There is no substitute for sound medical practice, based on a vast body of research, evidence, and experience. The musician Steven Tyler wrote about me in his autobiography. I received a call one day from his primary care physician, who asked if I'd ever heard of Tyler. I hadn't. He explained that he was the lead singer of Aerosmith, that he was very famous, and that he was sick.

When I went out into my waiting room he was surrounded, not just by other patients waiting to see me but also by our staff. I took a detailed history, performed a physical examination, did some tests, and a few weeks later performed a liver biopsy. A few weeks later I diagnosed him as having a mild case of chronic hepatitis C. At that time the success rate for treatment — which consisted of six months of interferon injections — was pretty abysmal, no more than 10 percent. The appropriate decision at that time was to defer treatment. I explained to him that there was substantial research into this disease being done in many academic centers throughout the world to refine treatments for his condition, and I recommended we wait and he see me on a yearly basis. Then I told him in very clear terms that he absolutely could not drink any alcohol.

"We have two eyes," I said, "two lungs, two kidneys and —" and before I could finish the sentence he interrupted.

"Yeah, Doc. One liver."

"You can't even look at alcohol." He was the rock star who couldn't drink. I would monitor his condition as we awaited refinement in treatment. He had the advantage of being perfectly fit; there wasn't an ounce of fat on his body. Over several years the treatment had evolved; with the strain of hepatitis C with which he was afflicted we had now reached a juncture where there was a 40 percent cure rate. This is how medical science marches forward.

"Steven, we should try the treatment now," I suggested. "Neither time nor the Ganges waits." There were side effects to consider: He would not be able to tour because he would need to see me frequently to be monitored, especially in the first three months because there were potentially significant and serious side effects. Those side effects included bone marrow suppression, nausea, vomiting, headaches, malaise, fevers, and hair loss.

Hair loss?

He was concerned about that. I assured him that my experience had been that hair always came back, and that it might even come back curly.

The treatment took a year. Steven was a dutiful patient. He kept every appointment. He adhered to the treatment. He was tenacious and handled the side effects very well. To reduce the discomfort I tell my patients they should be vigorously hydrated, try moderate exercise and massage, and then to help with the flulike symptoms caused by interferon, take up to four extra-strength Tylenol a day. When I talk to my patients about the Tylenol they are often astounded. Invariably they tell me that their primary care doctor warned them that Tylenol can cause liver damage and that they should never take it. That's true,

I explained, but only when taken in much larger doses. You can take up to two grams a day, the equivalent of four extra-strength Tylenol. I insist that they record how much they take and when they take it, to prevent them from accidentally taking more than those two grams. Interferon can also cause some befuddlement, a mind fog, and I don't want to chance any of my patients losing track of their dosage. Medicine is a science but also an art. That is the beauty of it.

The only chronic viral infection in human beings that we can eradicate is chronic hepatitis C. Every other chronic virus we can suppress but not eliminate. For example, if a patient had chicken-pox as a child, it lives dormant in ganglion cells and under certain circumstances it can reappear as herpes zoster, commonly known as shingles.

After a year of treatment there was no detectable hepatitis C in Steven Tyler's blood. More importantly, twenty-four weeks after stopping treatment his blood came back again with no detectable virus. In medical terminology this is called a sustained virological response, but what it really means is that the virus has been eradicated. Perhaps the most fulfilling thing in medicine is sitting with a patient who has been saddled with a chronic disease for years and had lots of concerns about cirrhosis, liver failure, the possibility of having to have a liver transplant, the possibly of developing cancer in the liver, a patient who has fought through a year-long treatment with side effects including sleep disturbances, irritability, a mental fog and being able to tell him, "Mr. Tyler, you're cured. You don't need to see me again."

That's an amazing word, "cured," and it is the best of what modern medicine can offer. And while I appreciate the potential benefits of integrative medicine, I will continue to practice the medicine that I know works best.

The best doctors in the world offer compassionate care for their patients whether they are rich or poor. Over the years I've been privileged to care for rock stars, royalty, and famous CEOs, while I've also been privileged to take care of poor patients who had no insurance and for whom I and the hospital I work for provided free care. Some years ago a patient of mine with chronic hepatitis C that had progressed to cirrhosis of the liver and had not responded to treatment asked me on a visit, "Dr. Chopra, do I need a liver transplant, and what does it cost?"

I told him he didn't need a liver transplant at the moment. He might need it down the road and we would take care of it.

He persisted: "But what does it cost?"

I answered truthfully. "Between one hundred thousand and a quarter million dollars."

A week later he returned to the office and told my assistant that he did not have an appointment and wanted to see me for a couple of minutes. He walked in with a big smile.

"Dr. Chopra," he said. "For more than ten years you have taken good care of me. You've done liver biopsies, all kinds of tests, and you even got me three months of treatment from the drug company on a compassionate basis. You've always treated me with dignity and respect even though I don't have insurance." He then handed me a baseball signed by the great Red Sox pitcher Pedro Martinez as well as an autographed photo. He told me he worked part-time in the dugout at Fenway Park and Pedro had walked up to him and said, "You don't look good, you look pale. Is everything all right?"

My patient told him that he had chronic hepatitis C, cirrhosis of the liver, and had failed treatment, and that he might need a liver transplant. Pedro asked him who his doctor was and then signed the baseball and photograph for me. But the best part of the story is that he then turned to my patient and said, "Don't you worry one bit about that liver transplant. If the time comes, I'll take care of it."

Subsequently Pedro Martinez moved to New York to play for the Mets, but kept in regular touch with the patient, who miraculously did well for years.

It's experiences like this that are truly rewarding and fulfilling.

American Dreaming

Deepak

Deepak and President Bill Clinton, Oval Office, 2005. Deepak gave a
lecture to the White House transitional staff.

WHEN YOU TURN AROUND to glance over your shoulder, your children are looking back at you, only now they are adults. My cultural genes were tossed into the air and landed to form new patterns. My son changed his name from Gautam to Gotham so that Americans could pronounce it. He liked the echo of Gotham City, where Batman swoops down from the night sky, just as Rita and I once liked the echo of the Buddha when we named our baby boy. My daughter, Mallika, earned an MBA and married a venture capitalist from India, even moving back there for a time to experience how it felt to live as an Indian. Now much of her energy is devoted to using social networking for furthering goodness in the world. She has inherited her mother's quiet grace.

There is no genome for the soul. If there were, we'd have the real code of life. Gotham is bemused by my soul. As a budding filmmaker, he decided to follow me around for a year, and the result is a documentary entitled *Decoding Deepak*. No father can fathom what his son really thinks about him. Gotham, who narrates the film, begins by saying that people have asked him all his life what it's like to be the son of that spiritual guy. His answer: "It's strange." The person whom other people point to in airports is just his dad, a constant around the house since he can remember.

A celebrity, so it's said, is famous for being very well-known. On the frequent-flyer list of United Airlines there were thirty-seven Deepak Chopras the last time I checked, but when I walk down the street and someone yells, "Hey, Deepak!" I know that I'm the one who should turn around and smile. Opinion polarizes around me. I've won the Ig Nobel Prize for the most ridiculous misuse of science and I've published an article in the *Journal of Cosmology* (the title was "How Consciousness Becomes the Physical Universe," and one coauthor is a chaired professor of physics). I've received book endorsements from the Dalai Lama and been excoriated by a conservative Catholic website as "the dress rehearsal for the Antichrist." Rita was asked a question about *The Seven Spiritual Laws of Success,* a book she hadn't read yet, and she commented with a smile that if the whole world followed me, my family wouldn't. That is a blessing she has created, so why was Gotham left with such a sense of strangeness?

When Gotham was seven or eight, he looked at me out of the blue in an uncanny way and said, "We're having it good this time around, aren't we?" I had a sudden visual image of two old men standing on a bridge in a mountain valley below the Himalayas, superimposed over a suburban doctor patting his son affectionately on the head.

In *Decoding Deepak* his viewpoint begins tongue in cheek. Carrying a handheld camera, Gotham says, "Shh, my dad is meditating." He cracks the door open, and I am found stretched out on the floor roundly snoring. I get my head shaved to enter a Buddhist monastery on a retreat in Thailand, and as I pad away in my monk's robe, I say to him, "Remember to text me." I'm a cell-phone-addicted, middle-aged man tramping through the snow in New York City, hardly looking up as taxis nearly graze me.

Midway through the film, the viewpoint begins to shift, and so does Gotham. He assembles a mental picture of his father that he can absorb into himself. We are back at Haridwar, where I cremated my own father, and I unfurl the scrolls that contain the greetings written by our family ancestors. The fragrance of old souls fills the air. Gotham finds himself choking up, as if some dormant cultural genes have kicked in. He has always gone his own way. He wanted to be a Boston Celtic as a kid, a dream he kept alive even after it was clear that his height was a foot or two shy of what professional basketball players need to be.

In another segment he has coaxed me into his backyard in Santa Monica, where there is a basketball hoop. I look owl-eyed with bewilderment as he points out that he has dressed me in a LeBron jersey while his own jersey is a Kobe. Who? The following dialogue takes place:

Son: Do you have a life purpose?

Dad: Yes, this. (Attempts a free throw facing backward from the hoop. A swish!)

Son: What makes you joyful?

Dad: Scoring everything in life with effortless spontaneity. (Attempts a shot sitting in lotus position. Another swish!)

Son: Do you believe in God?

Dad: I think we're all God in drag.

The swishes were camera tricks (except for one that I made accidentally), but in his sideways journey Gotham has always been paying attention. I don't pretend to see the invisible bricks that are building a self for him. How could I when I can't even see my own?

While Gotham questions every step of the way, Mallika has never voiced any spiritual doubts. He has mastered the image of the carefree guy who loves sports; she is effortlessly kind and caring. If the ancient rishis are right, our relationship goes back hundreds of lifetimes, which makes their journeys as wise as mine — and just as unknown.

Later in the documentary Gotham asks, "Do you really think you can change the world?"

I reply, "Me personally? No. But the world is changing, and I'm part of the transition team."

When I stepped away from the pack, I realized that you can't be a lighthouse without also being a lightning rod. Certain things must be said, as loudly as possible and in public. Become the change you want to see in the world. There is no way to peace — peace is the way. Slowly but surely a separate culture, almost a separate world, has grown up around the truth. As part of the general skepticism that has corroded our confidence as human beings, people bristle at the word "truth," as if a capital T is silently implied. There should be a capital T, I believe, but not for a set of dogmatic beliefs. Instead, there must be recognition of truth as universal. I remain deeply moved by a quote from the great Bengali poet Rabindranath Tagore: "Love is not a mere impulse. It must contain truth, which is law."

Tagore had a famous meeting with Albert Einstein in 1930 inside Einstein's small house outside Potsdam, Germany. It lasted three days, and their conversation became world news, with reporters anxiously waiting on the steps to record what had been said inside. Tagore cut an exotic figure in his white robes and long snowy beard; Einstein wore his professor's suit and wise expression, topped by the familiar whirlwind of hair. Their meeting was billed as a great soul comparing notes with the world's greatest mind. Despite cordial exchanges, neither could reconcile his world view with the other. Tagore spent most of the time arguing that physics had missed the most important thing about creation: We live in a human universe. It is through us that creation lives and breathes. Everything that happens is happening in the mind of God. Therefore God is thinking through each of us, right this minute.

Nazism was already on the rise in 1930, and the Great Depression had begun its devastating spiral. In the midst of terror and hardship, no one was likely to accept a philosophy of divine love. Tagore's prestige, which was immense after he won the Nobel Prize for Literature in 1913, quickly waned. Human beings were too busy savaging one another to think about our role in the cosmos. For me, however, Tagore has been an abiding influence, one of the first to awaken me to a world where you don't have to pray for transformation — it is happening all around you. The transition team is worth joining, no matter how ugly the evening news looks.

I wrote a book called *Peace Is the Way,* which addressed the whole issue of overturning the aggressive behavior that causes wars. People don't wake up in the morning wondering how to kill their enemies, but societies devote blood and treasure to doing it for them. Krishnamurti was once asked how to end war, and he gave a blistering reply. "Sir, war begins in you. Find out why. Until you do, trying to end war is a self-indulgent illusion." It's a sober answer that marks out a rigorous path of self-examination. I wrote in the book that people can develop peace consciousness along an easier path. The essential question is how the nonviolent people in the world, who amount to billions, can acquire enough power to overthrow the power devoted to violence.

The answer lies in three words that begin with the letter *S*, inherited from Sikhism, one of the newest faiths to branch off from Hinduism. These are *Seva, Simran,* and *Satsang.* These three Sanskrit words describe the ideal life of a spiritual person as service (Seva), remembrance of your true self (Simran), and being part of a community based in truth (Satsang). But these things need to reach a critical mass. If practiced by very large groups of people, they unlock a power that materialism can't defeat, as a rock can't defeat the rain even though one is hard and the other soft, as a tree can't defeat the wind, even though one is solid and the other invisible.

A daily way of life is implied by peace consciousness.

Seva: Your actions harm no one and benefit everyone. Seva brings the joy of knowing that your daily actions support life as a whole. You become part of the planet's evolution, not its wholesale destruction. You live in peace with your conscience because you have fulfilled your duty to be a steward of every aspect of Nature, down to the most sacred level.

Simran: You remember your true nature and your purpose for being here. Simran brings the satisfaction of expanded possibilities. You are not limited to being one individual lost in a sea of humanity. You find your authentic self and your authentic truth. A unique path to mastery is opened for you and you alone.

Satsang: You join in the community of peace and wisdom. Satsang brings the satisfaction of having no enemies. You are at home in the world. The rest of the human family is part of you. Older and younger generations are no longer separated by a gap but work together toward the vision of a world without poverty, ignorance, and violence.

None of these are hopeless ideals. Behind the welter of violence that makes headlines, each of these behaviors is a strong trend in the world already. What is most useful is for you, as a peaceful person, to see that you matter and that you are not alone. In 1988 a housewife walking in the rain to get bread in the shadow of the Berlin Wall might have had no idea that her suppressed will to be free was more potent than the wall. What is will compared with bricks, machine gun towers, and barbed wire? Will is an inner force, and that is its secret strength. Will is an aspect of consciousness that cannot be destroyed, and the trend of time must obey consciousness whenever it decides to change.

Which is why I loved making a fool of myself shooting baskets with Gotham in my LeBron jersey. I knew that walls were about to fall.

When he was a teenager and the first Iraqi War was underway, I asked Gotham what he and his friends thought about the whole issue of going to war.

"War?" he said in bewilderment, as if the word didn't compute.

I had arrived in New Jersey at the height of Vietnam and the antiwar movement. I'd seen guns, attack dogs, and tear gas turned against kids not much older than my son was then. But something invisible had shifted. We sat down and had a talk. I discovered that, in so many words, war was inconceivable to him. When asked why she didn't join the antiwar movement, Mother Teresa of Calcutta replied that she would join a peace movement, if one ever came about. An antiwar movement is fueled by righteous anger. A peace movement would look very different. It might need no parades or demonstrations, hardly a voice at all. It is based on the growth of peace consciousness, one person at a time.

Some dreams come true before people realize that they are waking up.

Tell me the meaning of one word, and I can probably tell you how your life will turn out. The word is "destiny." For many people destiny means something like being rear-ended when you've stopped at a red light — an unexpected force shoves you from behind and makes you go forward. For others it's like winning the lottery, one chance in a million that fortune will pluck you out of an ordinary life. Or is destiny simply a mystery that cannot be solved?

Anyone could fairly say that my life has been shaped by destiny.

The Seven Spiritual Laws of Success had a quirky birth. The publisher of a tiny unknown press asked if she could turn a lecture of mine into a little book. The proposed title was *The Seven Spiritual Laws of the Universe* — substituting the word "success" came about at the last minute. The little book did nothing for a year. We all forgot about it. Then out of the blue a business writer at the *New York Times* began an article with the sentence, "If you only read one business book this year, it should be *The Seven Spiritual Laws of Success.*" This, from a newspaper that has reviewed only one book of mine in twenty-six years. (When I had two books on the *Times* bestseller list, my exasperated publisher called up the editor of the book section to ask why neither had been reviewed. The editor's tart reply was, "We review books that people should read, not what they do read.") Within a week the *Wall Street Journal* also mentioned *The Seven Spiritual Laws of Success,* and after that the inexorable American media machine did the rest.

It felt like organized serendipity. It felt like being a bug under a magnifying glass, except that the light didn't burn. The ingredients of destiny do not form a confused jumble; they fall into a pattern. The mystery lies in figuring out what the pattern is showing you. What feels like pure chance might be inevitable. Without coming from India and being trained in medicine, there would be no foundation for all that unfolded in my future. When destiny shapes a life, it arises from the tiniest details. At the beginning of my speaking career, I'd hear muttering that some in the audience couldn't understand my accent. What if the accent had been a little thicker? The whole auditorium might have cleared out. This is more than "everything happens for a reason." As a famous South Indian guru said, "You must realize that the entire universe has to collaborate in order for this precise moment to happen."

The real question is how to respond to destiny, because its influence isn't as simple as being rear-ended at a stoplight. Destiny is a mixture of accident, predisposition, desire, intuition, and the unconscious. You find yourself acting on a whim, only to discover that your whim was one link in an iron chain of events. There is no map to follow. The wisdom of uncertainty enters into the picture, and yet you cannot live your days in total uncertainty.

I can only conclude that destiny is like a spark. In India there's an aphorism that I've carried around in the back of my mind for decades: One spark is enough to burn down the whole forest. The implication is spiritual. Once you are touched by the spark of self-awareness, the forest of ignorance will eventually be destroyed. When I refer to "the process," what I mean is that consciousness snowballs, starting from a speck of motivation and building up, year after year, until you look around, and in all directions what you see is eternity.

I got a chance telephone call in February 2008, just as I was stepping outside the door to go to dinner. A friend at the other end asked if I had heard the news. Maharishi had just died. I sat down heavily, looking out the window at the snow falling over Manhattan, pure white flakes that had no thought of how dirty they would soon be when boots trampled on them. My life is modest compared with that of a man who grabbed destiny by the throat (or was it the reverse?).

As a young college student Maharishi liked to visit the saints, just like my uncle Sohan Lal. One evening he went to a home where he had heard a great saint would be staying for a few days. It was growing late, and in the dark he sat in an upstairs room beside a meditating swami. From the road outside, a passing car's headlights swept the room.

The beams of the headlights fell on the meditating swami, and at that instant, Maharishi recounts, he knew that he had met Guru Dev, his great spiritual teacher. Within a year of graduating from college in 1942, the young Mahesh had become a monk working as his master's assistant — as it turned out, Guru Dev was the most eminent spiritual figure in northern India. Maharishi's future was set in place by a glance.

His funeral took place in India, although I didn't go. For a flashing second the glare of fame returned to him. I saw photos of the body arranged in lotus position surrounded by acres of flowers. Word came to me through old TM connections that Maharishi had anticipated his passing. Two weeks before, he made a conference call to all the TM centers declaring that his life's work was done, that he had accomplished what needed to be achieved for the good of the world. It is part of the lore of the enlightened that they undergo a conscious death, known as *Mahasamadhi*. The meditative state is samadhi, to which the word "great" (maha) is added, indicating that wherever the enlightened one goes when he shuts his eyes, this time he will never return.

In my family we wonder if my father took mahasamadhi. The night that he died, when he entered my mother's sickroom to kiss her good night, she thought it was like a final farewell. Or maybe not. Indians, like everyone else, love to fit events into sentimental patterns, the difference being that our sentimentality is spiritual.

Thinking back I see that it was never an either/or decision to walk out on Maharishi. A short while later, after I had definitively moved on, he called the house in Boston. Rita answered the phone. Hearing that I wasn't home, Maharishi told her that I had to reconsider coming back. He would give me "the whole kingdom." I would be his spiritual heir. Taken aback, Rita minced no words and told Maharishi that I had no interest in his offer. Eventually Maharishi caught up with me on the phone, and I repeated in my own words what she had said. When he was finally convinced that I had left for good, Maharishi's last words were, "From now on, I will treat you with indifference." One could hear an iron gate come down.

I was unconsciously following the same maverick pattern that crops up again and again in my story. Unconsciousness is the true enemy of destiny. Awareness is its greatest ally. Destiny awaits everyone, because each day brings a spark, which is to say a clue about higher reality. The best are clues that indicate something better than everyday life: a sudden surge of joy, a feeling that you are safe and cared for, a sense of lightness in the body, a sudden intimation that time is standing still. The poet Wordsworth called these interruptions in daily existence "spots of time," but they could be called spots of eternity. Our minds yearn to know the truth. Sometimes that means that the clues coming our way are painful, because untruth hurts, if only at a subtle level. Feeling drastically unsafe, alone, uncared for, and empty is not just a pain that you wish would go away. If you take the longest view, such feelings are hints that you have taken a wrong turn; negativity is a detour from the truth. Destiny helps anyone who picks up the clues that the soul strews in our path. The fact that accidents are mixed with desires, obstacles with open roads, is irrelevant. Reality uses whatever it takes to get people back to dharma, the force that upholds life absolutely.

An article about my work that *Time* magazine published in 1996 began with the story of a doctor, a Florida internist, whose daughter, coincidentally, had been the publicist for *Quantum Healing.* He had leafed through the book but put it aside. Its message was not for him. Then he was diagnosed with advanced, inoperable prostate cancer. The standard hormone therapy at the time had a patient survival rate of about two years. According to *Time,* "He retrieved the Chopra book, which claimed that meditation, the right diet, and a Westernized version of Hindu mysticism could prevent or even reverse disease. [The man] became a Chopra maniac. He meditated thirty minutes a day, prayed for five, and recited Chopra's ten Keys to Happiness . . . and then he got well. The tumor disappeared. Tumors sometimes do that, of course. But he knows who to thank. 'My professors would be turning over in their graves,' he says with a grin. 'It's a shame more doctors don't listen to him.'"

Will there ever be a time when such a story becomes normal? If so, it won't be because of "a Westernized version of Hindu mysticism." Instead, the body will become transparent to the mind. The intent to heal will not be blocked; a way to reach into the diseased area will open at the touch of consciousness. I've called this vision reinventing the body, because as long as the body is a dense package of matter, we will be moving in the opposite direction, making consciousness appear to be no more than a ghost in the machine.

My medical partner, David Simon, never stopped pushing the standard model of the body, and at the Chopra Center he worked on all fronts. He went deeply into Ayurveda. He proved to the California licensing authorities that our brand of medicine met the standards for courses in continuing medical education (CME) that doctors take annually to recertify their boards. Slowly but surely the legitimacy of integrative medicine advanced. David tirelessly taught courses at the center, wrote books, and kept faith that a new model of healing was emerging.

All diseases are multifactorial, and often when you reverse the detrimental factors in their lifestyle, people get better. You can't have physical well-being in someone who is unemployed, for example, who spends all day stressing about what he's going to do with his life. He's going to get angry at his situation, perhaps drink or eat too much, even smoke a cigarette to calm his nerves. Well-being requires a balance between all the elements of a person's life, but society poorly prepares us to think in holistic terms. David used to say, "If the only tool you have in your toolbox is a hammer, then everything looks like a nail."

At the Chopra Center he and I set out to provide people with a complete toolbox. We particularly focused on what we considered the three pillars of ancient wisdom, Ayurveda, meditation, and yoga, which were broken down further into the areas of physical healing, emotional well-being, and spiritual awakening.

The signature course that we created is called Journey into Healing, which is intended for the general public as well as health care professionals. It opens the door to the mind-body techniques that can affect their own and their patients' lives. When the course was certified by the American Medical Association for twenty-four hours of CME credits, we felt that a historic breakthrough had been made. CME credits are a stamp of professional approval. We had arrived. Journey into Healing continues to expand. At first it was taught by David and me, but now there are eminent guest speakers who cover everything from lifestyle prevention for heart disease to mind-body therapy during pregnancy.

Once the gates opened, there was no limit to what we wanted to teach. The Seduction of Spirit is a week-long dive into meditation; Perfect Health is a five-day course in which participants consult with our doctors for personalized care, then spend the next few days learning the essentials of mind-body care for themselves. Several years ago it became clear that calling ourselves holistic made little sense if any us-versus-them thinking existed. Walls had to be knocked down so that every field could see the light in every other.

From that impulse a yearly conference sprang up called Sages and Scientists. Ten years ago anyone who called himself a scientist would have circled anyone who called himself a sage like two wary cats. The very word "consciousness" wasn't a respectable field of research. Being conscious was a given. It meant that you weren't asleep or knocked over the head. But creeping gradualism is a powerful force. The thing that crept in was my old ally, quantum physics. If the basic building blocks of the universe were invisible, mere possibility waves in an infinite quantum field, how can anyone maintain that any part of the physical world isn't affected?

The question can't be begged, but people did, all over the place. Doctors weren't the only guilty parties, although most would shake their heads to hear that the placebo effect, for example, might have quantum roots. How? Through the well-established observer effect. In the standard model of quantum physics, there must be a way for invisible possibility waves to turn into physical objects. The observer seems to be the pivot point. Insert an observer into the system, and suddenly the infinite quantum field undergoes a transformation (known as the collapse of the wave function) by which all the properties of matter emerge.

Applying this knowledge to medicine meets with strong resistance, as I well knew. But there were dog fights over such newborn concepts as quantum biology as well. The moment Sages and Scientists was announced in 2009, I was astonished to discover that a considerable number of farseeing scientists were willing to risk derision by coming forward. In small groups that kept gaining in strength, consciousness had become a genuine topic of research. Holes in all kinds of standard disciplines needed filling. Quantum biology set out to build a solid chain from the quantum field to the cell. Derision wasn't a threat in the safe setting we provided, although an open door was left for skeptics.

The mind field, which was once as dangerous as a minefield, is blossoming. The wait has been long. Max Planck, the German physicist who is credited with starting the quantum revolution more than a century ago, also foresaw the mind field when he made a mysterious remark: "The universe knew that we were coming." Consciousness, in other words, is at least as old as the universe. To me these aren't rarefied speculations. Human beings exist in three states: unconscious, aware, and self-aware. Years ago, while I was still at the VA in Jamaica Plain, I treated a patient with chronic obstructive lung disease. He was on a ventilator for two weeks before we finally managed to wean him off so that he could breathe on his own. He had a hole in his throat from the permanent tracheotomy that had been performed to assist him in breathing the next time his blood oxygen fell dangerously low.

Two days after he was discharged, I walked into a store down the block from the hospital and saw this man smoking a cigarette through his tracheotomy. The power of addiction was at work, certainly, but there was something more fundamental. If you light up your fifth cigarette of the day without thinking, you are doing something unconsciously, as is the nature of habits. If you see yourself lighting up the cigarette, you are aware of what you're doing. But self-awareness goes further; it says, "What am I doing to myself?" Posing questions, reflecting on your behavior, taking your life seriously — these are all self-aware behaviors. The promotion of self-awareness is how we can take the next leap in well-being. The fact that the universe is self-aware makes the argument even stronger. It would mean that to live unconsciously is like throwing away our cosmic birthright.

In the midst of all this progress, which was very heartening, the starkness of medicine's life-and-death choices arose. In 2010 David began to have a defect in his sight that led to a minor automobile accident. He decided to go in for a CAT scan, and looking at it, he made a self-diagnosis.

"I have sad news," he told me on the phone. The scan had found a fast-growing malignant tumor known as a glioblastoma. The irony of the diagnosis was extraordinarily painful — a brilliant neurologist having a fatal brain tumor. His disease, as far as we know, has no specific risk factors. But later I learned that as a child David and his sister had both received heavy doses of radiation to treat enlarged tonsils. No one at the time recognized the long-term effects of radiation exposure (the Fifties saw groups of tourists being bused from Las Vegas to watch atomic bomb tests from a "safe" distance, protected with only sunglasses). As an experimental treatment, some children with swollen tonsils had their heads put under an X-ray machine that radiated the tonsils until the swelling shrank. I can't escape the thought that David's brain tumor was related to radiation; it was telling that his sister had died of cancer.

As an Ayurvedic physician trained in Western medicine, David used the best of both worlds to fight his disease, including surgery. He knew that the tumor was largely inoperable, but he was haunted by the prospect of leaving his family behind. He long outlived his prognosis, which originally gave him only a few months. He fought with his usual optimism and joy. Before his first operation, he told me, "I hope more light comes in than goes out."

David continued to teach courses at the center even when he was nearly blind as a consequence of his treatments. On January 31, 2012, he died. He referred to death as taking off a temporary disguise. I did my best to write a tribute, although his passing was an incalculable loss: "David has been my friend, partner, teacher, trusted colleague, and younger brother for more than twenty years. He touched my heart, influenced the way I think, and expanded my spirit. David approached life from a place of unlimited possibilities. His wisdom, courage, and love will continue to inspire all of us for decades to come."

I'm a compulsive notetaker, and in one notebook, under "Chinese fable," I see an old entry about a spiritual master who is walking in the evening with a disciple.

The master is discoursing on a familiar theme, that the world is an illusion. Reality hides behind a mask, sending us invisible messages.

We will never be free until we tear the mask away and see what lies beyond.

The disciple is baffled and resistant. "I believe in the world that I can see. Why shouldn't I? It makes no sense to say that the world is a dream."

The master replies, "It will, once you realize that you are the one being dreamed."

This parable comes to mind because the dream that we all read about, the American dream, is actually a massive defense against dreaming. In America materialism rules, and this country's enormous advances in science refute any spiritual nonsense about life as a dream. Walk in front of a bus and you'll see how much of a dream it is. The oldest texts on this issue date back to the Upanishads of ancient India. As America sits at the head of the world's banquet table, it must be annoying that anyone from the Third World, as it was once called, would defy the very notion of materialism.

But it's not a question of defiance. It's a question of what is. Every day offers a chance to find out what's real; every day offers a chance to reinforce illusion instead. When you go to sleep at night, your dreams aren't a threat, because even if a tiger is about to eat you, you will wake up from the dream. If the ancient rishis are to be believed, they must show us how to wake up from the dream we call waking existence.

Despite its faith in materialism, America is the best place to wake up from that dream, even better than India in its glory days of the great sages. An untouchable who cringed in the dirt as the Buddha passed by would have been astounded to have the Buddha stop to bless him. His heart might have burst; his whole existence could have changed in an instant. But for ages the turn to spirituality was forced, because the alternative was miserable poverty, ignorance, disease, and the rigidity of social authority. In America, where everyday existence is lavish by comparison, the choice to be spiritual isn't forced. It's free, and free choices are the ones that we can abide by for a lifetime.

Every year I return to an inspired book called *I Am That,* by the South Indian guru Nisargadatta Maharaj. He was always poor, and he had a completely unschooled background. As a boy plowing the family plot behind a bullock, Nisargadatta had spiritual yearnings. He sought out a teacher, and the teacher said, "For you the path is simple. Whenever you are tempted to think that you are a person, remind yourself, I am That." Nisargadatta took his teacher at his word. In the Indian tradition, "That" (*tat*) is the unnamable essence, the infinite source that cannot have a name since it permeates everything. It is sometimes called the unknown by which all things are known.

Nisargadatta went home and kept reminding himself that he was not anything that has a label. If he started to think "I am a man," "I am a poor farmer," or even "I am a person thinking this thought," he would stop and substitute the same phrase, "I am that." Extraordinarily the seed must have fallen on incredibly fertile ground, because without any other practice or discipline, he became enlightened. Devotees began to gather, and spontaneously this illiterate peasant uttered wisdom of the highest order.

India may look like a country of credulous believers, but Nisargadatta had more than his share of cranky, cantankerous followers. His book mostly consists of conversation with querulous visitors. One of them says, "I don't see anything spiritual about you. We are just two old men sitting in a room waiting for someone to bring us our lunch."

To which Nisargadatta gives an answer that brings tears to the eyes: "You see two old men waiting for lunch because that is your reality. It is made of your experience and memories. Such a reality is closed and private. My reality isn't private. It is built from infinite, unbounded consciousness, and fortunately it is open to all."

The visitor isn't mollified. "If you live in such a superior world, why do you bother being in mine?"

Nisargadatta replies, "Because it brings me joy to help others wake up."

There is really no arguing with that, and no one has ever reached a higher reality, a better world, or God except through the joy of living.

Misery isn't a stairway to heaven. The miracle is that waking up never ends; it's a universal experience. "The process" is about nothing else. The real impediment is drowsiness.

One of the most brilliant opening sentences I've ever read is in a book that had its heyday in the early Eighties, *A Course in Miracles:* "This is a course in miracles. It is a required course. Only the time you take it is voluntary." The soul doesn't push anyone to abandon their reality. The time must be right for each person.

Everyone has moments when the veil falls away. We sense that there is more to life than a random existence presided over by physical laws. The universe is purposeless according to physics, yet no one can tell us how purpose entered into the scheme. Living things can't survive without a purpose, even when it is as primitive as needing to eat and breathe. Human beings have gone much further. We exhibit all the qualities that physics insists on excluding from the cosmos: meaning, beauty, truth, love, intelligence, and creativity. Science can delete those things from its data, but to turn around and say that the data explains who we are strikes me as delusional.

I've gone head-to-head with numerous defenders of materialism, and the most blinkered ones insist that everything that makes life worthwhile — love, beauty, creativity, and all the rest — must have a physical explanation. This "must" is their blind spot. It took centuries before Kepler discovered that the planets in the solar system move in elliptical orbits because under the Ptolemaic system, which viewed geometry as divine, planets "must" move in a perfect circle. For people who pride themselves on rationality, scientists can become overheated when you encroach on their belief in "must." I've seen Nobel laureates sputter with rage at the proposition that the mind creates the brain and not the other way around.

The argument usually starts with smiling confidence on their side, and a hint of pity for me. They declare that no one can possibly doubt that the brain creates the mind. Just look at any brain scan showing different areas of the brain lighting up when thought occurs.

I reply that radio tubes light up when music is played. That doesn't mean that radios compose the music. This meets with a shrug. So

I press the point. I say that the brain can't possibly create the mind because brain cells don't think. People think. There's a big difference. My opponent looks put out. It's ridiculous to state that brain cells don't think. That's all they do, if you are talking about the cerebral cortex, or higher brain.

Really? I point out that the brain is fueled almost entirely by glucose, or blood sugar. The chemical makeup of blood sugar isn't very different from sucrose, the sugar we spoon into our coffee. Is he saying that a sugar cube can think? This doesn't even get a reply. Signs of sputtering are beginning to show.

If the sugar in my coffee can't think, I say, then show me where in the chain of chemical events inside the body did glucose start to think. In fact, where in the vast scheme of cosmology, going back 13.7 billion years, did the step occur that created consciousness out of totally unconscious ingredients? A challenge like that usually brings the sputtering to a full boil. But materialism can't abandon its "must." Falling back on the demand that mind must come from matter, science tends to kick the can down the road. All the mysteries that cannot be answered today will surely be answered sometime in the future.

If that turns out to be my opponent's final position, I say, "In the meantime, you believe in pure animism." Animism is a quality of so-called primitive religions that attributes spirit to trees, totems, and ancestral shrines. If science is attributing mind to sugar molecules, isn't that the same thing?

Before Einstein there were explorers of consciousness who made earthshaking discoveries; they were Einsteins in the inner universe. One of their most fundamental discoveries is stated by Lord Krishna in the Gita when he declares, "I am the field and the knower of the field." There's a double meaning here. God is addressing a great warrior on the field of battle, which has a literal meaning. But he also means the field of life and, beyond that, the field of divine existence. In a few words, Krishna points to who we really are: multidimensional creatures, spanning the physical, mental, and spiritual fields.

Even simpler are two words from the Vedas, "*Aham Brahmasmi*" ("I am the universe").

To get to that point, to be able to look at yourself as a multidimensional creature, you must creep out of drowsiness. Drowsiness is a comforting state, and we can't be naïve. Many people don't want to wake up; others will vituperatively defend the reality they espouse. But the dream comes with built-in defects that cannot be ignored. I've already touched upon two — war and the aging process — but the greatest defect is subtle. We don't really know who we are. Human beings are engaged in forgetting their true nature as privileged children of the universe.

People tell me that the age of the guru is past. The new age demands that each person become their own guru. I'd be happy if that happened, but how? Someone in India posed the same question a hundred years ago. His name was Aurobindo Ghose, and he probably lived the most exciting spiritual life of anyone in history. Aurobindo grew up at the height of empire, and he was sent in the 1880s to get a proper English education. But faced with prejudice at Cambridge despite his brilliance, Aurobindo returned home. He became a fighter for Indian independence, and when the British jailed him once and threatened to do it again, he fled to the French-controlled state of Pondicherry. He renounced politics for spirituality, which he pursued as Sri Aurobindo, one of the most widely known gurus in the first half of the twentieth century.

An extraordinary idea was seeded in Aurobindo's mind. Human beings, he declared, were not a final product. They were in transition, moving toward the goal of God-consciousness. He was zealous to bring his extraordinary idea to the world. Everyone must be told that, like a gentle rain, higher consciousness is descending on the world. Its influence will change humanity forever.

This story comes to mind because I look at myself and wonder: For all my sense of being a separate person running after his own dreams, perhaps I am merely being raised by the same wave of consciousness that Aurobindo spotted. I'm a cork on the ocean who thinks he's a yacht. It would come as a relief, actually, to know that I am not a final product, that this jerry-rigged construction I call a self is transitional. There's something tragic about finding a dried-up cocoon that has fallen to the ground, knowing that a butterfly will never emerge from it. Every butterfly automatically gets a second birth when it breaks free of the larval stage and spreads its wings in the sun. Human beings must choose. As long as you have a personal stake in the world, you can't have a second birth in spirit. You will be too busy dealing with the aftermath of your first birth.

Ever since I became a professional outsider, I've tried to expose the outworn beliefs that hinder the next leap in consciousness. Science holds out hope. If our species keeps evolving, maybe we'll become more conscious. Spirituality holds out certainty. If we become more conscious, we'll keep evolving. A dying planet waits with bated breath to see which course we choose. My stake in the game is clear. When "I am the universe" isn't a religious belief but a statement of fact, all my personal dreams will have come true. I will then be ready to break out of the cocoon. What kind of light will greet me?

Sri Aurobindo died in 1950, and very soon miracle stories swirled about him. At one stage he was furiously occupied writing about his vision for mankind. He churned out thousands of pages in relatively few years. A disciple recalls walking in during a heavy monsoon rain. Aurobindo was sitting at his typewriter before an open window, the curtains blowing wildly. The rain should have come in all over his desk, but instead, the desk, the typewriter, and Aurobindo himself were completely dry.

There are a few parallels with him that send a hint of a shiver. His father, like mine, was a doctor who went to the British Isles for his training. Aurobindo tried to become completely Westernized before India reclaimed him. And I certainly know what it means to write furiously. But if it should happen that I'm sitting in front of an open window with my laptop and the rain begins to blow in, so far it's very likely that I will get wet.

24
....

Peak Experience

Sanjiv

Sanjiv on a golf pilgrimage to St. Andrews, Scotland, 1997.

IN 1985 AMITA AND I went on a pilgrimage to the legendary Amarnath Cave in Kashmir. This is a famous pilgrimage made by many thousands of Hindus every year. One has to traverse the most challenging mountain terrain to arrive there. There is a renowned Shiva shrine at the cave. This is situated at an altitude of 12,756 feet. According to legend, the god Shiva explained the secret of life to his divine consort, Parvati, at this sacred site.

Getting there was indeed quite difficult; the cave is located in a narrow gorge high in the mountains. We had to travel the last few miles to the cave on horseback, led by a mounted guide. The path we followed up the mountain was only about four feet wide. There is no railing, no protective guard of any type, and at various points it is a sheer drop of several thousand feet. For some reason the horses like to walk along the edge, as far as possible away from the mountain. It is quite dangerous and very frightening. We arrived at the Amarnath temple in the early evening. Amita went inside the inner sanctum and prayed for a long time; for her this whole journey was much more spiritual than it was for me. For me it was more of a beautiful and scenic trek. By the time we finally were ready to begin the trip back to our camp it was about midnight.

We were physically exhausted. As we started back Amita noticed a large tent. It belonged to a couple of large families, and the folks inside were very welcoming to us. Amita thought it might be a good idea to stay in that tent for the night. No way, I said, asking her to step outside. It had rained earlier in the day and the sky had been covered by ominous clouds. But now the storm had passed, the clouds had disappeared.

"Look at the stars," I told her. "What a beautifully brilliant night it is. In fact, I have never seen stars this luminous. They look so close it feels as if you could extend your hand and literally snatch one out of the sky. The clouds are all gone. That's a message. God has lit our path and you and I can walk now. We will go back to our base camp, where we have a comfortable room and beds with warm blankets."

It was at least ten miles back. Amita looked shocked.

"You're nuts," she said. "It's too dangerous."

But I was insistent. It was too dangerous to ride the horses through the gorge at night, I decided, so instead we would walk. Our guide would lead the horses. We set out at about two in the morning. As I walked along this narrow mountain path, beneath a starlit sky, I thought, oh my God, we really are a long way from Boston.

We walked through the night and the following day, arriving at our camp in the early evening. At one point during our arduous journey, I looked nervously over the edge at the sheer drop.

"If you fall," I asked the guide, "how far do you go?"

"Sir, you would go all the way to America."

We laughed at the image that answer had evoked, of course, but clearly I understood the thought. It really was a long journey from India to Harvard Medical School — although definitely not as dangerous or as quick as the one from the mountain to the valley below. Certainly it was as good a metaphor for the distance we had traveled in our lives as I had ever heard.

My path, my dharma, has taken me from my home in India to America. In our upbringing Deepak and I had been taught to respect and uphold our dharma. Very early in my career it had become obvious to me that my dharma is to teach, to be a mentor. It is not something that I believe I should do, it's something that I cannot help but do. I had so many amazing role models. I was fortunate to have a good memory. I could embellish my teaching with many mnemonics and alliterations.

In the last two decades I have received numerous teaching awards. Deepak and our parents and family were very proud and supportive of all these accomplishments. In May 2012 I was honored by the National Ethnic Coalition of Organizations with the Ellis Island Medal of Honor, which is given to a number of people each year in recognition of their contribution to America "while continuing to preserve the richness of their particular heritage." When I received this award I began wondering how different my life might have been if I had stayed in India or returned there after completing my education. I suspect every immigrant thinks about this at some point.

Had I stayed in India I have no doubt I would have lived a comfortable life. I would have had the same moral compass as I do now, and I would likely possess the same core values that had been instilled in both Deepak and me when we were young children. Almost certainly I would have been successful in my career; my father had a thriving medical practice, he was the physician to the president of India and I would have joined him and, in later years, he, Deepak, and I might very well have opened our own hospital. I would have been happy in India, there are so many wonderful things about my homeland; we would have had a lot of servants, maybe less pressure and even my golf game might have improved. Indeed there are scores of golf courses all over India, a legacy of British rule, and the second oldest golf course in the world is in Calcutta.

Deep down I knew too well that as Amita and I got older we would have aspired for our children to go to America to study. Ironically, early in our careers in the States, when we would return to India we would spend time with our classmates from medical school who had decided to stay behind. They often would ask us what was so wonderful about America, and then suggest — sometimes vehemently — that we should return. But almost inevitably sometime later during that very same conversation they would ask us if we could help their children get into a good American university. It was not envy on their part and we never mistook it for that, but rather the acknowledgment that the intellectual stimulus and opportunities based on hard work and achievement that were found in America were quite different from those in India. They wanted to offer these unique advantages to their children.

It wasn't just those friends who asked, either; we were asked several times by the cook and the chauffeur, "When will you take us to America? How can we qualify for a job there?" These people were not well educated. They knew very little about the real America, but they equated it with hope. The only thing they knew about this place called America was that people who lived there had an opportunity to improve their lives and they wanted to go there.

If I had returned to India after completing my education I would have missed all the amazing, awe-inspiring, mind-expanding experiences I've had since we arrived in 1972 with eight dollars and Amita wearing her brand-new expensive Italian sandals. My dharma didn't just bring me to America, but more specifically to Boston, which as far as I'm concerned is a mecca of medicine. I could just as easily have ended up in Nebraska, or North Dakota, or anywhere else, working at a fine institution, but for whatever reasons that wasn't my path. Working and living in Boston I have had the opportunity to listen to lectures by Nobel laureates, to work alongside some of the most respected people in modern medicine, to learn firsthand from researchers who have spent their lives investigating the mysteries of the human body. I have been challenged to be better every single day — and I've been given the responsibility of passing along a great body of knowledge to physicians around the world.

Maybe the most difficult thing for many immigrants to deal with is the fact that they have left their country, their tradition, behind. There can be some guilt attached to that thought. People deal with that feeling in many ways. Deepak has a foundation that sponsors orphanages in India and makes sure young people can go to school. I like to feel I have contributed to my homeland in several meaningful ways. When I received that honor on Ellis Island I reflected, "Harvard Medical School Department of Continuing Medical Education should not only be the best academic CME department in the world, it should be the best academic CME department *for* the world." With my dedicated and talented colleagues, we have taught CME courses to medical professionals from around the world. We have instructed them in critical lessons, but I also believe there has been a modicum of inspiration. We have provided tools — such that they can not only acquire and retain the new knowledge but can also incorporate into their practices, thus improving the lives of their patients.

Perhaps more than other areas, science and especially medicine have the utmost ability to have a worldwide impact. Communications, entertainment, the legal field, teaching, sports — while all of these areas may make a huge impact on a country, generally they do not translate internationally. Medicine is different; a discovery anywhere in the world will impact the lives of patients everywhere in the world. I feel I have the privilege of informing and inspiring colleagues. I believe through our work that many of the attendings leave informed and inspired, and do so with a renewed commitment to cherish all that's glorious and best about the medical profession.

I also serve as the editor in chief of the hepatology section of *UpToDate,* an electronic textbook that directly reaches eight hundred and fifty thousand physicians in one hundred and fifty countries around the world, informing them of the latest developments in that branch of medicine. I've also published numerous articles and published five books, including *Live Better, Live Longer,* with my colleague Alan Lotvin, which provides the scientific evidence to the most interesting questions being asked about modern medicine.

I don't believe I would have had many of these accomplishments if I had stayed in India, and it is my conviction that what my colleagues and I do benefits people from all around the world, including India.

The excitement of America is that there is always more to be discovered. That is also true of India. The India of today is not the country that we left decades ago, a country in which tradition and status still dominated the nation's economic life. While there still are remnants of that, as a result of the availability of a free education India has become more of a partner with America than ever before in its long history. But as Amita and I discovered when we came here, probably more than any country on earth, America rewards hard work and dedication. In a very singular and remarkable way this country is blind to anything except results. The system for advancement is based on the ability of each individual rather than seniority or nepotism. We found the opportunity to fulfill our dreams here.

And while I still speak with a slightly pronounced Indian accent in just about every way I consider myself an American. An American of Indian descent, but an American. I think the thoughts of an American, and when we have problems I worry about my country. Sometimes when I'm traveling, for example, I find myself complaining about "the partisan politics we have in my country." That's the phrase that I use, "my country," and that's the way I feel about it. I have learned to appreciate what I found here and to love the best parts of America. I remember being called to jury duty once and actually being somewhat excited about it. When someone I know found out that I had been summoned, he told me I could simply tear it up, since it wasn't sent by certified mail, and claim I had never received it.

"You don't have to serve," he told me. Apparently the court actually factors in a percentage for people who will not respond. "I've never served," he continued in a proud voice.

"Why are you proud of that?" I asked him. "I want to serve. You should be chagrined, because it's a wonderful system to be tried by a jury of one's peers." So each time I've been called I've packed up my reading material and showed up at the court bright and early, ready and willing to serve.

As American as Amita and I have become, our children have known no other home. Priya was born in India, but Kanika and Bharat were born in Boston and consider India a foreign country to which they have some attachment. As they were growing up we took them to India as often as we could afford; we wanted them to know their family there. That way they would know where their parents' roots were.

Between Deepak and me we now have five grandchildren; they have Indian names, and we can see their heritage in their faces, they are every bit as American as the ancestors of people who came here on the *Mayflower*. In fact, Deepak's grandson is American, Indian, and Chinese; he speaks English, Spanish, Hindi, and Mandarin. Deepak and Rita call him a masterist, the global identity of the future made possible by instant communications and social media tools. Our grandchildren love to wear Indian clothes to show their classmates and they read the comic books about Indian mythology, but they are American. In only two generations the transition has been complete.

In 1973 Amita and I decided we would take my parents and our young children to Disney World. Mickey Mouse has always had universal appeal. We had very little money, so we had to drive there in our Volkswagen. We had only a brief vacation, so we drove as quickly as we could, stopping only when it was necessary. I remember stopping in Charlottesville, Virginia, to fill the gas tank, use the restrooms, and ask for directions. The gas station attendant we spoke to had such a thick southern accent I had no idea what language he was speaking. Was he speaking English or a totally different language? He was exasperated when I kept asking him to repeat directions to the restroom, until he finally escorted me there.

When we finally got to Disney one of the first rides we went on was called It's a Small World. This is a boat ride through an exhibition in which dolls dressed as children from all regions of the world sing the "It's a Small World" song. We never forgot it. That ride and that song had a special resonance for us. We had come from another country, but we believed at heart we were all the same.

At the end of our first day in this wonderful amusement park we were watching the electric parade and the amazing fireworks display, and my mother turned to me and said, "This is the closest I have come to heaven." That was quite a comment and I've never forgotten it. And in some respects, at least, that was the way we felt about living in America.

Decades have passed since then, and Amita and I have seen both the very best and the not so good about America, about our country. It's impossible to determine exactly when we started thinking of ourselves as Americans and not Indians living in America. The actual feeling of being "home" is very difficult to describe; every poet in history has tried to do it. To me it means this is where I belong and this is where the things that matter to me are. Amita and I really didn't know what we would find in America when we came here, and whatever illusions we once held are long gone.

In some ways Amita and I feel we are very much American. We celebrate the Fourth of July and Thanksgiving and always exercise our responsibility to vote. America is truly an amazing country and a melting pot. People from different countries and cultures can feel they belong and make a difference. Just the other day I was reflecting on the time a delegation from the Gastroenterology Division from the Beth Israel Deaconess Medical Center was invited to present an update in gastroenterology and hepatology in Greece. This particular group of American physicians had been selected because of our expertise in gastroenterology and hepatology. We were going to present lectures and engage in workshops with academic Greek professors, fellows, and residents.

At the airport I bumped into Dr. V. K. Saini, an eminent cardiothoracic surgeon in Boston. He had gone to medical school in India and then immigrated to England. There he had risen to the post of registrar in surgery, but then, despite his multitude of accomplishments, he encountered the proverbial glass ceiling. Frustrated, he moved to Boston and had to start his training all over again as a resident since none of his British degrees were recognized by the American Board of Surgery. He toiled hard and, interestingly enough, during his residency, while in the operating room, the senior cardiothoracic surgeon would often ask his advice because he had accrued so much experience in the United Kingdom. One of Saini's sons went into medicine and rose to the rank of professor of radiology at Harvard Medical School.

In a sense this was ironic but telling in that when I looked around at my colleagues who formed this American delegation to Greece, I realized that none of the six of us had been born or gone to medical school in America. Two of us had been trained in Irish medical schools and had emigrated from Ireland, one member was born in and had trained in Switzerland, another doctor was Greek born and educated, and myself and one other physician had been born and trained in India.

It actually was remarkable; all six of us, the entire American delegation, were first-generation Americans. We had all come here at different times but all of us had come for the opportunity to advance our careers in America and were now in Boston and working at Harvard Medical School. It struck me that America is not only a great democracy but also a meritocracy. Individuals climb up the success ladder based on ability, talent, and hard work. We had all reached the pinnacle of the medical profession, and now we had been chosen to represent the best of American medicine internationally. Subsequently as a group we traveled to a number of other countries. From time to time I realized that I always felt a great pride and sense of belonging in my chosen country on such occasions.

Interestingly the chief of the Division of Gastroenterology and Hepatology had also been invited to be part of our delegation. He was the only native-born American, but he could not participate because of preexisting commitments.

More recently, early in 2012, while I was away at another conference, our daughter Kanika invited Amita to join her and her husband, our grandchildren, and Kanika's in-laws on a trip to Disney World. As it turned out, the very first ride they went on was, coincidentally, It's a Small World. It hadn't changed very much in all that time; it is still a fascinating journey around the world as children in native dresses sing the song in their mother tongue. As Amita told me about it, she said that being there transported her back in time to our first visit, when America was still such a novelty for us. "I had tears in my eyes when I saw those dolls," she said. "Our young grandchildren were watching them with their eyes wide open with wonder just the same way we had seen those dolls from each part of the world, including India, decades ago. The stars in their eyes were the most beautiful thing to see."

When you start on your path there is no way of knowing where it will take you or even where it will end. It's just the natural way to go. Growing up, I couldn't have ever guessed that being a doctor and a teacher would take me to Harvard Medical School in Boston, Massachusetts. Or that I would follow my brother to America, that he would become famous around the world by embracing some of the oldest Indian traditions, and I would become a respected teacher of medicine and pursue my passion. I am reminded what the French philosopher De Montaigne once said, "The great and glorious masterpiece of man is to live with purpose."

None of this ever would have happened without the education we received in India, the core values instilled by our parents and grandparents, and by the remarkably gifted and generous contributions and nurturing by our senior colleagues and mentors. And, of course, my wife, Amita, who was the anchor of our family and has continued to inspire me in countless ways.

Amita and I have followed our passions and done so as easily as drifting on a river. Each part of it has been fulfilling, rewarding, and humbling. Most important, we still wait with bright-eyed excitement to see what is around the next bend.

Postscript

Deepak

President Obama and the Chopra family,
defining the new America, 2012.

A S THE BEST PREDICTOR of America's future, I'd pick a cab ride in any big city. The driver will be an immigrant, and he'll take a few seconds off from talking on his cell phone to ask where you want to go. Unless you know Arabic, Russian, or the tongues spoken in Haiti and Nigeria, you won't have any idea what your cabbie is saying into his cell; you'll just sit back with annoyance and pray that he doesn't rear-end somebody.

But he is binding the world together. Most immigrants are talking into their cell phones about one thing: how to get the rest of their family to America. If that has already happened, they are talking business and money. Driving a cab is on the lowest rung of the American dream, but at least it's a rung. Better to be an invisible "brownie" renting a taxi in New York City than wondering if your neighbor back home has his sights set on you when civil war breaks out. America is the most hated country in the world, and the one that foreigners most want to move to.

I'm repeating a cliché, behind which are two realities battling for supremacy. Someone dubbed it the war between the iPod and the mullahs. Modernism is openly clashing with tradition. A younger generation tunes into the future via Facebook while their elders nurse the bitter grievances and sweet nostalgia that prevent forward motion. If we're lucky, all those voices talking into cell phones will become one voice — or as close to one as we need to save an imperiled planet.

The beauty of such a merging is reflected in my story and Sanjiv's story. Neither of us drove cabs, but when I was moonlighting in ERs around Boston, I could read what many of the patients were thinking when I walked into the room. *Jesus, not another Indian doctor.* The first thing I ever wrote publicly was a letter to the *Boston Globe* protesting the prejudice against physicians with foreign training. Sanjiv and I brought Indian genes to a country highly adapted to Western science.

As brothers, we claimed the right to be our own selves. But the bond of dharma didn't get Americanized out of us. The Chopra brothers could have taken their brains and their background to another country and succeeded. What I celebrate is that in America you can climb the ladder of opportunity or kick it out from under you and still succeed beyond your wildest dreams.

Another cliché? More like a fading hope. If the worst in human nature prevails, the horrific wars of the twentieth century will only be a prelude to an entire planet put in jeopardy. Sanjiv and I followed the family dharma by becoming doctors. Lavish reward seemed like our due. Will our grandchildren be the clean-up crew for our luxury and waste? If so, how will we look in their eyes? Between them, China and the United States produce 40 percent of the greenhouse gases responsible for global warming. When he was being scolded about this, a young Chinese man was quoted as saying, "The West has feasted at the banquet, and when we show up for coffee, you tell us to pay for the whole meal."

There is much gloom about the future and only slender hopes. To be doomed feels meaningless when the cause of your destruction is the piling up of garbage. I think hope lies in nothing we can see. It lies in a new evolutionary trend, not survival of the fittest or the richest but survival of the wisest. We are in a phase transition, which is always turbulent. Human beings are self-correcting. We create problems and then evolve to solve them. It's a messy process but somehow necessary. I have three grandchildren, ages five to ten, and their curiosity far outstrips mine at their age. One asked me, "Who made God?" when she was barely four. Because Gotham's wife is of Chinese extraction, their son is growing up speaking Mandarin, English, a smattering of Hindi, and Spanish. He learned the Spanish from the maid who comes to clean; between them they crack jokes behind his parents' back.

Without immigrants, you'll never get global consensus. The alternative is more of the same toxic nationalism that leads directly to a toxic planet as each country demands "More for me—who cares about you?" My grandchildren live with the protection of privilege because Sanjiv and I succeeded and passed on the fruits of success. But this country is more anti-immigrant than I ever remember. Income inequality has become much wider, leading to the corrosion of social bonds. As an immigrant, I see clearly what native-born people may miss. America is an idea, and when Americans lose confidence in the idea, the seed of destruction has been planted. The idea that is America wears an official face. It's freedom, democracy, all men created equal. I'm not sure that such nobility impacts daily life very much. Maybe the idea should be voiced more like a command: "Keep the contradictions coming." I'm grateful to be included in the contradictions. America would be a moribund society fated to perpetual blandness if the melting pot ever succeeded.

Now the whole world needs to be an idea. This new idea is sustainability. Different societies will remain who they are, but unless they find a sustainable way of life, creeping disaster is imminent. The Maldives are an island nation composed of twenty-six atolls off the Western tip of India. The average elevation is four feet above sea level. The melting of the polar ice caps might as well be happening next door. Survival is a matter of car emissions in Beijing and smoke stacks in a coal-firing power plant in Arizona. But in actuality, the Maldives' greatest peril lies in the absence of a global idea that everyone will agree to.

A revolution in communications is making it possible for ideas to sweep the world in record time. Every cell phone tower is a neuron in the global nervous system. Therefore, I never want the cabbie's phone to go dead, and if his words are angry and resentful, that's the chance we have to take. A nation that spends more on defense than the next sixteen nations combined has more than a little wiggle room for tolerance.

The irony is that immigration is still salvaging the American way of life. Immigrants have a higher birth rate than whites. They lower the mean age in this country. Without that advantage, Japan and Russia are staring at a shrinking population that is aging inexorably. With diminishing resources, Europe will have to provide care for millions of seniors who have ended their productive years in the economy. Even as immigrants are railed against by callous politicians, racists, and a white majority that is threatened by losing its dominance, the demographic blessing that America will enjoy for the next fifty years is a gift from the brownies.

I want my grandchildren to know that I loved them; at the same time I want them to believe that my life was an example of *Ahimsa,* which in Sanskrit means nonviolence (*Himsa* means harm or violence). The meaning spreads much wider than that. Ahimsa is Gandhi's peaceful form of civil disobedience. It is Albert Schweitzer's reverence for life. It is awe before the mystery of life. As you go deeper and deeper, the doctor's oath to "first, do no harm" opens up the possibility for a higher reality to descend to earth.

Meanwhile I can take my grandkids to see the sights. Our cab is too hot inside. The cabbie shrugs his shoulders when I ask him if he has air-conditioning. So I roll down the window, and if I'm lucky, I won't get a blast of fumes from a passing city bus. No matter. A breeze is good on your face as you look up at the sky and the lovely light shifting throughout the day.

Why do we love the light, after all? Because it's the wind that moves the soul toward its secret destination.

Acknowledgments

This was a one-of-a-kind project, and I must thank my brother, Sanjiv, who urged me to participate, and David Fisher, whose first draft inspired me to launch much further on my own than I could have otherwise. The time spent with him was a great creative spur.

To David Moldawer and the team at Amazon, thank you for your faith and encouragement. I learn from every editor, but never more than from you.

Since this book is about family, I offer loving gratitude to five generations of Chopras, from my grandparents to my grandchildren — your presence was with me on every page. To my wife, Rita, I can only say that you added a beautiful Chopra to the mix. I feel very fortunate.

DEEPAK

This was a remarkably delightful project. Working with my older brother, Deepak, was both an inspirational and a rewarding journey. Reflecting on our lives growing up in the enchanting country of India and our journey to the West where we have taken roots and raised our families brought back memories galore. This treasure trove of experiences has shaped the way I think and work. Deepak and I were blessed to have the most loving and compassionate parents, from whom we learned many life lessons in our early formative years. Our grandparents, uncles, and aunts regaled us with myriad stories. Truly incredible storytellers!

To my wife, Amita, I want to say with all my heart that you have led and nurtured our family with dignity and compassion. You have been a great source of wisdom and strength. You inspire and motivate me daily in countless ways. To my children and granddaughters: what an absolute joy it is to be with you. You keep adding charming stories and insights constantly.

David Fisher, I am grateful to you for the three books that we have written together and for inspiring Deepak and me to take on this memorable project. I very much cherish our friendship.

SANJIV